SOCIALISM
AND THE
COMMON GOOD

T0346561

SOCIALISM AND THE COMMON GOOD
New Fabian Essays

Edited by
PRESTON KING

FRANK CASS
LONDON

First published 1996 in Great Britain by
FRANK CASS & CO. LTD.
Newbury House, 900 Eastern Avenue,
London IG2 7HH

and in the United States of America by
FRANK CASS
c/o ISBS, 5804 N.E. Hassalo Street
Portland, Oregon 97213-3644

Transferred to Digital Printing 2004

British Library Cataloguing in Publication Data

Socialism and the Common Good: New Fabian
Essays
I. King, Preston
320.531
ISBN 0-7146-4655-5 (cloth)   0-7146-4255-X (paper)

Library of Congress Cataloging-in-Publication Data

Socialism and the common good : new fabian essays / edited by Preston
King.
   p.   cm.
Includes bibliographical references and index.
ISBN 0-7146-4655-5 (cloth)   0-7146-4255-X (paper)
1. Socialism. 2. State, The. 3. Collectivism. I. King, Preston
T., 1936–   .
HX73.S617 1996
335'.14 – dc20   95-24863
                                                         CIP

Typeset by Vitaset, Paddock Wood, Kent

Contents

List of contributors

ANTHONY ARBLASTER, Reader, Department of Political Theory & Institutions, University of Sheffield

BRIAN BARRY, Professor of Political Science, London School of Economics

G. A. COHEN, Chichele Professor of Social & Political Theory, University of Oxford

IAIN HAMPSHER-MONK, Reader, Department of Politics, University of Exeter

MARTIN HOLLIS, Professor of Philosophy, University of East Anglia

PRESTON KING, Professor of Political Philosophy, Lancaster University

LESLIE MACFARLANE, Fellow, St John's College, University of Oxford

ONORA O'NEILL, Principal, Newnham College, University of Cambridge

BHIKHU PAREKH, Professor of Political Theory, University of Hull

RAYMOND PLANT, Master, St Catherine's College, Oxford

DAVID WINTER, Reader, Department of Economics, University of Bristol

Preface

This book brings together a set of writings by some of the leading social and political thinkers at work in Britain today. Its object is to place before the public some seminal discussions of what is largely a single theoretical issue, together with its practical ramifications: the role of the state, from a socialist perspective, in achieving the common good, or social justice, in modern market systems.

These essays raise many questions. Is state ownership essential to the common good, or is it only one among other theoretically feasible means of securing social justice? Is state ownership an exclusively socialist project, or is it equally a characteristic of conservative policy, in conditions of electoral competition and majority rule? Can a rationalist and egoistic contractualism serve as an adequate model for modern society, or is it at bottom descriptively inept and morally anaemic? Is communitarianism a threat to civil liberty in social democratic states, or is it a necessary condition for efficacy and fairness? How far should the citizen's community of allegiance extend? Up to the borders of his/her class? Nation? State? Beyond? And on what grounds? The authors of these essays reflect a variety of responses: they follow no single line. But they are remarkably uniform in their rejection of the cult of choice and of rational egoism, and in their promotion of a more robust and inclusive notion of community and of social responsibility.

It is commonly claimed that socialism is one or a set of social movements that basically originated in a positive concern to promote the common ownership of property. It is not so commonly recognised that it arose from something simpler and more negative: repudiation of the character and consequences of monopolistic private ownership and control. Where socialism is identified with the positive quest for common ownership, the question that arises is whether the theorem of public ownership can only be legitimately satisfied by direct and active state control, or equally legitimately by various less-engaged forms of arms-length, state regulation. A parallel question that arises is whether common ownership is better read as a part of the *meaning* of social justice, or by contrast as only one among other theoretically possible *means* to achieving the common good. This debate has been sharpened by the extraordinary celebration of market principles – which has largely meant both protecting and deepening the inequities of the market – since the first Thatcher government in 1979, and the first Reagan administration in 1980.

There are some who place the very highest value upon egalitarian community – upon strong individual identity grounded in a rough equality of social, economic and political condition. By contrast, many of the same individuals contend that common ownership, as a means to such a community, issues in state monopoly; and they conclude that this, if too encompassing, is not only inefficient, but also under-mines the very equality of condition which common ownership was originally intended to secure. The historical record is rather complex – for, while many socialists have been strong advocates of state owner-ship, many others (such as P.-J. Proudhon and Eduard Bernstein) have firmly promoted forms of private ownership. What is reflected in this volume is the importance both of community and individuality, and of the need for a better balance between them – in the interest of the common good and social justice.

Most of these essays were discussed by members of the Socialist Philosophy Group (SPG) of the Fabian Society in the period since 1990, either in their original or in modified form. Over half of them are entirely new and are published here for the first time, including the three opening chapters of Part One. Virtually all date from the period since 1990 (over the time that I served as Convenor of the SPG in succession to my colleague, Brian Barry). Two of these essays (Barry and Plant) were earlier published as independent tracts by the Fabian Society, but their limited circulation fully warrants republication. Three others (Hollis, Hampsher-Monk and Cohen) have been pub-lished elsewhere, and one of these (Cohen) is reproduced here in abbreviated form. The papers comprising Part Four have not been published hitherto. All of the authors, save one (Plant), have been cumulatively involved in some or all of these discussions, and most of the paper-writers have been influenced in some degree and fashion by the positions staked out by their colleagues and friends. The writers have been guided by no brief, but their essays do seem to establish a pretty coherent, but of course, pluralistic, coherence.

I take this opportunity to thank collectively the contributors, both for their essays, and for the re-direction of the royalties from these to the Fabian Society, which has sponsored and promoted this volume. Thanks are due to Simon Crine and to Giles Wright of the society for the support they have given throughout for the SPG meetings in Dartmouth Street and elsewhere. I should also like to note the helpful contributions of – among many others – Tony Beck, Geoffrey Bindman, John Carrier, John Champneys, Robin Cohen, Diana Coole, Nicholas Deakin, G. M. Dillon, David Donnison, James Doyle, Barbara Goodwin, Roger Hadley, Patricia Hewitt, Patricia Hollis, Paul Hirst, Ann Holmes, Sally Jenkinson, Ian Kendall, Kelvin Knight, R. D. McKinlay, Charles Marquand, David Marquand, Liam O'Sullivan, Anne Phillips, Alan Playdell, Margherita Rendel, L. J. Sharpe, Raewyn Stone, Sally Tomlinson and Peter Wilkin.

Preston King
Auckland, 27 January 1995

Introduction

PRESTON KING

This book supplies a set of essays on overlapping problems of contemporary political and social philosophy. A number of themes criss-cross throughout, such as individualism, communitarianism and collectivism; the common good, common ownership and social justice, rational egoism, friendship and citizenship, identity, constituency and local government, incentives, entitlements and obligations. Underlying all these is the central concern with socialism: its distinctiveness, its ends, means, community of inclusion, and most importantly its relation, not so much to capitalism, but to the market, the profit-motive, and to rational egoism. These papers appear fairly consistent both in their acceptance of the market and equally of the need to constrain it. Where writers of an earlier era – Bodin, Hobbes, Spinoza, Kant – used to celebrate the State, attributing to it an unquestionable autonomy and supremacy, so many writers of our own age – Hayek, Friedman, Nozick – have been disposed to celebrate the Market, attributing to it a similarly magical autonomy and independence. These papers demonstrate sophisticated evolution well beyond both such false enthusiasms, and will contribute significantly to the evolution of a vibrant social democracy appropriate to our age.

Part one: principles and constituencies

The first three essays of the volume are introductory and tend to concentrate upon choice, constituency and the question of common ownership.

Anthony Arblaster, author of the opening paper, is troubled by the question of choice, and by implication with the distinguishing features of socialism. He argues that all socialisms, Fabian or communist, belong to the same current of thought and owe a debt to Marx. He contends that socialism is a communitarian movement whose *raison d'être* was and is to check the rampant social atomisation produced by capitalism. Arblaster believes that every society must project a common good – placing a limit on the extent of its pluralism or tolerance. He accepts the importance of freedom, but believes that the promotion of competition and 'the cult of choice' in recent times has been carried much too far: competition, for example in the choice of doctors, hospitals and schools, merely has the effect of ensuring that those who are most disadvantaged will be further disadvantaged. Arblaster takes it that some compulsory practices, like universal health insurance and pension arrangements, are actually better than parallel non-compulsory schemes. He does not perceive the position of the individual as necessarily improved just because government leaves him or her more money in take-home pay. Lower taxes may mean less adequate social provision – as in transport or parks or education or museums. While Arblaster accepts the legitimacy of some communitarian claims, he does not nominate and need not intend that public ownership (that is, nationalisation) is the sole or even predominant means of achieving the common good which he seeks.

Where Arblaster never directly refers to common ownership, this is L. J. Macfarlane's exclusive concern. He traces this idea from Aristophanes and Plato right up to the present. His concern is to show not only that the notion of common ownership is not a new idea, but also that it comes in several distinct varieties. It may be restricted to a particular class; or merely consist of radical redistribution from rich individuals/classes to poor individuals/classes; or apply to some sectors of the economy, not all; or be driven by conflicting purposes – perhaps to make a conservative government more stable (by attracting popular support), equally perhaps to remove constraints on the emergence of excellence, et cetera. Two contrary hints are contained in Macfarlane's analysis. The first is that socialism is nothing without common ownership and that it abandons its soul in abandoning this strategy. The second, however, is that common ownership (as for Bismarck) in no way necessarily furthers the objective of a socialist morality. Arblaster's strategy is to begin with the common good as an end. Macfarlane's strategy is to begin with common ownership as a standard mechanism or means. Because this mechanism of common ownership is not distinctive – being appropriated both by socialists and non-socialists – Macfarlane, I think, is in turn implicitly forced back upon some notion of a socialist morality – that is, back upon a more abstract and comprehensive concern with the common good.

In the third paper I argue that it is a piece of misdirection to attempt to distinguish between socialist and conservative parties in terms of the volume of choice that each will allow or deny. For every communist Rumania or Albania there are very many more capitalist Germanies (Hitler), or Zaires (Mobutu) or Nicaraguas (Somoza). This paper argues that choice is always in any setting circumscribed; that each choice taken must close the door on some other that might have been; that each choice refused, of itself opens up fresh possibilities. This paper contends that governments do not enhance choice as such, but are only able to supply better or worse options; thus governments are not to be judged on the number, but on the quality, of the choices they allow. Choice is only the ground of morality; it cannot be its object. Markets are no more to be identified with freedom than are states; they create some possibilities, but always at the cost of killing off others.

The paper argues that the distinction between socialism and conservatism, whatever else it may be, is not a matter of one standing for monopoly and the other for competition. If government is itself a species of monopoly, and if all parties sanction government – as they appear to do by competing to win it – then in this they also all sanction some form and degree of monopoly. The appropriate question accordingly is not whether or not there should be monopoly, but rather what are the appropriate techniques for regulating it (oversight), and how far should we allow it to extend (limits). The state is of course dangerous. But then so is the market. And they are not always distinguishable. The market is not a mere collection of individuals, any more than is the state. The bulk of the market consists of giant private collectives. Some private collectives (General Motors, Sony) are infinitely more powerful than most public collectives (Bahamas, Nepal). If we are concerned to curb the one, it is inconsistent to omit constraints on the other. In any event, it is argued, the Right proves itself to be only rhetorically, not practically, opposed to government – even big government. The Right only perceives its elaborate use of government as 'natural', while recourse to government by opponents is 'tyranny'.

How far then should government monopoly extend? Government itself, in one form or another, is always with us. The tasks it sets itself are constantly evolving. The question whether government should nationalise the economy wholesale is not on the agenda. But it is suggested that some theoretical light may be thrown on this question by at least distinguishing between ownership and management, and between management and regulation. By cross-mapping ownership and management, the conclusion is reached that the only really common feature of socialists is their firm opposition to Monopolistic Private Ownership and its consequences. In response to the claim that it is highly damaging to socialism to remove from it doctrinal support for Centralised Public Ownership, the paper observes that too much attention may be paid to formal doctrine, and not enough to live constituencies.

Part two: collectivism and markets

The next three essays are more detailed and focus more narrowly on problems of collectivism and the market.

Brian Barry, like Arblaster, is suspicious of the cult of choice. He cogently replaces, however, the notion of a common good with something larger: social justice. The common good of course always reduces to some sort of social norm. This might be liberty or equality, but neither works on its own, and justice is larger than either. So Barry settles for socialism as a combination of social justice and collectivism, the latter being a selective form of common ownership. Barry might have constructed social justice as the end of socialism, with collectivism as its means. But he does not directly say this. Moreover, he does build 'collectivism' into the very meaning of socialism, which may imply that collectivism is itself for him an end. In any event, Barry's collectivism clearly excludes any simple anti-individualism.

Barry carefully distinguishes between (a) individualism and holism, (b) individualism and solidarism, and (c) individualism and collectivism. Under (a), Barry accepts individualism as a methodological principle and rejects holism. Under (b), he takes *solidarism* to imply a natural obligation to provide for the welfare of all members/citizens, simply because they are members/citizens; he takes *individualism* to imply that obligation only arises if it is artificially or contractually entered into; and he ends by rejecting both as models of duty. Under (c), Barry treats individualism as either classic (the nightwatchman state) or as left liberal (the equality-of-opportunity state), contrasting both with collectivism, which means joint action, standardly through the state, to achieve common goals; and here he accepts collectivism and rejects individualism. Barry accepts as plainly true that markets must be controlled and in some cases replaced. He takes it that markets betray no natural tendency to eliminate inequities along the lines of gender and race and otherwise. He also concludes that natural monopolies are best publicly owned, since in private hands there is no incentive to provide 'cheap and efficient service on standard terms to all'.

David Winter's paper constitutes a limited comment on Barry's, whose plea for methodological individualism he accepts. Winter, however, thinks the case of the New Right to be strongest, not in regard to the deficiency of *information* available to central planners, but in respect to inadequate *incentives* to central planners to respond to the interests of their citizens/clients. Winter does not believe that the behaviour of administrators is merely to be reduced to motives of self-interest. But he is chary of the idea that 'the man or the woman in Whitehall not only knows best but behaves best as well'. Winter insists that a centralised or collective system of health provision need not necessarily be either just or efficient, nor that decentralised or even private systems must necessarily be the reverse.

Winter is anxious to establish that collective provision cannot be viewed as *essential* to the socialist project. He thinks it cannot be essential at least for the reason – noted by Macfarlane – that it is not distinctive. Winter contends that the New Right prefers decentralised over centralised provision, and competitive over monopoly arrangements – always preferring of course to place monopolies in private hands where monopoly cannot otherwise be avoided. Winter extends the point by insisting that there is wide, cross-party acceptance of collective provision in most advanced industrial states, at least in such key sectors as education, health and transport, so that a collectivist programme, at least in these areas, must fail to set socialists apart from most other parties.

Raymond Plant directly accepts, with Hayek, that centralised planning is impossible and a threat to civil liberty. But he also accepts that the market can be managed or regulated in important ways – as by dispersing concentrations of capital, extracting from industry provisions for long-term training of the labour force, maintaining genuine competition and a plurality of economic institutions (including unions), policing the external effects of production (such as pollution), and in general by imposing upon the market a framework of civil responsibility. Within such regulatory limits, Plant accepts the value – or the common values – of a mixed economy. Indeed, he accepts the market, not as 'some amoral force', but as a part of a just society, as long as it is kept under constraint and in the public interest. By implication he appears to favour some form of effective decentralisation, which is not only administrative but also economic. He seeks to move socialism from a class to a citizenship basis, and thus to create a common moral community between owners of capital and purveyors of labour. He urges the adoption of a comprehensive citizenship perspective, which he believes will allow movement beyond sectionalism, rigid defence of interest groups, and class war.

Plant takes the comprehensive notion of citizenship to go hand-in-hand with some form of individualism and freedom, as long as it is understood that any effective freedom must have a positive dimension, requiring 'a feasible collective programme' which will satisfy the needs of agency. For Plant, a needs-based policy is essential, and the costs of sustaining it are not to be viewed as open-ended. If the costs of defending positive freedoms (welfare rights) are open-ended, then they could not be distinguished in this from the costs of enforcing negative freedoms (civil rights). For *all* entitlements have and are constrained by costs. The trick is simply not to allow the costs of any rights to become open-ended, so as to avoid over-extending government, and attendant threats to liberty. A part of the solution to the problem of costs may be to link rights to duties. The citizen has a duty to pay tax, and taxation is coercive. There is no reason why the redistribution of tax *qua* welfare should not have a matching element of coercion – in the minimal sense that receipt of welfare may be conditional, in appropriate circumstances, on the preparedness of recipients to produce – that is, to work.

Plant accepts the Rawlsian principle that the basic goods of citizens 'are to be distributed as equally as possible unless a more unequal distribution would produce more resources for the worst off'. In short, he accepts the principle of incentives for the better off. This principle, at least in terms of its practical effects, is one with which Cohen will be found to experience serious difficulty.

Part three: the poverty of egoism

The next three essays concentrate upon the logic of incentives and the morality and externalities of market arrangements.

Martin Hollis distinguishes between friendship, citizenship and, in effect, contract. Friendship is a loyalty which is not sullied by considerations of personal gain and is such that it may cut across allegiance to the state. Citizenship is erected upon duties to the state but purged, as in the case of friendship, of cost-benefit calculations. Contractualism involves rational egoists establishing agreements solely on the basis of mutual gain. These are three distinct principles and it is conceivable that a society as a whole could take its lead from any one of them. What we remark in our own time is an excessive affection for contract. Contractualists will view welfare entitlements as benefits or rights and civic responsibilities as costs or duties. Hollis observes the peculiar difficulty that attends the attempt to explain, for example, British politics in terms of the contractualist, or consumerist, model. If citizens did comprehensively behave contractually (as consumers), which is to say that if they actually did insist on minimising the costs of their membership, then they should necessarily avoid or severely restrict any form of voluntary (unpaid) public service. A strictly self-interested consumerism simply leaves no room for such disinterested behaviour. And yet, local government in Britain is marked by the entry of thousands of individuals who serve without remuneration. There is an argument for local government – and democracy at the local level – being ultimately more important than the more distant variety located at Westminster. Hollis views this as enough to show that contractualist consumerism is not altogether the aptest model for civil society.

Neither is Iain Hampsher-Monk enamoured of the contractual or consumerist model of rational egoism. He is concerned with the way in which the model of rational egoism produces, as a norm, behaviour which it seeks to predict as a fact. Hampsher-Monk argues that, from a rational egoist's perspective, if one can inoculate oneself individually against infective disease, there can remain no justification for universal, publicly supported inoculation of everyone. Similarly, if the rational egoist can afford to buy his or her own bottled water, there can remain no justification for public subvention of potable water from the tap. And so on – with transport, radio, transport, radio, TV, etc. To rigidly pursue the strategy of rational egoism, one must attempt to reconstruct all public goods from – or reduce them to – the interactions of self-interested egoists, whose sole object is the pursuit of personal gain. It is clear enough that humans are not all like this. But it is easy enough in an association to inculcate such an 'ideal' of egoism as that to which members may be encouraged to conform.

Hampsher-Monk takes it that the strategy of rational egoism breaks down as a possible way of making sense of certain types of public good. He mentions group games, like football or hockey. But we could easily add such other activities as participation in a choir or band or orchestra or theatrical play or Scottish reel or wedding or fete – where the goodness of the good precisely consists in the fact that it is jointly engaged and enjoyed. Hampsher-Monk, with Bernard Crick in mind, wants to extend such cases to the seminal circumstance of politics itself. Here, politics is fostered, not as something you do just for something you gain (for example, Lasswell's notorious 'Who Gets What, When, How'), but because it is a good whose goodness consists in the joint engagement and enjoyment. The point is not that the political hasn't its instrumental side. The point is that that is not its only side. The political, in short, is a form of activity which is not reducible to simple market relations. For Hampsher-Monk, though politics are not reducible to markets, they are threatened by them. Markets, despite advantages, are not benign. Unregulated, they threaten politics, and liberty itself. For the rational egoism which they feature has the effect of atomising populations and eroding social groupings – such as trades unions, voluntary associations, local government. So just as Hollis can see no way for rational egoism to account for vibrant and unremunerative local government, neither can Hampsher-Monk extract from it any Crick-like understanding of politics as an autonomous engagement.

Just as Hollis and Hampsher-Monk oppose contractarian theory, dipped as it is in rational egoism, with instrumental motives, so does Gerry Cohen. What appears common to all three essays is some form of commitment to community. For Cohen there are different types of community. That in which he displays the greatest interest is what he calls the justificatory community. This community is bound by common norms, capable of justifying policies on an interpersonal basis, irrespective of the unequal advantages that might mark the different classes, estates or fractions within that community. For there to be a justificatory community, following Cohen, there must also be a capacity for those who enjoy unequal benefit to justify the benefit to their fellows who are compelled to go without. Modern states basically pretend to be justificatory – that is, egalitarian – communities, featuring equality of consideration and respect for the Other, but they are rarely so.

Cohen finds that in advanced industrial states, the rich characteristically affect to share a justificatory community with the poor. The rich or their representatives commonly attempt to justify their advantage to their deprived fellows on the grounds that the lure of excess wealth acts as an incentive for the rich to work harder – the consequence being greater product. Cohen sees in this mere pretence. He compares the condition of the rich to that of a kidnapper, who says to parents from whom he seeks to extort a ransom: children ought to be with their parents; I shall not return your child unless you pay me; so you ought to pay me. What is to be noted about this procedure is that the kidnapper treats himself as an impersonal force, not as a human agent. From the kidnapper's perspective, taken as a moral agent, the point cannot be that the parents ought to pay, but that the kidnapper ought not to be holding and threatening harm to the child in the first place.

Cohen suggests that the rich individual is in a similar position when he or she says, in effect, to the poor or unemployed or disabled: people ought to work hard; I shall work less hard if tax is not reduced from 60 per cent to 40 per cent; so you ought to vote for a lower tax. From the perspective of a justificatory community – where members stand on a footing of equality with one another and have a shared concern for their mutual well-being – the point cannot be that the poor ought to vote for a lower tax so as to encourage the rich to work, but that the rich ought not to think to withdraw their labour in circumstances where their needs are being perfectly comfortably met while the most elementary needs of so many of their distressed fellows are not. In this, I confess that I cannot adequately convey the richness of Cohen's argument. But it is distinctive in bringing to life the interpersonal implications of a normally impersonal account of incentives.

Part four: the enrichment of identities

The final essays focus upon the plasticity of citizenship and the diversity and complexity of identity within and beyond the boundaries of modern states.

Bhikhu Parekh reformulates the question of political obligation, so as to ask, not: Why should I obey the law?, but rather: What obligations do I incur by virtue of citizenship of my state? This is in part an exploration of identity, and of its extent and limits. Citizens have multiple obligations, of which the political is but one. How these obligations mesh is a complex matter, but certainly political obligation must be sensitised to respect parallel obligations – as to an agent's kin, religion, ethnic community, not to omit humanity in general. One's obligation to the state, Parekh argues, is not only to obey it, but also to question it, and more than this, to disobey it – where appropriate. Parekh argues that one's obligations are not characteristically the result of a command or a contract but largely follow from one's elemental humanity. These obligations at least – if not one's citizenship – must be recognised to extend to the world at large.

We are citizens of states, but not only of states. We may have duties to states, yet certainly not to these alone. Just as our identities are more complex (multiple) than is often supposed, so might we expect states – which are a most significant feature of personal identity – to be less rigidly framed than is commonly the case. State boundaries are not normally open to question, being simply taken for granted. When we do seek to justify them, it is not uncommon to do so on grounds of nationality – that is, of the ethnic homogeneity of the folk residing within the territorial bounds of the state. Onora O'Neill draws it to our attention that we have little justification for this. She reminds us that every nation-state contains other nations – which is to say that it contains 'minorities' that are somehow culturally or otherwise distinct. The presence then of 'nationhood' neither explains nor legitimates the boundaries of virtually any state. For no state is as culturally homogeneous as all that, nor is it likely that a state could or should succeed in securing such homogeneity. When a nation seeks to form itself as a state, it always willy-nilly overleaps itself and ends up incorporating other nationals. When a state that is already formed has its contours contested by distinct and dissident national components (Kurds, Tutsis, Somalis, whoever), it reflexively resists the dissolution of the frontiers that seem to make it what it is. O'Neill is not dismissive of state boundaries. But she has no passion for them. She would be happy to see them drawn, like identities, in multiple ways, for multiple purposes.

The question of citizenship and national boundaries is a vexed one for modern socialists. Since socialists seek social justice, the question arises as to whom it is they seek this for. Is it only to be for those who happen to share the same national identity, or state boundaries? As David Winter remarks, if socialists only see their community of allegiance in terms of their nation or state, they will exclude from their collective concern all those other communities – producers of coffee in Brazil or cotton in Egypt or pyrethrum in Kenya – on whom their own well-being often exploitatively depends. Socialists may see themselves as such in two distinct ways: on the one side in terms of the principle of redistribution which they embrace; on the other, in terms of the community of inclusion (and thus exclusion) they accommodate. To stress technique of organisation or redistribution does not of itself touch the question of exclusion/inclusion.

If the community of inclusion is limited to one's state, then just distribution or provision is sought only within its confines. This excludes consideration of just provision for those who lie beyond the territorial bounds of one's state, but who none the less enter crucially into, and are typically controlled by, the very same chain of production by which one is sustained nationally. Communities are not just structured nationally, but also internationally. This is not just a matter for world religions and dispersed kinsfolk. It is more vitally a matter of and for production itself, which has today entered into a thoroughly encompassing, global phase. We are left accordingly with two very important problems. The first has to do with what we are to understand by socialism – that is, the sorts of principles and techniques we think it to require. The second problem has to do with that raised by Parekh and O'Neill, but also by Winter: who is to be included and how? It is obvious that a crude socialist centralism or nationalisation or common ownership will prove inept. But we must also consider that an unduly restrictive socialist nationalism – which has nothing to do with a national socialism – will simply prove unjust.

Part One:
Principles and Constituencies

1

Socialism and the common good

ANTHONY ARBLASTER

It is striking how little reaction there has been in social democratic circles and parties to the sudden and, as far as I know, barely predicted, collapse of European communism and the Soviet Union. I am not referring so much to the pathetic failure of the British Labour Party to adjust its 'defence' or foreign policy to these momentous changes – it was only too typical of the Labour leadership to embrace nuclear weapons at exactly the historical moment which made them irrelevant – as to the lack of discussion about the meaning and implications of these historic events.

What this reflects, I suspect, is the belief or assumption that social democracy has nothing in common, politically or intellectually, with communism; or at least the determination that it should not *appear* to have anything in common with communism. The claim that 'what happens in Eastern Europe' – even when it is good news – 'has nothing to do with us' is one more way of distancing social democracy from communism and Marxism; and that has, of course, been a prime concern of social democrats since 1917, and especially since 1945. Thus the Italian socialist and social democratic parties always co-operated in operating the first rule of post-Fascist Italian politics, which is that the Italian Communist Party (PCI) should never be allowed to form part of a government, despite being for more than 40 years the country's second largest party. Better a coalition with the Christian Democrats than the Communists, no matter how moderate and constitutional the latter became.

Historically and intellectually, all this is mere pretence and pretension. All forms of socialism, even the most moderate and diluted, owe a debt to Marx and Marxism whether they like it or not.

Historically the split between revolutionaries and reformers represented the partition of a single stream, and it is one which has never in

fact been complete or absolute. I would be happy to support these
assertions if it was thought necessary; but one need only look at the
tone and style of *Fabian Essays* of 1889 to see how different were
relations then between these gradualists and their revolutionary contemporaries such as William Morris, compared with the hostile and
dogmatic feuding that developed in the period after 1917.

More important for my purposes is to note the *de facto* degree of
mutual dependence which existed between social democracy and
communism. On the one hand social democracy could be perceived as
reassuringly moderate – a sensible middle way, avoiding both the
excesses of modern capitalism as epitomised in the decay and violence
of urban America, as well as the bureaucratised authoritarianism and
inefficiency of communist regimes and economies. On the other
hand, communism acted as a magnet, pulling the whole spectrum of
politics to the Left, and compelling reformist parties in the capitalist
world to devise policies which, they hoped, would undermine the
appeal of communism by echoing its good points and abjuring its bad
ones. It was also the case that the international role of the Soviet
Union acted as a usually unacknowledged restraint upon the foreign
interventions of the United States – so it was so much easier for the
United States to make war on Iraq once it was sure that the Soviet
Union would not obstruct such an enterprise. Now this pole of attraction and source of restraint has vanished, leaving the poor world
dangerously exposed to American threats and interventions – as in
Somalia – and leaving social democracy more isolated and vulnerable
than it has been for many decades.

The insecurity of the Left within the capitalist democracies has
been compounded by the coincidental revival of militant and merciless
capitalism which dominated the 1980s in much of the West, and
which has now been taken up with enthusiasm in the ex-communist
countries of Eastern Europe, where the very word 'socialism' is likely
to carry deeply negative overtones for a good many years to come.

None of this is meant to imply that the social and economic and
political order which has now disintegrated into rubble *was* an
embodiment of socialism, as it always suited the Right to assert. But it
was a tribute to the power of the Cold War ethos that most of the
Western Left was afraid to admit that those societies had *any* socialist
virtues at all, or that the Soviet Union played any positive role in
international politics. But now these things *can* be admitted, and are,
in some quite surprising quarters;[1] and we can see that the collapse of

communist authoritarianism, welcome as this was in itself, has not turned out to be an unmixed blessing, nor a prelude to unmixed blessings either.

Intellectually its impact in the Western world has been dreadful. We have been told yet again that 'Marxism is dead' by all kinds of people who had never willingly conceded that it was alive. And the corollary of this is the claim that 'we are all liberals now', and even that liberal capitalist democracy is the final political and economic goal to which all human history has been leading. The revival of liberal economics from the mid-1970s onwards has now been compounded by the proclaimed victory of capitalism over communism, or liberal democracy over socialist dictatorship. Given all that, given the particularly acute problems of the British Labour Party, which many people have argued, perhaps correctly, for more than a decade, is in long-term decline; given the general tendency of social democracy to forget if not openly renounce its original objectives and drift rightwards towards a would-be comfortable accommodation with capitalism – given all this, is it any wonder that social democrats are no longer clear in their own minds what socialism actually is or means, and are apt, or prefer, to think about it in the terms of established liberalism? It was surely entirely typical of these developments that when Neil Kinnock was asked why there was no mention of socialism in Labour's 1992 election manifesto, he replied by saying that everything in it was based on our fundamental socialist belief in the liberty of the individual (or words to that effect).

That belief or value is, of course, the central value of liberalism, not socialism; and it would have been perfectly possible for both Ashdown and Major to invoke it as central to their conception of liberalism or conservatism. In other words, it tells us nothing about what is distinctive about socialism, as opposed to what it may have in common with other ideologies. It is true that the 'New Liberalism', from T. H. Green onwards, did revise and enlarge the concept of freedom, and indeed the philosophy and agenda of liberalism, in ways which pushed liberalism towards socialism; so that there is, as Roy Hattersley showed in *Choose Freedom*, a way of thinking about freedom which does then distinguish socialism from traditional, conventional liberalism, which still views state or public action with some suspicion, still tends to think of freedom as 'the silence of the laws' or as 'an area of non-interference'.

But even allowing for all this, a socialism which elevates freedom or liberty to the position of its supreme or central value is conceding too much to liberalism. For, however sophisticated the conception of freedom that is employed, what it implies is that the central political aim is to increase the autonomy of the individual, and that no other goal is as important as, let alone more important than, this. This raises a whole range of questions – about both the desirability and feasibility of ever-growing individual autonomy and, at another level, about the very concept of the individual which, as Iain Hampsher-Monk points out in his essay, is called in question by a variety of ways of thinking about people and society, some at least of which would seem to be much closer to socialist thinking than the liberal individualism which underpins the preoccupation with personal freedom or autonomy.

One of the most obviously debatable assumptions inherent in John Stuart Mill's attempt to combine liberalism with utilitarianism is the assumption that freedom and happiness, or if not happiness then some kind of profound personal sense of fulfilment, go together, both for the individual and for society as a whole. Freedom is the pre-condition of progress; but the autonomous person also derives deep satisfaction from the fact that she or he is autonomous, in control of his or her own life. Now these are both empirical propositions in principle – which is not to say that we could ever finally prove them to be clearly true or false, of course. I think we can safely admit that both propositions have a lot of truth in them. But neither is as self-evidently true as Mill seems to have thought. All the relationships we enter into, and especially family relationships, carry with them obligations, commitments, ties, which entail very considerable losses in freedom and autonomy in all kinds of very obvious ways. Why then do we involve ourselves in them if not because we know that such relationships, although they often bring pain and misery, are also the source of the deepest and most durable happiness and personal security? Autonomy, self-direction, freedom make a strong appeal to those, especially perhaps young people and many women, who feel themselves to be trapped or cramped within established institutions, communities or networks which do not allow them the scope to 'be themselves'. But consider, on the other hand, the plight of both the very young and the very old in the more anonymous urban environments. Consider the old-age pensioner living alone in rented accommodation which has a generally transient population. He or she would probably appreciate a good deal *less* autonomy and freedom because in this situation they are effectively synonyms for emptiness, social isolation and neglect.

Of course one can construct counter-examples – of the gay man or lesbian who escapes from the censorious intolerance of family and village or small town to the relative freedom of the same big city which is so harshly indifferent to the lonely pensioner. I am not, of course, denying the value of freedom and autonomy. I am saying that they are not in themselves an adequate prescription for personal happiness or even self-realisation, and socialists cannot afford to believe that they are. Socialism cannot afford to lose sight of those other dimensions of the good society to which it was classically committed, and which its founders and creators well understood.

Nor can socialism be built upon the foundations of individualism, whether ontological or ethical. The concept of the individual is neither neutral nor banal. The idea that it is a kind of obvious truth was well expressed by that classic liberal writer, E. M. Forster:

> ... as for individualism – there seems no way of getting off this, even if one wanted to. The dictator-hero can grind down his citizens till they are all alike but he cannot melt them into a single man ... they are obliged to be born separately, and to die separately ... The memory of birth and the expectation of death always lurk within the human being, making him separate from his fellows ...

But about three hundred years earlier John Donne put quite a different construction upon death. Because it is the one destination to which we all travel, it reminds us of our common fate, not our separateness:

> that privat and *retirid* man, that thought himselfe his owne for ever, and never came forth, must in his dust of the grave bee published and ... bee mingled with the dust of every high way ...[2]

I think I am right in saying that the ancient Greeks had no word corresponding to 'individual', and that the privacy which is of such importance to modern liberalism did not seem to them to be an important or privileged condition. It was in fact one of deprivation, as Hannah Arendt pointed out, indicated by the word itself. The word 'idiot' signified a purely private person, and it was the public sphere which was the area of freedom.[3] And we need only turn to the opening pages of Aristotle's *Politics* to see that what we think of as essentially a rather too fanciful, if not actually sinister, metaphor – that of the body politic and its members – is for him a perfect image of the relation between the single human person (or man) and the community of *polis* to which he belongs. You could not be a human being outside

society. You would have to be either sub- or super-human, either a
beast or a god.

Bentham disliked this metaphor intensely – rightly from his own
point of view. 'The community is a fictitious *body*, composed of the
individual persons who are considered as constituting as it were its
members.' Note the 'fictitious' and 'as it were'. This is not an image
that Bentham wishes to endorse in any way. 'The interest of the
community then is, what? – the sum of the interests of the several
members who compose it ... Individual interests are the only real
interests.' When Mrs Thatcher announced that 'There is no such thing
as society. There are only individuals and their families', she was, apart
from the revealingly inconsistent reference to 'the family', closer to
Benthamite or liberal atomism (of the methodological individualist
kind preached by Hayek, Popper, Berlin and others) than she was to
traditional conservatism, as represented by Burke: 'Individuals pass
like shadows, but the commonwealth is fixed and stable.'

Liberal individualism thus does not represent a universal perception
of the relations between persons and society, as so many of its
advocates fondly imagine or assume. On the contrary, it is, if anything,
the historical exception to the general rule which sees men and women
as essentially social beings, caught up in the web of relationships and
institutions which compose a society, and unavoidably dependent
upon social interaction for their very existence as human beings.
Socialism and communism, as the very terms suggest, belong to that
family of ideologies. And they were in origin an attempt to create a
modern, post-industrial vision of community which would not only
replace nostalgia for the hierarchial pre-industrial society praised and
upheld by Burke and the conservatives, but also provide an alternative
to the miserably atomised and conflict-ridden conglomerations which
capitalism was producing in place of the old feudal order.

I do not myself see how socialism can convert its basic view
of the world into one which embodies or reflects essentially the
liberal individualist perspective without ceasing to be socialism. This
may not worry practical politicians, but it ought to worry socialist
philosophers. And, in fact, it ought to worry the politicians as well,
because the gap between philosophical fundamentals and the attraction
of public support is not the gulf which they, in their more anti-
intellectual moods, may suppose it to be.

There is, I think, plenty of evidence, perhaps including the result of
the British 1992 election, to suggest that the public do respond to

parties which clearly stand for something basic and big. They want a clear image of a party, and that means knowing what values or principles a party stands for. For example, take Crosland's view that the core of socialism is 'equality': socialism is about equality. That may not be an adequte definition of socialism, and it may not be one with which everyone will agree. But it has two virtues. One is that it is simple and easily grasped and remembered. The other is that it is distinctive. No liberal or conservative leader is likely to copy it. Indeed conservatives are more likely to proclaim their perennial belief in *in*equality. The point of this digression is a simple one: a party needs a clear and distinctive set of values in order to command popular support and allegiance. Philosophy and political effectiveness are not so far apart as might be supposed.

So individualism, and a consequent stress on personal freedom and free choice, do not offer anything distinctive for the Labour Party or the Left, and the temptation to embrace them, just because they became the stock-in-trade of the Right-dominated 1980s, should have been, and ought still to be, firmly resisted. To fight on this terrain is to fight on the enemy's ground.

I would like to add a word here against the current cult of *choice*, which is obviously seen and presented as the embodiment of increased personal freedom. This is, at first glance, difficult to do. To deny choice seems to be arrogant and authoritarian. And perhaps in one version of the ideal world, one of abundance and unlimited resources – a world which looks less and less possible for ecological reasons if no others – there could be choice right across the spectrum of human needs and desires. But in practical terms the pursuit of choice is in many areas not only delusory, but actively damaging. Parents ought to have a choice of schools to which to send their children, it is suggested. Fine, if this was a choice between different educational patterns and philosophies offered by equally good, well-funded and well-supported schools. But that is not the way it is, or will be. Choice of schools means choice between markedly better and worse schools within the state system, or between the state system and private schools for those who can afford the latter. Choice then enhances the benefits and advantages already available to the rich and privileged, leaving the children of the poor and the working class even more disadvantaged than they were before. And even if that were not so, even if the choice between good and less good schools was open equally to working-class parents and children, it would still be the case that those who lost out in this process of choice would actually lose because of the wide disparities between schools in the state system. Personally, as a parent, I do not want a choice of schools: I simply want a good local school to which my children can happily go.

The same applies in areas like health care. I do not want or need a choice of doctors, hospitals, consultants. I simply want the local provision to be adequate to deal with such health problems as may arise in my family. The focus on choice and competition, in this area as in others, even without its predictable, inevitable, class dimension, means that some people will lose out, will have to make do with second- or third-class care, attention and facilities; and that runs against the principles of fairness and social justice which are supposed to underpin public services like the National Health Service and state schooling.

In some cases I think we should go further, and recognise (and publicise) the virtues of compulsion. I am thinking in particular of the system of National Insurance. The Major government, following the Thatcherite agenda, is clearly working towards a situation in which each individual is responsible for his or her own insurance in respect of health, benefits and pensions. It would be a matter of free personal choice, and the person who chose not to save or insure against old age would simply have to face the consequences of that choice – destitution or dependence on such charity as might be available. This was the nineteenth century situation, and it is the utopia of the more whole-hearted economic liberals. For all I know, that might have been the situation approved of by Mill, who held as a general principle that it was always better that something is done voluntarily rather than by compulsion or by the state. For my part, I know very well that I am not capable of putting aside money voluntarily towards an old-age pension, for both personal and economic reasons. I suspect that most of us are in the same position. We ought, therefore, to be profoundly grateful that we are *compelled* to make this provision. It seems to be a clear, classic case of a situation in which enlightened self-interest is, or is likely to be, in conflict with our immediate desires and interests, and where the state and the law act on our behalf, in our own long-term interest.

A good deal of law and regulation – traffic regulations, for example – can surely be justified in the same way. All of us benefit, overall, from speed limits, parking regulations, traffic lights, etc., even if there are particular occasions when they are a hindrance to our purposes, which may even be good ones (we are rushing someone to hospital).

And the element of compulsion is welcome, because we could not trust ourselves always to comply with a general rule which was voluntary, even if we recognised its rightness and wisdom. If this is correct, then I think it follows that a good deal of nonsense is talked about the supposed virtues of voluntarism. Choice and competition do not necessarily and in all circumstances benefit the user, or society as a whole. I suspect that there is little or no evidence that the imposition of choice in relation to local bus services since 1986 has resulted in improved services, let alone lower fares. And as for railways, one only has to compare the relative rationality of the oligopoly/monopoly situation that emerged in twentieth-century Britain with the costly and destructive absurdities of nineteenth-century competition, when two or three different companies would all construct their separate routes and run their separate trains between, let us say, Nottingham and Sheffield, or even London and Manchester. Similarly, if we had genuine competition between the various private telephone companies, they would presumably all be digging up the roads to lay their separate cables to their customers. Thank God for regulation and quasi-monopoly.

So strongly has the current run against 'statism' and planning in recent years, even on the Left, that it has become difficult to say a word in defence of the conscious rationality of planning as opposed to the supposedly self-regulating freedom and democracy of market choice. It is time, and past time, to buck this absurd trend, and to reassert the principle that there are many situations in which publicly owned and controlled monopoly – with whatever safeguards and mechanisms are necessary to provide for accountability and openness – is the best way of ensuring fair and efficient provision for the public.

The pernicious effects of individualism can also be perceived in the definitions of well-being, or well-offness, which Labour as much as the parties to its Right has employed in recent years. The claim, during the 1992 election, that eight out of ten families would be better off as a result of Labour's tax plans simply accepted the conservative (and Conservative) definition of being better off in terms of having more money in your pocket or pay packet. But it is and always has been of the essence of social democracy – let alone anything more radical – to put forward a definition of well-being which is *not* so crudely and narrowly defined, which recognises that you can be better off in real terms, in terms of having a better standard of living, even if, as a result of taxation, you have less money in your pocket. Money in your pocket will not, unless you are phenomenally rich, buy you a park, swings and a slide, or an art gallery or museum, let alone a clean water supply or drains, or paved roads, or street lighting, etc., etc.

All this is elementary, and was understood more than a century ago by the first Fabians. It is understood well enough in principle even by today's Labour Party; and it is understood by the people who have shown, in countless surveys, that they are in principle willing to pay higher taxes as the price of better public services, and who also responded positively to what I thought was the Liberal Democrats' admirably open policy of proposing to add a penny to income tax to pay for improvements in education. It is therefore all the more regrettable that the Labour Party, which ought to and probably does know better, should have conceded so much – and in vain – to crude individualist definitions of well-being in terms of post-tax money incomes.

But the most important choice is not that between alternative definitions of individual well-being – a way of thinking that might, and in the case of a minority actually does, lead some people to calculate, perhaps correctly, that they are better off with more money, since they can always buy better education, more prompt health care, and so forth, while relying on taxation to provide them with drains, roads, street lighting, museums and other services. So long as one is content to argue on the terrain of self-interest, there is no answer to such calculations; and in real politics, it has to be accepted that in radically unequal capitalist societies there will always be substantial numbers of people who will think and act on such a basis.

The only long-term hope for socialism or even social democracy lies in persuading significant numbers of people to look beyond simple and basic calculations of self-interest, and to consider how their own good and welfare, in general terms if not specific ones, are bound up with the good of society as a whole – in a word, with the common good; to the extent that they will even be prepared to put that good before and above their own immediate interest and benefit, provided always that basic principles of fairness and social justice are being observed. That cumbersome and qualified statement reflects, in a rather unsatisfactory way, some of the difficulties which nevertheless attach to any idea of the general interest or the common good.

Everyone is aware of the ways in which such concepts or phrases are exploited and abused. In British politics these usually take the form of invocations of 'the national interest', in the name of which wages have to be kept low, or public expenditure has to be cut back, or pension and benefit increases withheld or postponed. Invariably these sacrifices are called for from, or imposed upon, those who have least in absolute terms to sacrifice but most, proportionally, to lose. All too often it has been a Labour Government which has required such sacrifices.

People are rightly cynical, or at least sceptical, about such rhetoric. It is the kind of thing that gives 'the common good' a bad name, and it prompts the kind of questions that Bentham undoubtedly would have asked. Who gains, exactly, from 'the national interest'? Which individuals actually benefit, and how many? There must be a relationship between such supposed general benefits and actual tangible benefits to actual people.

On the other hand, this line of scepticism can easily be carried to individualist extremes. Thus Isaiah Berlin has quoted Bentham with approval on the absurdity of preferring 'the man who is not to him who is', and of 'torment[ing] the living, under pretence of promoting the happiness of them who are not born, and who may never be born'.[4] The idea that those who are yet unborn are some kind of 'metaphysical' invention, who ought to be disregarded by the 'empirical' liberal, is not only absurd – it is irresponsible in the extreme. We have to bear in mind the interests of future generations and make provision for them; and in fact this *is* done, however inadequately. Ecologists and 'greens' have rightly drawn our attention to how much more needs to be done in this respect, how we can no longer continue to exploit and abuse the natural environment of the planet without endangering the very survival of the human species. This may mean sacrifices in the present for the sake of that future. Such sacrifices cannot be called for or justified in terms of the self-interest of existing persons, but only in terms of some such concept as the common good. So, although it is undeniable that such ideas are exploited in unjustifiable ways by unscrupulous politicians, it is nevertheless also the case that they are meaningful, and cannot be dispensed with by any enlightened or far-sighted politics.

Not long ago I got involved in an argument in the press with a free market opponent of public subsidy for opera (which happens to be a particular interest of mine). He summed up my position (I quote from memory) as 'Mr Arblaster thinks that other people should pay for his pleasures'. He obviously thought this was a terrific put-down, but he was quite right. I do, just as I think that we, as tax- and rate-payers, should also pay for parks, and swimming pools and libraries, even if, as in the case of swimming pools, I do not myself use them. The logic of his approach is a mean-minded self-interest: 'why should I pay for facilities and services which I do not personally use or benefit from?' Thanks to the revival of economic liberalism, this kind of petty selfishness is now far more common in British society. In the end it would mean that those adults who are not parents or whose children have derived all the benefit they could from the educational system, and who had done the same themselves, would claim that they ought not to be supporting the education of other people and other people's children. The healthy person would resent helping to pay for the care of the chronically sick. And so on. Mean-minded examples can easily be multiplied.

I do not believe we can have such a thing as a society at all without the recognition that there are certain common goods which have to be provided collectively and without accepting that the provision of these common goods may well benefit some people, or some groups, more than others. The second point is important because it implies a recognition of the plural character of society. It avoids the trap of identifying the common good with the good or benefit of all or of the majority. It simply asserts the principle that society accepts that there are a range of institutions and services to which it commits itself collectively, whether because, as in the cases of health, education and clean water, they are indispensable to any decent human life, or because they are part of what makes up 'the quality of life' – as is the case with libraries, theatres and opera companies.

I have argued that individualism – at least of the kind portrayed here – is destructive of the general good and even, in some cases, of personal happiness. I also want to suggest that pluralism does not offer us a way of avoiding the notion of the common good. Of course it is important, as was indicated in the previous paragraph, that the variety of interests, cultures and life patterns within any large-scale modern society should be recognised and accepted as legitimate. And in fact even the established democracies of the West continue to resist the logic of pluralism in many ways – for example in claims that Britain is essentially a Christian country, or that the United States is essentially an English-speaking society.

Much more could be said along those lines. But still, when all is said and done, there are some questions of value which have to be resolved collectively in one direction or another. A society cannot be totally pluralistic or totally tolerant without disintegrating. For example, it has to make some collective decisions about the kind of education it wants its children to get. This issue is currently raised by the demand that the state should legitimate and subsidise Muslim schools as it does Anglican, Catholic, Non-conformist and Jewish schools. Put that way, it sounds like a reasonable demand, given that, unlike the United States, we do not require education to be conducted on a secular basis. But the problematic aspect of the demand lies in the kind of education that strict Muslims may want to give their female children. If it is an education in direct conflict with the principle of genuinely equal opportunities for men and women, then it is not a kind of education which this society can permit.

There are plenty of other issues of this kind. Abortion is another obvious case, which is dividing Irish society in a very sharp way. It is an issue which has to be resolved one way or the other. You either have a society based on Catholic principles, which disallows abortion under all or most circumstances, or you have a liberal society which accepts that there is at least a limited right to abortion for those who do not have moral or religious objections to it. Certain decisions have to be made by or on behalf of the whole society – and a referendum may be the effective as well as the most democratic way of making such decisions. These decisions then represent that society's most central or fundamental values, its own perception of its common good. Pluralism does not enable us to evade those decisions and commitments.

The argument here is that no society, even the most liberal, can dispense with some conception of the common good, which will be an expression of its collective values – values that will probably not be universally shared. My further argument has been that this is not, as liberals, and certainly economic liberals, may think, a necessary evil, but a positive virtue in society. Only a society with a strong and positive conception of, and commitment to, the common good can avoid declining into the jungle which is produced by the dominance of individualism. That jungle exists, more or less, in the United States and, for all I know, in other advanced capitalist societies. Some parts of the jungle are quite attractive. It is possible to construct – quite literally – protected enclaves within which life can be pleasant and prosperous. But the stockaded mansions of Beverly Hills and the well-guarded suburban housing developments are themselves an expression of a society which has been atomised and fragmented by the uninhibited pursuit of self-interest, with all the callousness, ruthlessness and, ultimately, lawlessness that that implies. Outside the stockades there is squalor, decay, despair and crime. That is the direction in which Britain, under its Thatcherite and post-Thatcherite leadership, is steadily moving; and it is no wonder, as Martin Hollis points out in his essay, that the traditionalist and perceptive Tories are worried, and have made efforts to breathe life into the dying concept of 'citizenship'. But the jungle has no citizens, only inhabitants. To have citizens you need a city, a *polis*, a place with common goals and a sense of its collective common good. Despite the siren voices of the centrists who, in the wake of Labour's election defeat are urging – as they always do – *more* concessions to individualism and further dilution, if not outright renunciation, of collectivism, the purpose of socialism remains to tame and civilise the jungle, not to compete in offering tastier bait to the wild animals which inhabit it.

NOTES

1. See the citations from the *Financial Times, The Economist,* and *The Spectator,* by Robin Blackburn in 'The Ruins of Westminster', *New Left Review* 191, (January–February 1992) p. 8.
2. I have here and in what follows recycled some material from my *The Rise and Decline of Western Liberalism* (Oxford, Blackwell, 1984) pp. 15–16 and 22.
3. See Hannah Arendt, *The Human Condition* (Chicago, University of Chicago Press, 1958) p. 38.
4. Isaiah Berlin, *Four Essays on Liberty* (Oxford, Oxford University Press, 1969) footnote, p. 171.

2

Socialism and common ownership: an historical perspective

LESLIE MACFARLANE

Though the words 'socialism' and 'communism' emerged in the 1830s in France and England to denote the distinctive nature of the doctrines of particular thinkers and their followers who aimed to rebuild society on the basis of co-operation and the collective furtherance of common interests, the conceptions which underlay such doctrines were many and varied. In this essay I am concerned with one of the most influential of these conceptions, that of common ownership, which has a long and chequered history spanning over 2,000 years and which became central to the socialist parties which emerged in the late nineteenth century.

Though my emphasis will be on the various conceptions of common ownership found in different periods and situations, I shall be particularly concerned with the movements and organisations to which these conceptions gave birth. What I aim to provide are historical insights into the impact of the concept of common ownership over the centuries and the problems which emerged with its incorporation into the doctrines of socialist parties. Geographically, I have restricted my attention, after a brief look at fifth-century Athens, to Western Christendom up to the the fifteenth century, Germany and Central Europe in the sixteenth century, England in the seventeenth and eighteenth centuries and to Britain, Germany and Sweden in the nineteenth and twentieth centuries.

Common sharing and common ownership

The conception of common ownership of the resources required to sustain the life of a community's members, as a natural and necessary condition of social harmony and well-being, is to be found in many cultures. The origins of these conceptions can rarely, if ever, be established, though they often find expression in myths of a Golden Age which may yet be capable of recall. Myths of this character were to be found in ancient Greece. Alfred Zimmern wrote of it as 'a world in which public ownership, and even complete communism, seem to serious people more natural and satisfactory and in harmony with the past than the "absolute rights" of the individual property owner.' What mattered, Zimmern argued, was not whether the Greeks in prehistoric times had actually lived in a state of communism, but that they believed this to be the case.[1]

Between the end of the fifth century and the beginning of the fourth century BC there was considerable radical speculation in Athens about the idea of communal property. Aristophanes' satirical play, *Ecclesiazusae*, held up to ridicule an Athens under a system of community of wives and property. More seriously Phaleas of Chalcedon proposed a model state based on equalisation of property in land to relieve the economic plight of the poor, which he saw as the major source of civil dissension, and on equality of access to a common form of education.[2] Phaleas' remedy of redistributing land from rich to poor was to be advocated on countless occasions during the succeeding centuries and was, almost always, far more attractive to landless labourers and poor peasants than common ownership.

In *The Republic*, Plato sketched a much more radical and original scheme than Phaleas had, based not on removing class barriers but on institutionalising a two-class system: a dominant class of Guardians, divided into rulers (women would be eligible) and warriors, and a subordinate labouring class of farmers and artisans. The Guardians would live in common barracks, eat together at common table and own no personal property of any kind. Male and female Guardians would mate together, under strictly controlled conditions, to ensure a sufficient supply of high-quality children to be brought up to serve as the future ruling élite. No child would know its parents and no parent its child. The Guardians, removed from the temptations and distractions of family and possessions, would be able to devote themselves exclusively to promoting the good of the state. Though *The Republic* is widely regarded as the most important early model of a society based on common ownership and common sharing (Koinōnia), the community of property proposed is restricted to the Guardian class. There is no common ownership of land or other property, all of which remains in the private possession of individual farmers and artisans, who are required to hand over part of their products to supply the Guardians' common table and other needs. Private, not communal, ownership is the economic basis of the state proposed in *The Republic*. Plato's concerns are quite alien to those of latter-day communitarians and socialists.

The growing impact of calls for common sharing and common ownership of property in western Europe during the centuries that followed owed very little to Plato's *Republic* (not translated into Latin until 1477) and almost everything to Christian teaching on wealth and poverty. This derived from Christ's own message in the Gospels that wealth was a barrier to salvation (Matthew 19:21), but even more to the espousal of common-sharing in The Acts of the Apostles. In Acts 4:32–35 it is recorded that those newly converted and baptised by Peter and John into the Judean Church 'were of one heart and of one soul: neither said any of them that ought of the things which he possessed was his own; but they had all things common ... Neither was there any among them that lacked: for as many as were possessors of land or houses sold them and brought the prices of the things that were sold: And laid them at the apostles' feet: and distribution was made unto every man according as he had need.'

Though there is no evidence, outside Judea, of Christian communities being set up on the basis of community of possessions, prominent Christian teachers later urged the need to return to the communal practices of the early church. Thus John Chrysostom of Antioch in the fourth century preached:

> For 'mine' and 'thine' – those chilling words which introduce innumerable wars in the world – should be eliminated from the holy church. The poor would not envy the rich, because there would be no rich. Neither would the poor be despised by the rich; for there would be no poor. All things would be in common.[3]

In a bizarre development, the force of Acts 4 was reinforced around 850 when a French monk incorporated them into a Fifth Epistle of Pope Clement, a first-century Bishop of Rome held to have been a pupil of St Peter himself. The Epistle fathered on Pope Clement a much earlier attribution to a Greek philosopher that 'just as the air cannot be divided up, nor the splendours of the sun, so the other things which are given in this world to be held in common by all ought not to be divided up, but really ought to be held in common.' The false Fifth Epistle had great authority and influence until it was discredited in the sixteenth century.

Mainstream early Christian teaching saw private ownership of property not as natural or God-ordained, but as a result of the Fall of Man from Grace. St Ambrose and St Augustine, two of the most celebrated early Church Fathers, held that God created the world in such form that Nature's fruits were available to all men for their common possession and enjoyment. It was private avarice and usurption of common rights which gave rise to private property (an assertion which Rousseau was to echo in a sectarian form fourteen hundred years later in his *Essay on Inequality*). Since there was no possibility of returning to the blessed natural condition of common possession that existed before the fall from Grace, those who possessed wealth had a strict Christian obligation to use it for the common good; in particular to relieve the poverty of the poor through charity. St Augustine wrote 'He who uses his wealth badly possesses it wrongfully and wrongful possession means that it is another's property. You see then how many there are who ought to make restitution of another's goods.'[4] In the twelfth century the most celebrated of all medieval Christian theologians, St Thomas Aquinas, was to argue that a man might openly or secretly take another man's property in case of need, whether of himself or others, since in a case of necessity all things are by natural law common.[5]

From the eleventh century onwards monastic communities were set up in many parts of Europe, with their members dedicated to leading a simple Christian way of life, of prayer, devotion and work, sharing under conditions of voluntary poverty such as the early Christians were believed to have practised. St Francis of Assisi's rule of 1221 for the Franciscan Order laid down that 'the friars are to have no property; Franciscan candidates should sell all possessions and give the money to the poor'; though it is unclear whether he intended the Order to renounce common as well as individual possession, retaining only what was necessary to keep themselves alive.[6] In the fourteenth century, controversy arose over the place of mendicancy and poverty in the Church, which became caught up in the deeper controversy over the relative roles of the ecclesiastical and secular authorities in Christian states. Marsilius of Padua in his masterpiece, *Defensor Pacis*, argued that the Franciscan notion of poverty should be applied to the whole Church, as part of his radical claim that the Church was subject to the coercive authority of law and government, with government itself regulated by law made by the whole body of the citizens.

In late fourteenth-century England we find John Wyclif claiming at Oxford to have proved that all things should be held in common. Only common ownership made it possible for all men to be in a state of grace, since in that state a man is master of the whole world and all it contains. In Cambridge the University Chancellor preached powerful sermons presenting the last judgement as the day of vengeance of the poor and weak against their rich and powerful opponents. Given this background it is not surprising to find the Revd. John Ball (reported by Froissart) delivering a sermon to the poor declaring: 'things cannot go well in England nor ever shall until all things are in common and there is neither villein nor noble, but all of us are of one condition', and another to the rebel peasant host at Blackheath in 1381 on the text of the traditional proverb 'When Adam delved and Eve span, Who was then a Gentleman?'[7]

In the fifteenth century millenistic religious movements and sects appeared proclaiming the imminent second coming of Christ. This would be immediately preceded by war, 'abominations of desolation' and 'afflictions such as was not from the beginning of creation', as foretold by Christ in Matthew 24 and Mark 13. Christ would appear with his angels and gather together the elect, a new Golden Age would dawn and the poor would inherit the earth.

A radical group of Hussites, called Taborites (or Saints), emerged in Bohemia who were distinguished from other millenarian groups by their belief that the way had to be cleared for the coming of Christ by a massacre of all sinners, the powerful lords, nobles and rich town merchants who oppressed the poor. When this purification had been completed in Bohemia, the warrior Christ would appear at the head of his army of angels to join the armies of the Saints to defeat the forces of anti-Christ and establish the Millennium on earth. In that blessed condition there would be neither authority nor government, neither taxes nor private property – 'all shall live together as brothers, none shall be subject to another.'

Since the Taborites believed that the day of the Lord was at hand, they saw their immediate task as being the establishment of communities of the elect based on common ownership and common sharing principles. Thousands of peasants and artisans throughout Bohemia and Moravia sold their possessions and paid the proceeds

into communal chests, forming communities intended to be completely egalitarian. The new Golden Age was inaugurated in 1419 in
the newly built fortress city of Tabor where Christ was to manifest
himself. Tabor became the spiritual centre for the whole Taborite
movement.

> As Mine and Thine do not exist at Tabor, but all possession is
> communal, so all people must always hold everything in common;
> and nobody must possess anything of his own; whoever owns private
> property commits a mortal sin.[8]

Although the experiment in communal living in Tabor had soon to
be abandoned, the revolutionary spirit of the Taborites spread to
France and Taborite armies penetrated into Germany. The movement
rapidly declined after military defeat in 1434, but the hopes it raised
lived on, finding striking expression during the German Peasants War
of 1524–5. The goals of the peasants, as set out in the oft-quoted
'Twelve Articles of March 1525', were restricted to the redress of
grievances on such matters as tithe payments, rents, labour services
and appropriation of common lands. But thousands of Thuringian
peasants followed the lead of the celebrated preacher, Thomas
Müntzer, who called on his League of the Elect to rouse the poor to
exterminate lords and princes who used the law to protect the property
they had appropriated from the common people.

Müntzer was captured and killed after a battle in which 5,000
Thuringian peasants were slain. His mantle was taken over by Hans
Hut, a leader of the militant form of Anabaptism which emerged in
this period. Hut added a chiliastic message to the social doctrine of
common ownership of property; a doctrine which all the 40 or so
independent Anabaptist groups saw as the ideal, and which some of
them practised within their own communities. Hut proclaimed himself a prophet sent by God to announce Christ's return to earth at
Whitsuntide 1528, when He would use rebaptised Christians (Saints)
to punish wicked priests and pastors, kings and nobles, to establish a
Millennium of free love and community of possessions. He was killed
in 1527, but militant Anabaptism spread, engendering ever-increasing
persecution. Many Anabaptists fled to join their fellows in Munster
and in a highly charged atmosphere of religious hysteria and apoca-
lyptic visions the town was taken over by the Anabaptists in February
1534. 'Godless' Lutherans and Catholics who would not accept adult
rebaptism were driven out, and their property confiscated and made

available to the poor. Over the next few months private ownership of money, buying and selling of goods and working for money were forbidden, residential property was requisitioned for billeting immigrants, direction of labour was introduced, the cathedral sacked and all books except the Bible burnt.

In April 1534, Jan Bockelson established himself as spiritual dictator and ruler of Munster, dedicated to realising a society in which 'all things were to be in common, there was to be no private property, and nobody was to do any work'.[9] Bockelson claimed divine revelation for the institution of polygamy in the New Jerusalem, as Munster was now called. Those who publicly opposed this flagrant violation of the rigid sexual codes of Anabaptism, rigidly enforced up to that point, were put to death. Bockelson soon had a harem of 15 wives. In September Bockelson had himself proclaimed as King of the New Jerusalem, revealed by God as the Messiah of the Last Days who would be the spiritual and temporal ruler of the whole world – 'One king of righteousness over all'. Bockelson, who was an adroit politician and an able commander, ruled the besieged city until June 1535 when it fell to the besiegers, who put to death all surviving Anabaptists. Militant millenarian Anabaptism declined rapidly and disappeared by the end of the century. Anabaptist communities, some based on common ownership, survived by reverting to pacifist principles and accepting the need to pay taxes to the authorities. In this form the Anabaptists presented no direct threat to the established secular order, but many Catholic and Protestant authorities held that mere adherence to heretical beliefs constituted a threat to society and continued to persecute them.

The English seventeenth-century Revolution and Civil War was a period of social, as well as of political and religious ferment; ferment which found expression in hundreds of printed tracts and pamphlets, and uniquely in the army debates at Putney in October 1647. For the first time, radicals had a forum which could be used to persuade the authorities to bring about major extensions of the franchise, opening up the possibility of securing social and economic reforms through a Parliament representing a much wider range of social groups.

In the Debates, General Ireton attacked the Leveller call for all free-born Englishmen over 21 to be given the franchise. The argument was that this would threaten property, since a Parliament composed of representatives of the propertyless could enact laws to 'vote against all property'.[10] Such a prospect was as unpalatable to the Levellers and their small-holding supporters as to their opponents. Subsequent Leveller declarations laid down that no Parliament would have power 'to level men's Estates, destroy Property or make all things common'. The Levellers criticised the existing Parliament, however, for failing either to open up recently enclosed fens and commons, or to put them to the benefit of the poor.[11]

The cause of common ownership was espoused by the Diggers, the True Levellers, under the leadership of the crusading pamphleteer, Gerrard Winstanley. Over the period 1648–51, he developed the idea of England as a true commonwealth, based on common property, the only remedy for the desperate position of the poor. 'And this is the battle that is fought between the two powers which is property on the one hand, called the devil or covetousness, or community on the other, called Christ or universal love.'[12] Community was the term used in England from the late fourteenth century to refer to a condition where property was held more or less completely in common.[13]

Winstanley hoped that the example set by the tiny scattered bands of Diggers taking over and cultivating waste land might spread throughout England, one third of which he estimated to be uncultivated since the Norman Power took it from the people after the Conquest. In his 'Appeal to all Englishmen' of March 1650, he called on them 'to take Plow and Spade, build and plant, and make waste land fruitful, that there may be no beggar nor idle person among us, for if the waste land of England were manured by her Children, it would become in a few years the richest, the strongest, and most flourishing land in the world.'[14] The True Commonwealth of Freedom based on common ownership which he portrays has an innocent anarchistic flavour – 'if everyone did but quietly enjoy the earth for food and raiment, there would be no wars nor gallows and this action which man calls theft would be no sin.'[15] The breaking up of the Digger settlements by physical force and legal eviction, and the failure of Parliament to redress the grievances of the poor, led Winstanley in desperation in November 1651 to petition Cromwell, as Protector of the Realm, to use 'the power in your hand … to see all burdens taken off your friends the commoners of England' by giving effect to the proposals contained in *The Law of Freedom in a Platform* which he presented to Cromwell.[16]

In the *Platform* Winstanley sets out for the first time a political programme for an alternative society based on common ownership and common sharing, to replace the existing society based on private property and greed. Though Sir Thomas More in *Utopia* had portrayed a society based on common possession, it was not a programme for action as Winstanley's *Platform* was.[17] In Winstanley's commonwealth all members would work in common fields or workshops under the supervision of elected overseers responsible for ensuring compliance with laws relating to such matters as the organisation and control of work and the conveyance of goods produced, and the running of the common storehouses and shops, to which all families would have free access. There would also be laws against idleness, buying and selling, and against hiring labour. Private property would be restricted to the family house and personal possessions. There was to be no place for clergy in the commonwealth, but a prominent role was given to education.

In his letter to Cromwell Winstanley states that the new commonwealth's land should be restricted to 'the ancient commons and waste land, and the lands newly got in by the Armies' victories out of the oppressors' hands' (that is, the Royalists) and be open to use by all who wished to come into the Commonwealth and obey its laws. Those unwilling to join would be left with their own lands and possessions 'till they be willing'.[18] Winstanley was, as ever, concerned to stress that he would not countenance violence or coercion to realise his goals. He relied on the power of reason and on the force of example to move men to follow the path of community and mutual aid laid down by God and by Christ, and to forsake covetousness and self-seeking which were the province of the Devil. His pleas to Cromwell were ignored and Winstanley and his writings disappeared from the scene, to be rediscovered and popularised in the late nineteenth century by, among others, the German Marxist revisionist, Eduard Bernstein. Significantly, Bernstein attested to the influence of New Testament teaching on common ownership in attracting workers and artisans to support the socialist case presented by German Marxist speakers.[19]

Though John Locke lived as a young man through the years of the Civil War and the Commonwealth his writings show little direct evidence of the experience. Locke's theory of property has been presented by Professor C. B. Macpherson as a justification for individual appropriation of property, providing 'a positive moral basis for capitalist society'.[20] But Locke's *Second Treatise of Government* not only echoes some of the demands put forward thirty years earlier by the Levellers for the franchise to be given to all men of property, but provides, in his concept of natural rights and his labour theory of value, foundations for radical proposals for redistributing wealth and relieving property, such as those put forward by Tom Paine in the 1790s and by Hall, Gray and Hodgskin in the 1820s.

Locke's justification of property was that, since the earth and all its fruits had originally been created by God and nature for the use of all men in common, each man was entitled to appropriate such fruits and land as were the products of his own labour subject to there being no waste and 'enough and as good left in common for others'. Although Locke claimed that the limitation of waste was removed by the invention of money, which enabled wealth to be stored, he provided no argument for the removal of the 'sufficiency-for-others' condition. It might, therefore, be argued that this condition could be brought into play if civil society, established to protect men's lives, property and estates, was unable or unwilling to secure to the mass of poor persons the means of sustaining themselves through their own labours. Locke himself asserts that the property rights established by law in civil society are necessarily subject to regulation by law, enacted with the consent of the majority and designed to serve the common good.[21] In these terms the redistribution of land or taxation of wealth through legal enactment could be justified as necessary to secure the elimination of poverty and insecurity, thereby furthering the common good.

The conception of the common good finds powerful expression in the writings of Jean Jacques Rousseau, who insists that it can never be realised until the gross inequalities of wealth, which divide society into the starving subservient poor and the idle dominant rich, are removed. A free political society requires that no man shall be economically dependent on another. The model society he proposes in the *Social Contract* (1762) is one composed of independent farmers and artisans, but with individual property rights where the common interest so requires. In his incomplete *Constitutional Project for Corsica* (1765) Rousseau appears to shift away from the model of a democratic society of small property owners when he declares 'Far from wanting the state to be poor I should like ... for it to run everything, and for each individual to share in the common property only in proportion to his services.' But the creation of a communal society would require the confiscation of the property of existing owners, which was unacceptable to Rousseau. 'No law can despoil any private citizen of any part of his property; the law can merely prevent him from acquiring more.'[22] Rousseau's bold espousal of the virtues of communal ownership is reduced to a modest proposal to build up, in each parish or region, areas of community land from reclaimed waste land, land purchases and through changes in the laws of succession. This community land would be made available either for private cultivation by individuals without land or for collective cultivation by members of the parish or region concerned. He remained committed, however, to the principle put forward in a *Discourse on Political Economy* (1758) that the rich should be heavily taxed to relieve the poverty of the poor and to reduce inequality.

In late eighteenth-century England radical reformers concerned to improve the economic condition of the poor believed that the remedy lay through political reform. John Thelwell, for example, claimed that 'the unrepresentative nature of Parliaments was responsible for the situation in which nine-tenths of the population were condemned to be beasts of burden in order to maintain the privileged position of the other tenth.'[23] Universal suffrage would result in representation of the poor and, in consequence, greater attention to their needs. The few radical social reformers, such as William Ogilvie and Thomas Paine, who saw the need to make changes in the English property structure, had no wish to replace private ownership by common ownership but preferred to redistribute wealth and land to the benefit of the labouring classes. Ogilvie proposed government purchase of estates for division into small farms for renting, while Paine advocated state action to secure a more even distribution of the burden of taxation and the curtailment of landed wealth.

In *Agrarian Justice* (1795) Paine uses the traditional argument that in the original state of nature the earth was common property, to claim that every man was thereby born to 'a joint life partnership in the property of the soil'. From this he deduces 'the first principle of civilisation ... that the condition of every man born into the world, after a state of civilisation commences, ought not to be worse than if he had been born before that period.' But, while private appropriation and improvement of land had bought about an enormous increase in overall wealth, it had left millions of Europeans worse off than the Indians of North America living in a state of nature. Since it was only the value of the improvements to land deriving from cultivation, and not the land itself, which could be claimed as private property, Paine asserted the right of each of those millions deprived of their natural inheritance to the land to indemnification for their loss. On the assumption that cultivation had increased the value of the land ten-fold, and using official figures of national capital value, Paine estimated that a ten per cent tax on the capital values of property would produce sufficient revenue to enable every person on reaching the age of 21 to receive £15, and every person over the age of 50, £10 a year (about half an agricultural worker's yearly earnings), as 'a compensation in part for the loss of his or her natural inheritance by the introduction of landed property'.[24] The ineffectual moral right of the poor to inadequate and ill-distributed charity had to be replaced by the state's assumption of a legal obligation to relieve poverty.

Thomas Spence was one of the few English radical social reformers to advocate the redistribution of the land from rich to poor as the remedy for poverty. Although his agrarian scheme provided for the land to be communally owned, it was not to be communally cultivated, as in Winstanley's scheme, but leased out as smallholdings to tenant farmers. Spence believed that once redistribution was completed England would be and remain a contented land of small peasant farmers. Like other reformers, of this period and later, he failed to take account of the growing importance of rapid commercial and industrial development and of population increase.[25] The promotion of small-holder tenant farming on state land found expression in Chartist programmes of the 1840s and in the objectives of European peasant movements. The radical 1906 programme of the ill-fated Russian Social Revolutionary Party, for example, demanded the appropriation of all privately owned land and its handover to local rural bodies for distribution amongst peasants and farm labourers on a needs basis.

The right to property embodied in the 1789 French Declaration of the Rights of Man and of the Citizen was seen by the leaders of the French Revolution as a right of all men to *own* the property they occupied, not as an entitlement of all men to *possess* property. It was a right which offered nothing to the poor, although the Jacobins took up their cause by demanding that the burden of taxes should be shifted entirely on to the shoulders of the rich. The defeat of the Jacobins, and the resulting disenchantment of wide sections of the urban poor with the outcome of the Revolution, encouraged Babeuf and his followers to plot a seizure of power to give effect to the radical proposals set out in the *Manifesto of the Equals* (1796). The *Manifesto* provided for all property belonging to corporations and enemies of the people to be taken into communal ownership and administered by locally elected officials. The right of inheritance to all remaining private property would be abolished, so that within a generation all property would be communal. Labour would be compulsory for all and the age-old division into rich and poor brought to an end. The plot failed miserably and the conspirators were executed or deported, but their revolutionary 'communist' ideas found political expression in the years after the 1830 revolution in France.

Socialism and socialists

As G. D. H. Cole pointed out in Volume I of *A History of Socialist Thought*, the terms 'socialism' and 'socialist' were first used in France and England in the 1820s and 1830s, the period of emerging capitalism, to apply to the doctrines and adherents of Saint-Simon, Fourier and Robert Owen. While all three asserted that the workers were victims of exploitation, none thought in terms of a new social order arising out of a class struggle between workers and capitalists, nor were they in favour of the expropriation of capital. Saint-Simon wanted workers and employers to co-operate together against the old privileged classes to bring about a new industrial order of large corporate enterprises, financed by the banks, and run by salaried managers in conformity with plans laid down by a central council of managers, bankers and experts. Fourier wished to see society reorganised in communities (phalanstères) where all work would be shared on a voluntary basis. To establish such communities he sought, in vain, to raise investment capital on which interest would be paid out of the proceeds of the work of the communities' members. Robert Owen, having failed to persuade his fellow English capitalists to follow his example and improve the conditions and status of their workers, appealed to rich men and public bodies for money to found his model communities, villages of co-operation, where the application of scientific knowledge would greatly increase output. Like Fourier he was willing to pay investors in his schemes a fixed limited return on their capital. By the late 1830s the terms Owenism and socialism were seen as virtually synonymous in England, leading the Owenites to adopt the name 'socialists' in 1841.

Socialism, wrote G. D. H. Cole, originally 'meant the collective regulation of men's affairs on a co-operative basis, with the happiness and welfare of all as the end in view and on the strengthening of "socialising" influences in the lifetime education of the citizens in co-operative, as against competitive, patterns of behaviour and social attitudes and beliefs.'[26]

The terms 'communism' and 'communist' appeared in France in

the 1830s and were associated both with the word *commune* as the basic unit of self-government and with the conception of a form of society based on a federation of free communes; and with the word *communauté*, of having things in common and of common ownership. It was in this latter sense that the terms *communisme* and *communiste* were applied to Etienne Cabet's theories and followers in the 1840s when the terms came into common usage. Cabet, who was strongly influenced by More's *Utopia* and the writings of Robert Owen, advocated complete socialisation of the means of production and a full communal way of life. The terms 'communist' and 'communism' were also applied retrospectively to Babeuf and his fellow conspirators and their *Manifesto of the Equals* of 1796.

In Germany the secret revolutionary association, the 'League of the Just', set up in Paris in 1836, changed its name in 1847 to the Communist League rather than the Socialist League, because of the former term's stronger association with revolutionary struggle, common ownership of wealth and the conception of government by commune. The celebrated *Manifesto* written by Marx and Engels in 1848 for the League was therefore a 'communist' not a 'socialist' manifesto.[27] But although in 1847–48 the term 'socialist' was commonly seen in England and France as middle class and respectable and the term 'communist' as working class and disreputable, there are dangers in making a sharp distinction between the two terms. The pre-eminent French 'communist', Etienne Cabet, was a Utopian socialist who hoped to realise his goal by setting up small communities overseas, financed by capitalist investment, just as Owen did. Yet in the *Communist Manifesto*, Marx and Engels characterise the theories of Saint-Simon, Fourier and Owen as 'Utopian socialist and communist systems'. Thirty years later Engels, in his highly influential *Socialism: Utopian and Scientific*, wrote of Owen's 'communist' theories. By the 1860s the term 'socialist' had become accepted as the appropriate one to apply to all those political groups and parties dedicated to replacing the capitalist private enterprise economy by the social ownership of the means of production. This remained the position until March 1918 when the Bolshevik leaders of the world's first socialist state changed the name of their party from the Russian Social-Democratic Workers Party to the Russian Communist Party (Bolshevik). A year later the Russian Communist Party organised the Communist International and set about the task of creating communist parties to combat existing socialist parties.

Owenism, Chartism and Marxism

The first reference to the word 'socialism' in England is to be found in a reader's letter to the Owenite journal *New Moral World* in December 1836 referring to that journal as 'the ORGAN OF SOCIALISM'.[28] The Owenite socialists, though in a number of respects heirs to the social radical tradition of Thomas Paine and Thomas Spence, were treading a new and different path under rapidly changing economic and social conditions.

Owenism emerged in the period of rapid industrialisation which followed on the end of the Napoleonic Wars, bringing in its wake misery, hunger, unemployment and discontent on a scale not seen before or since. The distress occasioned and the protest generated derived in particular from the impact of the new capitalism on factory workers and the hordes of displaced hand workers. Owenism took root because it held out the prospect of averting catastrophe by restraining, bypassing or transforming the invading capitalist economy. Following on Owen's failure to persuade his fellow capitalists to humanise capitalism, or to fund the creation of 'Villages of Co-operation' where the unemployed might work on the land to produce food, or at their trades to produce goods for consumption or exchange, Owen set off in 1824 to Indiana to find his own 'New Harmony' community. Though it was not a success, Owen remained convinced of the superiority of the co-operative principle to that of *laissez-faire* capitalism, if only the right conditions for operating it could be found.

The Owenite conception of co-operation appealed to many of the leaders of the trade unions which emerged in the 1820s and 1830s who were desperately looking for a way out of the calamities which had beset their members. The upshot in February 1834 was the decision of union delegates to come together in the Grand National Consolidated Trade Union of Great Britain and Ireland (GNCTU), whose immediate aim was to raise wages and reduce hours; but whose 'great and ultimate object' was to bring about

> A DIFFERENT ORDER OF THINGS, in which the really useful and intelligent part of society only shall have direction of its affairs, and in which well-directed industry and virtue shall meet their just distinction and reward and vicious idleness its merited contempt and destitution.[29]

The delegates resolved to take such measures as would 'afford to the productive classes a complete emancipation from the tyranny of capital and monopoly'. Supremacy of capital 'was to be replaced by the supremacy of labour'.[30]

For the Owenites the supremacy of labour meant the abolition of competition, with the workers in each branch of manufacture organised in national companies, running their own local factories and workshops, and exchanging their goods through labour exchanges, with values determined by their labour content. Small masters and employers would be welcome to join. Cole wrote that 'Owen went about prophesying the downfall of the old immoral order of society and the inauguration of the new within a few months, apparently expecting the employing classes to acquiesce in their overthrow in the face of the workers' refusal to go on working for them.'[31] The half-a-million members who joined the GNCTU in its first few weeks had their hopes quickly dashed, but the belief persisted that it ought to be possible to prevent the spread of the evils of the new unrestrained capitalist system. Their vision of a fairer more egalitarian society, in which all who worked would receive due reward for their labour, was to be realised not through the expropriation of the rich, but by the removal of the political and legal power of the ruling class to exploit the poor. Even in the years of deepest stress and most widespread agitation there were not calls for the mills of the hated 'steam-producing' class to be taken over. 'From the earliest writings of Owen to the last disintegration of Chartism', writes Christopher Hill:

> men thought they could escape from capitalism by building rural co-operative or Communist communities. The hold of this dream over the nascent working class surely owes much to the traditions of Anglo-Saxon freedom, of lost rights and lost property, and to those dying institutions which it was still hoped to revivify.[32]

But, while the Owenites challenged the very nature of the capitalist system of production based on competition and private profit, most workers directed their wrath against the 'capitalists' – an epithet employed at that time not to the whole class of employers, but to grinding, tyrannical employers in general and to the new cotton lords and 'millocrats' in particular. These sentiments found expression within the Chartist movement. As it happens, the First National Petition presented to Parliament in June 1839 was even-handed as between labour and capital, declaring that 'the capital of the master must not be deprived of its due profit' and 'the labour of the workman must no longer be deprived of its due reward'. None the less, at their own convention, delegates resolved that 'neither peace, comfort nor happiness can exist in this country, so long as this system [the new factory system] is allowed to continue'.[33] The factory system attacked by the Chartists and the GNCTU excluded small masters, shop-keepers and self-employed journeymen.

Though the Chartist Petitions of 1839 and 1842 embodied many of the demands and conceptions of late eighteenth-century radicalism, and found no place for the new Owenite socialist doctrines, socialists were active in the Chartist movement. Their influence grew in the 1840s as the movement declined, a decline reflecting an upturn in the economy and a change in the role of the state, which gradually distanced itself from unqualified commitment to *laissez-faire* and the imposition of repressive class legislation, in favour of the promotion of limited reforms beneficial to the lower classes. In these changed circumstances capitalism in Britain at the end of the 1840s could no longer be treated as a dreadful aberration which would either be bypassed and left to wither away or be overwhelmed by some great cataclysmic rising of the working masses with nothing to lose but their chains.[34] By the 1840s the more agrarian Utopian communitarianism which had prevailed within Owenite socialism in the 1820s and 1830s was displaced by the more industrial and worldly 'economic socialism'. Both Owenite conceptions had the same goal of an egalitarian, just and democratic society and both looked to its realisation through some form of collective ownership of the means of production. But whereas the communitarians sought to bring this about through the creation of self-governing co-operative communities, the 'economic socialists' took account increasingly of the new conditions prevailing in the 1840s, and looked to state regulation and control of the economy. The triumph of capitalism and the failure of communitarianism orientated English socialism in a state socialist direction.[35] The fight to displace capitalism would be long and difficult. Socialists would have to win over the working class to the cause of socialism and this would require that a socialist movement provide more than hopes for a new and better social order in the future. Socialists needed a set of demands for reforms in areas central to working-class interests and concerns, for implementation within the existing social order.

Two such programmes were drawn up by Chartist bodies after the fiasco of the Third Chartist Petition of 1848. The first was drafted in 1850 by Bronterre O'Brien for the newly formed National Reform

League and brought together ideas and proposals drawn from a wide range of traditional Radical, Spencean agrarian, Owenite co-operative and French socialist sources. Its most striking feature was the inclusion – alongside the widely accepted Spencean claim for land, as the source of all wealth, to be returned to the people – of proposals for the nationalisation of major utilities vital to the well-being of the whole community. The programme covered the reform of the Poor Law, work or maintenance on fair conditions, state purchase of land for settlement of the unemployed (either in Owenite co-operative communities or in O'Connorite land colonies of tenant proprietors), public credit to encourage co-operative societies and small scale businesses, the establishment of exchanges where the products of the various trades could be exchanged upon a labour or corn basis to replace 'the present reckless system of competitive trading and shopkeeping', government-funded public works, and the gradual nationalisation of land, minerals, mines and fisheries and later of railways, canals, docks, waterworks and other utilities.[36] The programme, written by Ernest Jones for the older and more influential National Charter Association and adopted at its 1851 Convention, was in many respects similar to that of the National Reform League; though with the addition of state support for the aged and infirm. Nationalisation, however, was to be restricted to the land, which was to be purchased by the state as it came on the market, and rented out either as small-holdings to individual tenant farmers, or, as Jones himself preferred, as large farms to agricultural co-operatives.[37] G. D. H. Cole characterises the National Reform Programme as 'a remarkable adumbration of the Socialist programmes of the revival period of the 1880s', while John Saville claims that the National Charter Association's programme was 'a blueprint for the social-democratic state, and its enunciation of principles and policies was not bettered until the twentieth century.'[38]

The socialism of Marx and Engels differed sharply from that of Owenite socialism in that, far from seeing capitalism as an aberration to be avoided if at all possible, they welcomed it as a necessary stage in the economic and social development of society, whose historic role it was to develop the forces of production to the level where everyone's needs were capable of being met. But that possibility could not be realised under a system of private capital ownership based on the exploitation of the propertyless working class. The only way to negate the capitalist system was for the working class to seize power, and to use it to create a socialist society based on the common ownership of the means of production of wealth. This scenario was not, however, seen as universally binding. In their introduction to the 1882 Russian edition of the *Communist Manifesto* Marx and Engels raised the possibility that a revolution in Russia against the Tsarist autocracy, complemented by a proletarian revolution in the West, might enable the Russian system of common ownership of land to serve as the basis for a communist society, avoiding the capitalist stage altogether. But for the countries of western Europe, where capitalism was becoming ever more firmly entrenched, the capitalist stage had to run its course since

> No social order ever perishes before all the productive forces for which there is room in it have developed; and new higher relations of production never appear before the material conditions of their existence have matured in the womb of the old society itself.[39]

In a few countries, such as England and the United States, it might be possible, Marx conceded, for the working class to gain power by constitutional means rather than through revolution; but even if this happened it would have to be prepared to use force against the capitalist class, who would resist any socialist government seeking to expropriate and socialise its capital assets. What form such appropriation might take was never laid down, so much would depend on the specific circumstances of the time. However in the theoretical chapter on socialism in *Socialism: Utopian and Scientific* (1880)[40] Engels stressed that both he and Marx were agreed that state ownership in itself did not constitute socialism, since under a capitalist system, state enterprises serve the economic interests of the dominant economic class. Only if the workers seized control of the state, and subjected all the means of production to social control upon a definite plan tailored to the needs of the community, could state ownership provide a basis for a socialist society.

The revival of British socialism and the formation of the British Labour Party

Interest in socialism began to revive in Britain in the 1870s and 1880s leading to widespread speculation as to how socialism might be realised and the form it should take. John Stuart Mill pointed out in the *Chapters on Socialism*, published six years after his death in 1879, that all the different schools of socialism agreed that the present economic and social order based on the principles of individualism, competition and private ownership of capital had to be replaced by one in which 'production is only carried on upon the common account, and the instruments of production are held as common property.' While sympathetic to these aims and sentiments, Mill rejects as 'chimerical' proposals for 'taking possession of the whole land and capital of the country and beginning at once to administer it on the public account'.[41] Mill favoured a gradual transformation of the capitalist system with exclusive private ownership and control replaced, on the one hand, by co-partnership and profit-sharing, and, on the other, by 'the association of the labourers themselves on terms of equality, collectively owning the capital with which they carry out their operations, and working under managers elected and removable by themselves.'[42]

Though Mill's 'conversion' to socialism was welcomed by socialists, his conception of a radically modified capitalism with a mixture of co-operative ownership and co-partnership with worker participation, rather than full socialisation,[43] found little support. The Marxist Social Democratic Federation (1884), the gradualist Fabian Society (1884), and the quasi-anarchistic Hammersmith Socialist Society (founded by William Morris in 1890) issued a joint manifesto on 1 May 1893

> to remind the public once more of what Socialism means to those who are working for the transformation of our present unsocialist state into a collectivist republic, and who are entirely free of the illusion that the amelioration or 'moralisation' of the conditions of capitalist private property can do away with the necessity for abolishing it. Even those readjustments of industry and admini-stration which are Socialist in form will not be permanently useful unless the whole state is merged into an organised commonwealth. Municipalisation, for instance, can only be accepted as Socialism on the condition of its forming a part of national and at last international Socialism; in which the workers of all nations ... can federate upon a common basis of the collective ownership of the great means and instruments of the creation and distribution of wealth.[44]

1893 also saw the formation of the Independent Labour Party (ILP) which adopted as its object 'the collective ownership of all the means of production, distribution and exchange'. Unlike the other socialist bodies the ILP was broadly based, with growing trade union support, and with its political conceptions derived far more from the Fabian

Society than from Marx. Like the Fabian Society, the ILP believed in gradualism, the possibility of securing partial reforms and improvements from bourgeois governments; though it never accepted, as did some Fabian leaders, that a Liberal Party permeated with Fabian doctrines would be a more effective vehicle for the gradual realisation of socialism than an independent party of the working class. The ILP promoted, with union support, the creation in 1901 of the Labour Representation Committee (LRC) to secure the election of independent Labour Members of Parliament. In 1906 the LRC changed its name to the Labour Party and in 1908 its Annual Conference passed a resolution that 'the Labour Party should have as a definite object the socialisation of the means of production, distribution and exchange, to be controlled by a democratic state in the interests of the entire community, and the complete emancipation of Labour from the domination of capitalism and landlordism.'[45] The principle embodied in this resolution was incorporated in Clause 3.1 (later Clause 4) of the Party's Objects at the February 1918 Labour Party Conference:

> To secure for the producers by hand and by brain the full fruits of their industry and the most equitable distribution thereof that may be possible upon the basis of the common ownership of the means of production and the best attainable system of public administration and control of each industry or service.[46]

The June 1918 Conference pledged the Labour Party to campaign for the immediate nationalisation of the railways, mines, canals and electricity generation.

State socialism and revisionism in the German Social Democratic Party

At the end of the nineteenth century it was not Britain but Germany which was the great centre of the socialist revival in Europe. In 1891 the German Social Democratic Party (SPD) adopted the Erfurt Programme drafted by Bernstein and Kautsky in consultation with Engels.

The Programme called for 'the transformation of the capitalist private ownership of the means of production ... into social ownership and the conversion of commodity production into socialist production.'[47] The programme laid down a list of immediate demands to be fought for in advance of the achievement of political power, a list which did not include proposals for nationalisation. Though this omission reflects Engels' general strictures against state capitalism, it derived more directly from the politics pursued by Bismarck in the authoritarian, militaristic German empire. In 1876 the SPD Congress opposed Bismarck's proposals for the nationalisation of the railways on the grounds that they would advance 'the interests of the class and militaristic state'.[48] Bismarckianism was at its height in the years 1878–90 when the anti-socialist laws were in force. The laws outlawed the SPD and associated SPD trade unions, banned the SPD press and resulted in the imprisonment of hundreds of SPD members and the self-exile of the leaders. Both Auguste Bebel, Party leader, and Eduard Bernstein strongly opposed a proposal, put forward by Engels in 1884, that the SPD faction in the Reichstag support Bismarck's proposed steamship subsidy in return for a similar subsidy to buy up empty factories and lease agricultural estates to set up workers' co-operatives, which would be given priority over capitalist firms in bidding for public contracts. Though Engels did not expect such a proposal would be agreed to, he claimed that its implementation could 'lead gradually to a transition of the total production into co-operative [production]'.[49] This suggested the possibility of using the capitalist state machine to open up the road to socialism, reminiscent of the proposals advocated by the German socialist leader Ferdinand Lassalle in the 1860s and bitterly opposed by Marx and Engels.

German state socialism was seen by Marxists as a reactionary doctrine advocated by conservative politicians and academics with the aim of winning over the working class to support the existing social structure of society, by state measures of social welfare and limited nationalisation or municipalisation of private enterprises, where this would be likely to increase efficiency. Bismarck's measures to give effect to these objectives in the early 1880s raised the question of state socialism inside the SPD, whose more moderate Reichstag members were attracted by the prospect of government legislation to improve the conditions of the working class. The majority view, advocated by Bebel and Bernstein, prevailed – state nationalisation or municipalisation would retard rather than advance the cause of socialism.[50]

Bernstein, unlike the other SPD leaders, was not permitted to return to Germany after the ban on the party was lifted in 1890. He remained behind in England, where he enjoyed friendly relations with leading Fabians and New Liberal radical intellectuals. In 1898 *Neue Zeit*, edited by Karl Kautsky, published a series of articles on socialism by Bernstein which were to rock the SPD to its ideological roots. Bernstein questioned the entrenched conception that socialism would be realised through an economic crisis of such magnitude and severity, generating such misery and hardship for the whole working class as to drive them into mass political action, bringing about the economic collapse of the capitalist system and the coming to power of a Social Democratic Government. If the SPD were to come to power under such circumstances the result would be chaos. It would be impossible, given the tens of thousands of economic enterprises involved, for an SPD government 'to abolish capitalism by decree, nor could it manage without it, but neither could it guarantee capitalism the security which it needs to fulfil its functions. This contradiction would inevitably destroy Social Democracy'.[51] Alternatively it would 'be forced to desert its proper course and act as a restraining rather than a revolutionary force'.[52] But the statistical evidence available provided no support for the thesis of an imminent capitalist collapse – 'bourgeois society is still capable of considerable expansion and ... can undergo a good many changes of form before it finally "collapses"', many years hence.[53] In the meantime the SPD should accept its role as an opposition party to secure reforms within the existing system.

> The steady expansion of the sphere of social obligation ... the extension of the right of society ... to regulate economic life, the growth of democratic self-government in municipality, district and province, and the extended responsibilities of these bodies ... mean development towards socialism ... or piecemeal socialism. The transfer of companies from private to public ownership will naturally accompany this development, but it can only proceed by degrees.[54]

Bernstein quoted from the Erfurt Programme: it was only through socialisation that the means of production could 'be changed from a source of misery and oppression of the exploited classes to *one of well being and harmonious development*'. He insisted that it was the well-being of the exploited, not socialisation, that was the aim of the socialist movement. 'But for this reason', he continued,

> the socialisation of the means of production is, from a socialist point of view worth pursuing only when, and to the extent that, we may reasonably expect it to lead to the fulfilment of this aim. In this sense I do indeed hold the views that a good Factory Act contains more socialism than the nationalisation of a whole group of factories.[55]

It is not surprising that Bernstein should have written of himself to Bebel in terms that might be paraphrased as 'a certain Marxist who went down from Berlin to London and fell amongst Fabians'.

At the Stuttgart Congress in October 1898, Kautsky, the party's leading theoretician, broke his silence and argued that Bernstein's espousal of a gradual peaceful transformation of capitalism into socialism was valid for England but not for Germany. England alone in Europe had no standing army, no bureaucracy and no peasantry and was the exception to the rule of proletarian revolution in 1898, as it had been for Marx in 1872.[56] Bernstein's revisionist theories were decisively rejected.

Throughout the period of the revisionist controversy, down to the German November 1918 Revolution, Kautsky maintained the position he had taken up in his 1892 commentary on *Das Erfurter Programm*. Proposals for the nationalisation of industry had no place in SPD policy since the modern capitalist state nationalises industries not 'for the purpose of restricting capitalist exploitation but for the purpose of protecting the capitalist system and establishing it upon a firmer basis, or for the purpose of itself taking a hand in the exploitation of labour and increasing its own revenues.'[57] The aim of socialism, on the other hand, was 'to place the workers in possession of the means of production' by establishing co-operative production under co-operative ownership in large industrial and agricultural enterprises. Small industrialists and small farmers could be left to their own devices, since small-scale production presented no threat to a socialist society and was, in any case, 'doomed to disappear' within a short time.[58]

Kautsky's opposition in principle to state socialist measures in Germany was criticised in 1892 by Georg von Vollmar, 'the first of the revisionists'. Vollmar argued that the SPD's objection to the class nature of the German state did not justify opposing all extensions of public enterprise. Socialisation measures, such as railway nationalisation, benefited all members of the community, not just the capitalist class.[59] Bernstein came round to this point of view and in the revisionist alternative programme, which he put forward in 1909 as a replacement for the 1891 Erfurt Programme, he called for the transfer of monopolies to social ownership and state control over all fields of production.[60]

Though revolutionary Marxism outwardly triumphed over revisionism at successive SPD congresses, the practice of the Party became increasingly reformist in character. This widening gap between theory and practice, though strongly criticised by Rosa Luxemburg, largely passed unnoticed by ordinary party members, the great majority of whom saw the growth in party membership and in the SPD vote in Reichstag elections (where the SPD was the largest party) as a firm indication that the party was working on the correct lines and would soon achieve political power. Marxist revolutionary theory provided the workers with a sense of solidarity and purpose against a capitalist society dedicated to their repression, but doomed to be superseded by socialism. Reformist practice was the 'here and now' activity of tens of thousands of party members in trade unions, local councils, and SPD social, educational, cultural and recreational associations, dedicated to improving the economic lot of ordinary working people. Marxist theory and reformist practice were compatible as long as reformism was accepted by the majority in the SPD as furthering the end of revolution. When the SPD split in 1917, however, the break was not a clean one between revisionists and revolutionaries, but between the majority who continued to support the German government in its prosecution of the war and those who wanted the SPD to reassert its independence as an opposition party. While some representatives of the radical Left remained with the majority SPD, both Kautsky and Bernstein joined the breakaway Independent SPD (Independent Socialists).

The November 1918 Revolution in Germany, following on the heels of the Bolshevik Revolution of October 1917, radicalised wide sections of the German working class. The provisional Government of Majority Social Democrats and Independent Socialists supported socialisation measures but urged that priority had to be given to getting the shattered economy working again. The workers' councils responded with the slogan 'No increased production without socialisation'. A Commission for Socialisation was appointed by the Provisional Government with Kautsky as its chairman. With the workers in power the way was now open, Kautsky believed, for the establishment of a democratic republic, 'the indispensable political foundation of the new collectivist order'.[61] Though Kautsky accepted that the revival of production, rather than the form of ownership of the productive forces, was the more pressing problem, this did not entail leaving socialisation until production had fully revived. The Commission endorsed Kautsky's conception and recommended the socialisation, with compensation, of monopolistic sectors of the economy, particularly coal and iron mining, large estates and forests, insurance companies and mortgage banks. The governing bodies of the new socialised undertakings should include elected worker representatives with 'a special and decisive influence in determining wages, working hours and conditions of safety' and access to company information.[62]

With the resignation of the Independent Socialist members from the coalition provisional government at the end of December, the government of Majority Socialists showed no interest in implementing the Socialisation Commission's proposals. The January 1919 elections failed to produce a socialist majority, and since the Independent Socialists refused to enter a coalition government with the Majority Socialists, the latter decided to form a coalition with the Centre Party and Democratic Party. The coalition was based on acceptance by these two parties of a republican form of government, severe measures against wealth and property in budgetary policy, and a far-reaching social policy to include measures of socialisation. In March 1919 the National Assembly passed a Socialisation Law empowering the State, by legislation and with adequate compensation, 'to transfer to public ownership such economic enterprises as lend themselves to nationalisation, particularly those involved with the extraction of mineral resources and the exploitation of natural power'.[63] Specific laws regulating the coal, potash and electricity industries were passed under the Socialisation Law provisions, though to little effect, and the provisions themselves were incorporated into the Weimar Constitution of July 1919. The SPD was never in a position to appeal to the Constitution as a basis for a thoroughgoing socialisation programme, as it was never elected to power during the life of the Weimar Republic.

In 1921 Kautsky visited Georgia, which had a Menshevik Social Democratic government, soon to be overthrown by the Bolshevik Red Army. The contrast between the policies pursued by Bolshevik Russia and Menshevik Georgia convinced Kautsky that socialist governments had to recognise that capitalism could not be abolished at a stroke (as the Bolsheviks had attempted until Lenin's inauguration, in March 1921, of the New Economic Policy). 'Socialist production,' Kautsky wrote, 'can only be introduced gradually, after careful preparation. If the wheels of production are not to come to a halt ... capitalist production must be kept going in those branches of production which are not yet socialised, and in some branches of industry it may survive for a generation.'[64]

The SPD reiterated its commitment to its Marxist principles at its

1921 Gorlitz Conference, calling for 'the progressive transformation of the entire capitalist economy into a Socialist economy operated for the common good, as the necessary means of freeing the working people from the fetters of the rule of capital, of increasing productive output, of leading mankind onward and upward to higher forms of economic and moral co-operation.' The negation of capitalism remained the final goal of the SPD throughout the period of Nazi rule and into the immediate post-war era. In a famous speech at Kiel in October 1945, Karl Schumacher, the most respected of the surviving SPD leaders, called for 'the abolition of capitalist exploitation and the transfer of the means of production from the control of the big proprietors to social ownership'. Schumacher prophesied that without 'drastic socialisation' and a planned economy, economic reconstruction would be impossible and that 'in this country capitalism and democracy cannot co-exist'.[65] The rapid economic and political progress made by Germany from the late forties onwards led the SPD to modify its strict adherence to the principles of Erfurt Marxism. It declared its commitment to 'small and medium scale private ownership' (1952) and to the principle of 'competition wherever possible, planning wherever necessary' (1954).[66] In the new Bad Godesberg Programme, adopted in 1959, public ownership is presented as 'a legitimate form of public control which no modern state can do without', but as 'an appropriate and necessary means' only where 'sound economic relations cannot be guaranteed by other means'.[67] The once-defiant bastion of revolutionary Marxism now proclaimed its adherence to democratic socialism as the 'fight for freedom and justice' within a mixed economy where capitalism could claim 'protection by society as long as it does not hinder the establishment of social justice'.[68]

Swedish socialism[69]

The Swedish Social Democratic Party (SAP) was set up in 1889. In 1897 it adopted a Marxist-oriented programme based on the 1891 Erfurt Programme of the German SPD, but with the important proviso that socialisation in Sweden would have to be carried out gradually and peacefully. Following on gains in the 1917 elections the SAP entered into coalition with the Liberals.

In May 1919 the SAP executive met to clarify how the party's commitment to the principle of socialisation might be translated into concrete measures. Most of the executive members were hesitant about embarking on specific projects because of doubts as to the economic advantages claimed for socialisation, and the political dangers of making socialisation a central feature of the next election programme. Even the two most ardent exponents of socialisation, Gustav Möller and Hjalmar Branting, accepted that such measures would be irrelevant and unacceptable unless they brought about increases in production necessary for the raising of working-class living standards.

Early in 1920 the Liberal-SAP coalition broke up and Branting formed Sweden's first Social Democratic (minority) government. It proceeded cautiously on socialisation, setting up a Socialisation Committee to examine the conditions for, and suitability of, public ownership or control of key resources and means of production. Branting stressed to the Committee the need not to seek the socialisa-tion of all production, but to aim to combine the best of private initiative with public ownership or control. At the 1921 Party Con-ference, however, a programme was adopted declaring that the party's fundamental aim was to entirely reconstruct the economic organisation of bourgeois society and bring about the social liberation of the exploited classes through 'the socialist organisation of society ... a new order of production planned on the basis of the real needs of society'. Though the Programme did not envisage a complete socialisation of all private concerns, it called for 'all necessary natural resources, industrial enterprises, credit institutions, transport and communication routes' to be gradually transferred to the state, and listed natural resources and banks as 'ripe' for early treatment.[70]

Meanwhile the Socialisation Committee continued its work, plod-ding on for 15 years with its voluminous investigations, deliberations and reports, unable to agree on any specific socialisation proposal, save the setting up of a state shoe factory to compete with existing shoe firms. Even this 'socialist mouse' of 1931 was too much for the SAP Executive to stomach. From the writings of Nils Karleby and Rickard Sandler, respectively secretary and chairman of the Socialisation Committee, there emerged a new Swedish conception of socialism as 'a socialised market economy'.[71] Karleby rejected the 'doctrinaire scholasticism' of the German SPD in insisting on socialisation of capital and central planning of production as the essential require-ments of a socialist society. Instead he argued the case for a gradual socialisation and redistribution of purchasing power, of educational opportunity and of property rights and the creation of a broad category of social welfare rights. These measures would enable the workers to be full participants in the benefits of free choice offered by a market economy. Sandler pressed for 'an idea of socialisation that in principle will preserve the goods market, the labour market and the capital market, although it will change the conditions under which markets currently operate,' with private enterprise required to 'accustom itself to the idea that the resources over which it disposes are in reality "public means"'.[72] Tim Tilton claims that Sandler elaborated one of the central but least understood conceptions of Swedish Social Democracy,

> the use of politics not to abolish or supersede markets, *but to make them work better*, providing 'the logic that underlines such distinctive Swedish policies as active labour market policy, investment reserves, solidaristic wage policy, public capital formation, and even ... wage-earner funds'.[73]

In 1944 the SAP issued a new radical party programme which declared the party's long-term aim to be 'the economic organisation of bourgeois society, so that the right of self-determination over production is placed in the hands of the entire people, the majority is liberated from dependence on a few owners of capital'. The SAP also issued a less radical *Post-War Programme* for the coming election. It promised socialisation of inefficient monopolies and industries and the creation of corporate bodies – representing government, private and co-operative enterprises and employers – to co-ordinate and plan pro-duction. Faced, however, with the unexpected problem of inflation, instead of the expected problem of unemployment, and a fall in the SAP vote in 1946, the SAP government abandoned the socialisation proposals of the *Post-War Programme*, though not the principle of socialisation as a long-term aim.[74]

In the years after World War II, Sweden, instead of being one of the poorest countries in Western Europe (as it had been immediately after World War I) emerged under Social Democratic government[75] as one of the richest and most egalitarian societies in the world. To maintain this enviable position, SAP governments had to promote economic policies which enabled leading Swedish companies to compete effec-tively in world markets, in the face of strong competition from the United States and increasingly from Germany and Japan. To this end Social Democratic governments in the 1950s modified their taxation policies, originally conceived to promote a redistribution of wealth

and deconcentration of capital, into one designed to dampen fluctua-
tions in the business cycle and encourage investment in Sweden's
largest and most successful companies.[76] Equally important was the
acceptance by the powerful Swedish trade unions and employers'
associations of a national solidaristic wages policy, which recognised
the need to increase economic efficiency and reduced wage differentials
to benefit the lower paid. This required workers in the most successful
industrial sectors to accept lower wage increases than their levels of
productivity would justify – forgoing short-term gains for the longer-
term benefits resulting from high growth and low inflation.[77]

Tage Erlander, Prime Minister of Sweden from 1946 to 1968, had a
major impact on SAP thinking during his period of office and beyond.
Writing in 1973 of the changes which had occurred since the publication of the 1944 Party Programme, he concluded that 'the demand
for socialisation has been pushed into the background. Let private
industry under society's control take care of what it can. Society
should not intervene unless it is necessary'[78] – an echo of the words
and sentiments of the Bad Godesberg Programme adopted by the
German Social Democratic Party in 1959.

Erlander underestimated, however, the continued force of the anti-
capitalist tradition within the SAP, which resurfaced in the radical
report put forward by Rudolf Meidner in 1976 and adopted by the
powerful Swedish blue-collar union (LO), but not by SAP, for the
creation of wage-earner funds. The Meidner Report proposed a 20 per
cent profits tax on private corporations to build up funds to be
administered by the trade unions and used to purchase shares in
Sweden's major companies. It was estimated that in 20 years the
workers' wage-earner funds would have a majority holding in such
companies. The LO trade union journal *FACK* wrote

> Power over people and production belongs to the owners of capital.
> With wage-earner funds the labour movement can repeal this
> injustice. If we do not deprive capital owners of their ownership, we
> can never fundamentally alter society and carry through economic
> democracy.[79]

The owners of industry bitterly attacked the plan as an attempt to
require them to work for their own expropriation, without compensation; while the SAP leaders were apprehensive about its electoral
impact on their more moderate supporters.

The wage-earner funds issue figured prominently in the 1976

election campaign, which resulted in the SAP losing office after 44 years in power, and again in the 1979 election when the SAP suffered a second defeat. When the SAP regained power in the 1982 election it was recognised that this was due principally to the ineptitude of the bourgeois coalition government, and in spite of SAP adherence to a modified form of wage-earner funds. The new SAP government was reluctantly compelled to introduce wage-earner funds legislation, as their proposals for economic recovery required union adherence to a policy of wage restraint. The legislation enacted in 1983 lacked the strength to pave the way to worker ownership of the commanding heights of Swedish capitalism. The funds were to be financed by a 20 per cent tax on profits in excess of 15 to 20 per cent, to allow an 'acceptable' return on capital, and by a small payroll tax. Fund investment in company shares would be limited to not more than 40 per cent in any one company, thereby precluding worker-fund 'takeovers'. The scheme was to run from 1984 to 1991, by which time it was estimated that between five and ten per cent of publicly held shares would be in wage-earner funds.[80]

The opposition parties promised to repeal the funds leglislation as soon as they were returned to office, but in the meantime private companies learned to live with the wage funds tax as just another tax, rather than a threat to their operations and their future. They were reassured, too, by the conciliatory policies adopted by the powerful Finance Minister, Kjell-Olof Feldt, who declared that the government was dependent on managers and employers 'to operate on their own terms, [to] strive for profitability, efficiency and rationality. That they as employers hold down wage demands and wage drift – in short we want them to function as good capitalists.'[81]

The Swedish Social Democrats were in power from 1982 to 1991, when a centre-right 'bourgeois' coalition was formed which promised a retrenchment programme on British Conservative lines, embracing major cuts in public expenditure and privatisation of 35 state-owned companies. No mention was made of the wage-earner funds, doubtless because the existing scheme would come to an end in 1991. In September 1992 the worst economic crisis since the 1920s engulfed Sweden and led to an agreement between the Conservative Prime Minister and the SAP opposition leader for major public expenditure cuts, including welfare benefits, VAT increases, and reductions in employers' social insurance and health contributions; in return for the postponement of privatisation of state companies and the abolition of capital gains tax. This political collaboration broke down in November when the SAP refused to support measures to cut employers' social security contributions still further, while increasing that of employees and reducing unemployment benefits.

Tim Tilton, in his masterly study of *The Political Theory of Swedish Social Democracy*, claims that the Swedish Social Democratic tradition 'has at its core not a vision of a socialist society, but a set of fundamental values, which it applies in an evolving critique of liberal capitalist society'.[82] He identifies five such values:

(i) *Integrative democracy*, directed to extending political democracy into economic and social areas of life with all participating on terms of equality and with a marked preference for consensual democracy.

(ii) *Folkhemmet or society as the 'people's home'*, involving the breaking down of all social and economic barriers which divide citizens into rulers and subjects, rich and poor, the privileged and the unfortunate.

(iii) *Compatibility of equality and economic efficiency*, the latter requiring worker co-operation in managerial decisions and a more solid-aristic wages policy.

(iv) *Property seen as a bundle of rights – functional socialism* – distinguishing which property rights require to be fully socialised, which subject to control or restraint, and which left in private hands to realise particular economic and social objectives.

(v) *Expansion of the public sector to extend freedom of choice*, since the provision of social security, social welfare, full employment and health care increase the opportunities for ordinary people to make meaningful life choices.

The British Labour Party and the path to power and socialism

The prospects of creating a new socialist society, which inspired the German SPD and the Swedish SAP at the end of World War I, also caught the imagination of the British Labour Party. In its 1918 statement *Labour and the New Social Order*, the party dedicated itself to ensuring that the individualistic system of capitalist production 'is buried with the millions whom it has done to death'.[83] In 1923 the Labour Party Conference unanimously resolved that 'the supreme object of the Labour Party should be the supersession of capitalism by

the Socialist Commonwealth'.[84] Philip Snowden moved a motion in
the House of Commons calling for 'the gradual supersession of the
capitalist system' by a new order based 'on the public ownership and
democratic control of the instruments of production and distribution'.[85]
The 1924 Labour government saw no opportunity even to nibble at
the roots of capitalism. Nevertheless, the 1928 programme *Labour
and the Nation*, which R. H. Tawney played a leading role in drafting,
was presented as the road from 'the bankruptcy of capitalism' to 'the
establishment of the Socialist Commonwealth'.[86] The limited proposals for the socialisation of land, coal and power, railways, docks and
harbours would, Ramsay MacDonald stated, occupy Parliament for
many years to come. His Left-wing critics, John Wheatley and James
Maxton, argued that the programme was based on the fallacious
assumption that the Labour Party could run capitalism better than the
Conservatives could. W. J. Brown asserted that the public ownership
measures proposed would serve to provide cheap services to private
industry: 'The result would be not Socialism, but a State-subsidised
Capitalism.'[87]

Following the failure and break-up of the 1929–31 Labour government, the Labour Party turned Leftwards, with Herbert Morrison and
Arthur Henderson at the 1931 Conference calling for less attention to
reform and more to changing the economic system. At the 1933
Conference, Henderson insisted that the capitalist system was breaking
down, facing the world with the alternatives of socialism or capitalist
economic dictatorship – 'We want the maximum socialism in the
minimum time.'[88] A resolution was passed by the conference con-
demning 'all efforts to discredit the practice of socialism in Russia',
whose 'Socialist rulers' were seeking to realise 'a similar economic and
social objective' to that of the British Labour Party.[89]

In 1945 the Labour Party achieved power for the first time as a
majority government. Its manifesto proclaimed its ultimate purpose
to be 'the establishment of the Socialist Commonwealth of Great
Britain, free, democratic, progressive, public-spirited, its material
resources organised in the service of the people'. Many small businesses
could be left alone to get on with their 'useful work'. Some big
businesses were 'not yet ripe for public ownership', but the basic
industries of fuel and power, inland transport, iron and steel, along
with the Bank of England, were 'ripe or over-ripe'.[90] In his report to
the 1947 Conference, Prime Minister Attlee declared that the government's aim in its five-year term of office was to lay the foundations of

the transition from a capitalist to a socialist economy. With the help of the party and the backing of the people it would carry on from there to achieve its long-term goal of a socialist commonwealth.[91] The assumption which lay behind this optimistic appraisal was the belief among party leaders and members that, at the end of its first term, the government would have brought about such improvements in the lives of working men and women that the Tories would never again get back to office. But this was not to be, as the government found itself facing mounting economic difficulties. At the 1948 Conference Morrison recalled: 'In my early days Socialists used to say ... capitalism had solved the problem of production and Socialism would solve that of distribution.' Unfortunately, he told his audience, the former was not true and the success of the Labour government and the prospects for socialism depended on its capacity to promote increased production over the next ten to fifteen years.[82] That increased production would have to come, in the main, from the private sector of the economy. But would successive Labour governments be able to secure continued co-operation from private companies and firms if such governments continued to pursue their declared aim of transforming a predominantly privately-owned economy into a predominantly publicly-owned one? The issue did not arise as the Labour Party suffered three successive election defeats in 1951, 1955 and 1959.

Revisionism and the Labour Party

The electoral defeats of 1951 and 1955 gave rise to renewed debate inside the Labour Party on the question of what had gone wrong with the party during its years in office and what changes should be made in party policy, especially nationalisation policy. The old gap between Left and Right opened up. The Left took the traditionalist stance that the party must rededicate itself to realising its socialist goal of the ownership of the means of production of wealth embodied in clause 4 of the constitution. The Right, the revisionists, argued that the 'nothingless-than-clause-4' approach was historically outdated, economically unnecessary and electorally a liability.

Anthony Crosland was the leading exponent of the revisionist case. In his major work, *The Future of Socialism* (1956), Crosland drew on the experience of Swedish social democracy. He saw Sweden as coming much nearer to the socialist ideal of the good society than any other in that 'it gives a higher priority to social welfare and the social services, it has a greater equality of wealth, it enjoys a harmonious and co-operative pattern of industrial relations, it is characteristically ruled by socialist governments, its cultural record is exceptional.'[93] *The Future of Socialism* was enthusiastically commended by Labour Party moderates and bitterly attacked by Left-wing socialists on its publication, nine months after the Labour Party's 1955 defeat which cost Crosland his own Parliamentary seat. Raymond Plant claimed that, just as Eduard Bernstein had made moral values the centre of socialist revisionism in the German SPD, so 'it was Anthony Crosland who placed the ideals of democratic socialism at the centre of the political agenda' of the British Labour Party.[94]

After a brief survey of the main schools of socialist thought, Crosland concluded that the only element common to them all had been 'the basic aspirations, the underlying moral values'. He identified five such values, all underlaid by a passionate belief in liberty and democracy:

(i) a protest against the poverty and squalor of capitalism;
(ii) a concern for the interests and social welfare of the needy, oppressed or unfortunate;
(iii) a belief in equality and a classless society;
(vi) a rejection of antagonistic competition in favour of the ideals of fraternity and co-operation;
(v) a protest against the economic inefficiencies of capitalism.

Of these five values, the first and the last were of rapidly decreasing relevance in Britain and other west European societies, since 'traditional capitalism had been modified and reformed almost out of existence' – an inflated optimistic assessment which Crosland was later to modify. Positive change had also taken place with respect to the fourth value – society was much less aggressively individualistic than it had been. Although the positive principle of co-operation had made relatively small progress, Crosland felt unable to include the co-operative ideal in what was intended to be a 'definite and practical statement of socialist aims'. His emphasis was, therefore, on aspirations (ii) and (iii). Socialists, he claimed, are distinguished from conservatives by their commitment to giving exceptional priority to the relief of poverty and the elimination of the squalor suffered by the needy, oppressed or unfortunate in society. The sharpest distinction, however, was to be found in the socialist dedication to social equality and a classless society. The socialist seeks a distribution of rewards, status and privileges egalitarian enough to minimise social resentment, to secure justice between individuals and to equalise opportunities; and he seeks to weaken the existing deep-rooted class stratification with its concomitant feelings of envy and inferiority, and its barriers to uninhibited mingling between the classes. This belief in socialist equality, which had been the strongest ethical inspiration of virtually every socialist doctrine, still remains the most characteristic feature of socialist thought today.[95]

Although the worst economic abuses and inefficiences had been corrected, there remained 'a significant residue of distress, resentment and injustice' in British society to be dealt with. It was 'the belief that further changes will appreciably increase personal freedom, social contentment and justice that constitutes the ethical basis for being a socialist'.[96]

The most contentious sections of *The Future of Socialism* were those on nationalisation and public ownership. The success of socialist governments in Sweden and Norway confirmed Crosland's own view 'that wholesale nationalisation is not a necessary condition of greater equality', or 'of creating a socialist society'.[97] The Marxist doctrine of the imminent collapse of capitalism, which almost all socialist writers had endorsed in the 1930s, had proved fallacious. Its adherents, like the majority of German Marxists in the 1890s, had refused to take account of the fundamental changes which had taken place in the character of Western capitalism. Ownership in the 1950s had little to do with economic efficiency or with economic control, and in consequence there was no case for advocating across-the-board nationalisation. Nationalisation should be proposed only where it could be justified to the electorate as likely to lead to economic improvement. The proper role for a British socialist government was to be ready 'to intervene negatively' to stop industry acting 'mani-festively against the public interest' and 'to intervene positively' to secure economic expansion by searching out the weak elements in the economy. 'If it fulfils this positive role of enlarging the industrial base ... the remaining 90 per cent of the economy can increasingly be left to look after itself, now that we are moving from a subsistence to an abundant society.'[98]

Crosland's revisionist thesis was enthusiastically endorsed by his close friend, the Labour Party leader, Hugh Gaitskell. At the 1959 and 1960 Labour Party Conferences, Gaitskell sought to give effect to these revisionist conceptions by amending clause 4 of the party's constitution which enshrined the party's commitment to the realisation of a socialist society based on common ownership of the means of production, distribution and exchange. The Executive Committee's *Statement on Labour's Aims*, presented by Gaitskell, though declaring Labour's goal to be 'a socialist community based on fellowship, co-operation and service', requiring 'an expansion of common ownership substantial enough to give the community power over the commanding heights of the economy', asserted that 'both public and private ownership have a place in the economy'.[99] In his speech to the 1959 Conference Gaitskell had accused his Left-wing critics of

> a fundamental confusion about the fundamental meaning of socialism … we regard public ownership not as an end in itself but as a means – and not necessarily the only or most important one – to certain ends such as full employment, greater equality and higher production. Our goal is not 100 per cent State ownership.[100]

With strong support from union leaders, the anti-revisionists forced the leadership to drop the proposal to incorporate the *Statement on Labour's Aims* into the party constitution. Instead it was accepted by the 1960 conference 'as a valuable statement of the aims of the Labour Party in the second half of the twentieth century'.[101]

The defeat of the revisionist attempt to provide the Labour Party with a constitution embodying a broader statement of fundamental aims, more in keeping with the realities of life than that adopted 40 years earlier, indicated how strongly entrenched among party stalwarts was the identification of full social ownership with socialism and of a 'mixed' economy with socialism's betrayal. This was not perhaps surprising, given that the acceptance of a permanent mixed economy involved the rejection of the traditional conception of socialism as the negation of capitalism. Since the majority of the Labour Party's leaders in Parliament and most MPs accepted the mixed economy as permanent for all practical purposes, tension was inevitable.

With Harold Wilson as leader, the Labour Party was returned to power in 1964 and re-elected in 1966. In both elections, socialisation proposals, apart from the re-nationalisation of the iron and steel industry, were restricted to the water supply and the aircraft industry. The emphasis under Wilson's dynamic leadership was on promoting a National Economic Plan operating through partnership agreements embracing the government, business and trade unions to promote the economic growth necessary to fund higher living standards, better provision of social welfare and the elimination of poverty. The 1966 devaluation crisis put an end to the National Economic Plan and to any attempt to promote a planned economy.

Many party members were deeply critical of the record of the Wilson government from 1964 to 1970. The leadership responded to this criticism at the 1973 Conference with a radically new economic programme embracing nationalisation (including North Sea oil and gas) and an Industry Act. These measures were intended to give the government power to offer financial assistance to private companies in return for a proportionate shareholding, and to seek agreements with companies over a wide range of issues, including prices, profits and investment programmes. Though Wilson spoke fervently of storming 'the commanding heights' of the economy at the conference, neither he nor his Cabinet colleagues, with the exception of Tony Benn, had any enthusiasm for the Industry Act, according to Ben Pimlott's account, and little use was made of it.[102] Given good will and more propitious circumstances, it might have played a useful role. That role, however, would not have been one of working towards a socialist commonwealth but towards a greater degree of partnership between the state and private enterprise with some union participation.

Following on Labour's electoral defeat of 1979, there was a Leftward swing within the party, exacerbated in this case by the breakaway of part of the Right wing in 1981 to form the Social Democratic Party. However, the calamitous defeat of 1984 under Michael Foot's leadership, and the limited recovery in 1989, prompted the Labour Party, with Neil Kinnock as leader, to adopt an ever more moderate economic policy, especially with respect to nationalisation. The 1981 conference, with NEC support, had declared 'there is no way forward for the working class within the framework of capitalism and pledges the Labour Government under Clause IV ... to bring into public ownership the commanding heights of the economy'. The 1982 Conference had agreed to re-nationalise all privatised public assets and to take at least 25 major private companies into public ownership. But the only provisions in the 1992 election manifesto were for the return to public control of the national grid and water provision. The whole thrust of the manifesto was the promotion of economic growth by assisting private companies to be more efficient and competitive. Labour promised to 'back British industry', 'to create the conditions for enterprise to thrive' and 'to ensure that the market works properly'.[103]

Appropriately, neither the word 'socialism' or the word 'capitalism' appeared in the text. Significantly, the Labour Party's third successive electoral defeat in 1992 did not result in a shift to the Left at the party's conference in October. A resolution declaring Clause 4 to be central to the philosophy of the Labour Party was defeated.

Socialisation and the future of socialism

Anti-capitalism was at the heart of the concept of socialism from its early nineteenth-century beginnings, when it was hoped that capitalism might be avoided or stopped in its tracks. That central negative element was complemented by positive co-operative elements, projecting stark contrast between the wretched, wicked world that was and the prosperous moral world which could be. This conception survived and found expression in the programmes adopted by the European socialist parties which emerged at the end of the nineteenth century in a period of rampant, unadulterated capitalism. In this period there was agreement among the major socialist parties that their task was to replace the capitalist economic system by a socialist economic system, through a process of socialisation. The new socialist society would eliminate the evils inherent in capitalism, poverty, unemployment, insecurity, inequality and injustice, and usher in a new age of enlightenment where all would enjoy full and meaningful lives, satisfying their material, cultural and spiritual needs.

Sidney Webb, writing on 'The Basis of Socialism: Historic', in the celebrated *Fabian Essays in Socialism* (1889), confidently asserted that 'The economic history of the century is an almost continuous record of the progress of socialism' in England, with 'the gradual substitution of organised co-operation for the anarchy of the competitive struggle' in every field of economic and social life. Webb presents the process of socialisation through regulation, limitation and supersession of private ownership of the means of production as an irresistible glide into collectivist socialism.[104] But what would become of the concept of socialism if the 'irresistible glide' slowed down or even ground to a halt, while the collectivist measures already undertaken substantially reduced the number of those in poverty and the depths of that poverty?

This issue was addressed by Karl Kautsky in *The Dictatorship of the Proletariat* (1918). Socialism, 'by which is meant the socialisation of the means of production and of [the processes of] production', is not itself the goal. The final goal socialists strive for is the abolition of every form of exploitation and oppression, whether it be that of a class, a party, a sex or a race (Erfurt Programme):

> If in this struggle, we set ourselves the aim of the socialist mode of production, it is because under the present technical and economic conditions, this appears to be the only means of achieving our goal. If it were to be shown that we are mistaken in this matter and that the liberation of the proletariat and of humanity could be achieved solely or most appropriately on the basis of private property in the means of production ... then we should be obliged to abandon socialism

in the interests of the final goal.[105] For Kautsky the goals of the abolition of exploitation and oppression are not inherent in, or distinctive of, socialism; other creeds and ideologies also espoused them. What was distinctive of socialism was the conviction that the abolition of exploitation and oppression could be realised *only* through the abolition of the capitalist system and its replacement by an economic system based on the social ownership of the means of production. If that conviction were found to be false, the case for socialism would collapse.

Crosland and the Labour Party revisionists were by the late 1950s convinced that the experience of the post-war period demonstrated that the gradual removal of exploitation and oppression could be realised within an economic system which was likely to remain predominantly based on capitalist ownership of the means of production. But they did not conclude from this that socialism was 'played out'. Crosland and Gaitskell denied that socialisation was a goal of socialism, it was simply one of a number of means to realise the 'basic aspirations, the underlying values of socialism' – social justice, equitable distribution of wealth and income, priority of the public interest over private interests, equality of all races and peoples, and the promotion of co-operation and fellowship.

In his studies of liberalism, Michael Freeden makes an impressive case for the claim that Labour Party theorists in the late nineteenth and early twentieth centuries were greatly influenced by radical New Liberal theorists. The two groups came to share a wide area of common aims and values in respect of social justice, social equality, abolition of privileges derived from birth or unearned wealth and the importance of the community to individual development. But in spite of so much common ground and the political co-operation between the radical Liberals and the Labour Party in Labour's early years, the two groups remained ideologically aloof from each other. The ideological source of this aloofness was the Labour Party's commitment to the socialisation of the capitalist economy. Hobson, who was sympathetic to many of Labour's aspirations, wrote that the aim of the New Liberals' 'Practicable Socialism' was

> not to abolish the competitive system, to socialise all instruments of production, distribution and exchange, and to convert all workers into public employees [the goal of 'Theoretical Socialism'] – but rather to supply all workers at cost price with all the economic conditions requisite to the education and employment of their personal powers for their personal advantage and enjoyment (*The Crisis of Liberalism*, 1909).

Freeden comments that this 'Practicable Socialist' aim was 'probably as radical as one could get within the existing system'.[106] But it was precisely the existing system's limits which the Labour Party at its 1909 and successive conferences dedicated itself to remove, by endorsing the 'Theoretical Socialist' goal of replacing capitalism with an economic system based on public ownership. Although the New Liberals were not opposed in principle to nationalisation (many supported nationalisation of mines and railways), the issue was a marginal one, to be decided on practical grounds in each particular case. It was not a core element in their ideological thinking. For the Labour Party, however, the replacement of capitalism through socialisation of the means of production was *the* core of their ideology, distinguishing it from the Liberal Party which it aimed to displace.

NOTES

1. Alfred Zimmern, *The Greek Commonwealth* (Oxford University Press, 1931) pp. 286–7.
2. E. Barker, *The Political Thought of Plato and Aristotle* (London: Methuen, 1906) p. 44.
3. Charles Avila, *Ownership: Early Christian Teaching* (Sheed & Ward, 1983) p. 86
4. Ibid., p. 133.
5. R. W. and A. J. Carlyle, *A History of Medieval Political Theory in the West*, Vol. V (Blackwood, 1928) p. 19.
6. Janet Coleman, 'Property and Poverty', in J. H. Burns (ed.) *The Cambridge History of Medieval Political Thought* (Cambridge, 1928) p. 19.
7. Norman Cohn, *The Pursuit of the Millennium* (Secker & Warburg, 1952) p. 210.

8. Ibid., p. 230.
9. Ibid., p. 288.
10. See A. S. Woodhouse, *Puritanism and Liberty: The Army Debates 1647–49* (J. M. Dent, 1938) 'Debate on 29 October 1647' pp. 38–95 and *An Agreement of the People* (First Agreement, 3 November 1647) pp. 443–5.
11. See *Second Agreement of the People* (15 December 1648) p. 363, *Petition to the House of Commons* (11 September 1648) p. 839.
12. Gerrard Winstanley, 'Fire in the Bush' (1650) (April 1649) in Christopher Hill (ed.) *The Law of Freedom and Other Writings* (Pelican Classics, 1973) p. 268.
13. Arthur Bester 'The Evolution of the Socialist Vocabulary', *Journal of the History of Ideas*, Vol. IX (June 1948).
14. George H. Sabine, *The Works of Gerrard Winstanley* (New York: Russell & Russell, 1965) p. 408.
15. Winstanley, *A New Year's Gift for the Parliament and Army* (June 1650) in Hill, op. cit., p. 192.
16. Winstanley, *The Law of Freedom in a Platform* (November 1651) in Hill, op. cit., p. 278.
17. There has been much dispute as to what More's purpose was in writing *Utopia*. His friend and contemporary, Erasmus, said it was to show whence sprang the evil of states, with special reference to the English state. Anthony Kenny thinks that More meant his English Christian readers to recognise that, in such matters as the treatment of the poor, they behaved worse than the heathen Utopians he portrayed. He points out that in coining the word 'Utopia' More was not ascribing to it the characteristics of an ideal but unobtainable society with which the word has since become associated. See Anthony Kenny, *More's Utopia* (Oxford University Press, 1983) p. 20 and pp. 100–1.
18. Winstanley, *The Law of Freedom in a Platform*, in Hill, op. cit., p. 290.
19. Eduard Bernstein, *The Preconditions of Socialism* (1899), ed. and trans. by Henry Tudor (Cambridge University Press, 1993) p. 160.
20. C. B. Macpherson, *The Political Theory of Possessive Individualism: Hobbes to Locke* (Oxford University Press, 1962) pp. 220–21.
21. In *A Discourse on Property: John Locke and his adversaries* (Cambridge University Press, 1980) James Tully writes 'It is remarkable that Locke has been depicted as a defender of unconditional private property in land', since his 'is a system in which private and common property are not mutually exclusive but mutually related' (p. 170).
22. *Rousseau: Political Writings*, trans. and ed. Frederick Watkins (Nelson, 1953) pp. 317–18 and p. 324.
23. H. T. Dickinson, *Liberty and Property: Political Ideology in Eighteenth Century Britain* (Weidenfeld & Nicolson, 1977) pp. 256–7.
24. Thomas Paine, *Agrarian Justice*, in *The Thomas Paine Reader*, edited by Michael Foot and Isaac Kramnick (Penguin, 1987) pp. 475–8. See also George Claeys, *Thomas Paine: Social and Political Thought* (Unwin Hyman, 1989) pp. 86–99 and 198–204.
25. Dickinson, op. cit., pp. 267–8.
26. G. D. H. Cole, *A History of Socialist Thought*; Volume 1: *The Forerunners 1789–1850* (Macmillan Press, 1953) pp. 4–5.
27. Ibid., pp. 7–8.
28. Reference found by the author and sent to *The Oxford English Dictionary* to replace earlier and less precise entry.
29. Sidney and Beatrice Webb, *The History of Trade Unionism 1666–1920* (Authors' edition 1919), Appendix II Rules and Regulations of the Grand National Con-

solidated Trades Union of Great Britain and Ireland, pp. 732–3.

30. Abstract of Proceedings of a Special Meeting of Trades Union Delegates held in London from 13–19 Feb. 1934, MSs G. D. H. Cole, Box 8 Nuffield College, Oxford.
31. G. D. H. Cole, *The Forerunners*, pp. 127–8.
32. Christopher Hill, 'The Norman Yoke', in *Puritanism and Revolution* (Secker & Warburg, 1958) p. 108.
33. M. Beer, *A History of British Socialism* Vol. II (National Labour Press, 1921) pp. 36–7, *The Charter*, 17 March 1839.
34. See Gareth Stedman Jones, 'Rethinking Chartism', in *Languages of Class: Studies in English Working Class History, 1832–1982* (Cambridge University Press, 1983) and T. Tholfson, *Working Class Radicalism in Mid-Victorian England* (Croom Helm, 1976).
35. Gregory Claeys, *Machinery, Money and the Millennium: From Moral Economy to Socialism* (Polity Press, 1987) pp. 184–95.
36. G. D. H. Cole, *The Forerunners*, pp. 154–5.
37. John Saville (ed.), *Ernest Jones, Chartist: Selection of Writings and Speeches*, Appendix III Programme Adopted by the Charter Convention of 1851; and editorials in *Notes to the People*, July 1851, 8 May and 5 June 1852.
38. G. D. H. Cole, *The Forerunners*, p. 154 and John Saville, *Ernest Jones, Chartist*, p. 45.
39. Karl Marx, *Preface to a Critique of Political Economy*, 1859.
40. Frederick Engels, *Socialism: Utopian and Scientific* was first published in French in 1880 and in English in 1892. It quickly became the most popular Marxist text, second only to *The Communist Manifesto*.
41. John Stuart Mill, *Chapters on Socialism*, published in the *Fortnightly Review* 1879 and reprinted in *John Stuart Mill: Collected Works*, Vol. III. See pp. 712–15 and p. 748.
42. John Stuart Mill, *Principles of Political Economy*, 1871 edition, p. 773.
43. The word 'socialisation' as used by Marx in *Capital* meant not nationalisation or social ownership but the supersession of individual businesses by larger capitalist enterprises.
44. 'What Labour Means', in Eric J. Hobsbaum (ed.), *Labour's Turning Point: Nineteenth Century Vol. II. 1880–1900* (Lawrence & Wishart, 1948) p. 59.
45. *Labour Party Conference Report, 1908*, p. 76.
46. *Labour Party Conference Report, 26 Feb. 1918*, p. 140.
47. Programme of the Social Democratic Party of Germany, Erfurt 1891, in Susanne Miller and Heinrich Potthoff, *A History of German Social Democracy* (New York: Berg) pp. 135–6.
48. Vernon Lidtke, *The Outlawed Party: Social Democracy in Germany, 1878–1890* (Princeton University Press, 1966) p. 60.
49. Ibid., pp. 198–203, quoting Engels' letter to Bebel, 30 Dec. 1884.
50. Ibid., p. 65.
51. Eduard Bernstein, 'The Struggle of Social Democracy and the Socialist Revolution, 2: the theory of collapse and Colonial Policy', *Neue Zeit*, 19 Jan. 1898, in H. Tudor and J. M. Tudor (ed. and trans.) *Marxism and Social Democracy: The Revisionist Debate 1896–98* (Cambridge University Press, 1988) p. 167.
52. Bernstein, 'Critical Interlude', *Neue Zeit*, 1 March 1898; ibid., p. 222.
53. Bernstein, 'Critical Interlude', p. 223.
54. Bernstein, 'The Struggle of Social Democracy', p. 168.
55. Bernstein, 'Critical Interlude', op. cit., pp. 213–14.
56. H. Tudor and J. M. Tudor, *Marxism and Social Democracy*, pp. 294–7.

57. Karl Kautsky, *Das Erfurter Programm* (1892) English translation published by Charles H. Kerr (Chicago, 1910), and reprinted in Irving Howe, *Essential Works of Socialism* (New York: Holt, Rinehart and Winston, 1970) p. 101.
58. Ibid., pp. 107–9.
59. G. D. H. Cole, *A History of Socialist Thought: The Second International* Pt. I, pp. 274–5.
60. Peter Gay, *The Dilemma of Democratic Socialism* (New York: Octagon Books, 1979) p. 251.
61. M. Salvadori, *Karl Kautsky and the Socialist Revolution, 1880–1932*, trans. Jon Rothschild (London and New York: NCB, 1979) p. 232.
62. Ibid., p. 235.
63. Miller and Potthoff, op. cit., p. 74.
64. K. Kautsky, *Georgia: A Social Democratic Peasant Republic*, trans. H. J. Stenning (Manchester, 1921) Ch. 8, 'Capitalism and Socialism' in Patrick Goode (ed.) *K. Kautsky: Selected Political Writings* (Macmillan, 1983) p. 128 and p. 132.
65. Miller and Potthoff, op. cit., p. 254 and p. 268.
66. Ibid., p. 166 and p. 275.
67. Ibid., p. 279.
68. Ibid., pp. 274–9.
69. This section owes much to Tim Tilton's *The Political Theory of Swedish Social Democracy: Through the Welfare State to Socialism* (Oxford: Clarendon Press, 1990).
70. Malcolm B. Hamilton, *Democratic Socialism in Britain and Sweden* (Macmillan, 1989) p. 161.
71. This is the term used by Tim Tilton, op. cit., Ch. 4, 'Nils Karleby and Rickard Sandler: The Theory of a Socialised Market Economy'.
72. Ibid., p. 98 and p. 101.
73. Ibid., p. 99.
74. Hamilton, op. cit., pp. 180–87.
75. The Swedish Democratic Party was in office, either alone or in coalition, from 1932 to 1972 and from 1982 to 1991.
76. See Sven Steinmo 'Social Democracy vs Socialism: Goal Adaptation in Social Democratic Society', *Politics and Society*, 16, 1988.
77. Henry Milner, *Sweden: Social Democracy in Practice* (Oxford University Press, 1989) pp. 106–12.
78. Tilton, op. cit., p. 174.
79. Steinmo, op. cit., p. 431.
80. Milner, op. cit., pp. 129–37, Steinmo, op. cit., pp. 431–4.
81. Tilton, op. cit., p. 244.
82. Ibid., p. 275.
83. *Labour Party Conference Report, June 1918*, pp. 3–4.
84. *Labour Party Conference Report 1923*, p. 244.
85. *Parliamentary Debates*, 20 March 1923, Vol. 161, col. 2472.
86. *Labour Party Conference Report, 1928*, pp. 13–14.
87. Ibid., pp. 207–8.
88. *Labour Party Conference Report, 1933*, p. 156.
89. Ibid., p. 230.
90. *Labour Party Election Manifesto, 1945*.
91. *Labour Party Conference Report, 1946*, p. 124.
92. *Labour Party Conference Report, 1948*, p. 130.
93. C. A. R. Crosland, *The Future of Socialism* (Jonathan Cape, 1956) p. 249.
94. Raymond Plant, 'Democratic Socialism and Equality', in David Lipsey and Dick

Leonard (eds.), *The Socialist Agenda: Crosland's Legacy* (Jonathan Cape, 1981) p. 137.

95. Crosland, op. cit., p. 113.
96. Ibid., p. 116.
97. Ibid., p. 485, and pp. 496–7.
98. Ibid., p. 510.
99. Twelve aims were set out in the Statement on Labour's aims: (i) rejection of discrimination, (ii) right of all peoples to self-determination, (iii) support for UN, (iv) duty of richer nations to help poorer nations, (v) social justice, (vi) socialist community based on fellowship, co-operation and service, (vii) class-less society, (viii) planned economy and subordination of private economic power to the interests of the community, (ix) industrial democracy in public and private sectors of the economy, (x) expansion of common ownership in variety of forms to give the community power over the commanding heights of the economy, (xi) protection of the freedom of the individual against the state and other sources of arbitrary power, (xii) political freedom as the basis of socialism and democratic institutions and as the vehicle for the realisation of party objectives (*Labour Party Conference Report, 1960*, pp. 112–13).
100. *Labour Party Conference Report, 1959*, pp. 111–12.
101. *Labour Party Conference Report, 1960*, p. 231.
102. Ben Pimlott, *Harold Wilson* (HarperCollins, 1992)) pp. 664–6.
103. *Labour Party Conference Report, 1982*, p. 99; *Labour's Election Manifesto*, April 1992: 'Building a Strong Economy'.
104. Sidney Webb, 'The Basis of Socialism: Historic', in G. Bernard Shaw (ed.), *Fabian Essays in Socialism* (Fabian Society, 1920), pp. 20, 33 and 56.
105. Karl Kautsky, 'The Dictatorship of the Proletariat' (Vienna, 1918), in Patrick Goode (ed.), *Karl Kautsky, Selected Political Writings*, p. 99.
106. Michael Freeden, *The New Liberation: An Ideology of Social Reform* (Oxford: Clarendon Press, 1978) p. 47.

3

Labour: a choice of constituency

PRESTON KING

An eternity of choice

We may oppose the individual to the community, and yet we know that individuals are, mostly if not always, dependent on communities. We may promote the ideal of communitarianism, and yet we know that the value of community is tenuous if the community contributes nothing to the lives of individuals. We must draw some form of line between individuals and communities. But we can see from the start that to make that line too sharp is misleading.

The discussion of individualism and communitarianism is sometimes unhappily caught up in the discussion of choice *per se*, as in commonplace suggestions that individualists are in favour of choice and communitarians against it. Conservatives and even some socialists often contend that the former are in favour of choice and that the latter oppose it. This is an absorbing piece of misdirection which it is well to put behind us. Communitarians will doubtless oppose individualism conceived as selfishness, but not, for example, as self-fulfilment. Their emphasis will probably not be upon choice as such, but upon particular sorts of choice. Where the Right and neo-conservatives will be disposed to celebrate choice *per se*, the Left and contemporary socialists are more likely to ask who is hurt and whose choices are subverted by a supposed enhancement of choice *per se*. The distinction between individualism and communitarianism is nothing to do with promoting or opposing choice. It concerns, rather, the moral quality of the choices which are presented. And the nub of the debate turns round the legitimacy of the preference, under certain conditions, for collective, as against individual, action.

Conservatives imply, for example, that when they give parents a choice between schools they increase choice absolutely. Such a hypothetical increase is at best a piece of self-deception. What actually happens is that some options are open to some parents and are simultaneously closed to others. Parents who are better off and/or whose children are better at exams may be given the choice of a school with a higher rating outside the local catchment area. But parents who are less well off and/or whose children are less good at exams, by the same token, must be denied the choice of a school with a higher rating, whether inside or outside the local catchment area.

An educational authority can provide schools in at least two different ways: (a) the authority supplies, say, one secondary school within each residential district, to which all parents of the district are entitled to send their children; (b) the supply of schools remains constant; each school is ranked against the rest throughout the borough or city; parents become entitled to send their children to any school outside the local district should the child's performance match the level of the school chosen. As it happens, no government can consistently operate both policies (a) and (b). The choice extended to parents under (b) can only work if the choice to send one's child to the nearest local school – formerly allowed under (a) – is annulled. Thus, if a government gives the nod to policy (b) over policy (a), and even if (for the sake of argument) it is right to do so, it cannot conceivably be right *on the grounds* that it is enhancing choice *per se*.

Again, Conservatives imply, for example, that when they give patients a choice between private health care and public health care, they increase choice absolutely – that they add to the total stock of choice available to the community at large. But this is not so. What they actually do is to increase the options available to some patients while decreasing those available to others. The choice which the specialist medical consultant, fully backed by governmental authority, offers the patient is that between (a) public care for no charge at point of treatment and (b) quick private care for extra money at point of treatment. It will be obvious that, if the medical personnel offering options (a) and (b) are the same, then to bring into play the one option must simultaneously exclude the other. To accelerate attention to some, for money, must delay attention to others who cannot pay, or who on principle refuse to pay. If Doctor D works both privately and publicly, and assuming that D's time is not infinitely elastic, then the time D devotes to public care is time deflected from private care, and vice versa. If there are some with means who are permitted to pay to accelerate treatment, then this fact of itself prolongs the discomfort of, or heightens the risks to, those without means whose treatment is in consequence deferred. To allow some to jump the queue is to impose upon others additional delay. The queue-jumping option involves no net addition to choice; it is merely a restructuring of choice, with one type of option replacing another.

A health authority might (a) allow general practitioners and local or district hospitals to treat patients on a strictly first-come-first-served basis, without pay, modified by the urgency of cases presented and possibly by other exceptions that do not infringe fairness, or (b) allow the first-come-first-served principle to be undercut not only by urgency but also by patients' ability and willingness to pay. Under policy (a), the patient with means is denied the choice of simply buying a position at the head of the queue. Under policy (b), the patient without means is denied the choice of being treated in turn. To promote (b) over (a) does not enhance choice as such. The choice secured at (b) to the well off only works by overturning the choice that is or might be secured at (a) to the less well off. To allow some to queue-jump itself stifles the tacit preference for earlier attention by those whose treatment is delayed as a result of queue-jumping. It may of course be argued that, should the desire prove strong enough, everyone is equally able to find the resources to pay for queue-jumping. But if everyone were *equally* able to buy their way, few or none would be able to succeed in doing so, to the point that queue-jumping would quickly become an irrelevance.

In such cases as the two so sketchily considered – education and health – the important question really seems to be nothing to do with whether government allows parents or patients either greater choice, or just the bare bones of choice *per se*. Every choice that a government may allow is twinned to some other choice(s) that it must kill. The most important thing about a government is the binding and compulsory character of its actions. It is disingenuous for those avidly seeking to capture government to do so on the grounds that they will either abolish or significantly diminish it. Mr Reagan and Mrs Thatcher were full of homilies about reducing the size of government (that is, numbers of employees and size of budget) but both left office leaving government far bigger than they found it. Governments may well decide to decentralise or not to interfere (as with women's rights to abortion). But 'non-interference' does not mean 'has no effect'. Decentralisation itself imposes new arrangements; these must be policed; it is a different form of government, not the abolition of government.

It beggars the imagination to suppose that trainees, fiercely bent on getting at the joystick of government, having secured take-off into the empyrean of power, should suddenly think to ditch their craft in sea or jungle. Talk of 'getting rid of government' is essentially a rhetorician's device for 'taking over the controls'. It is also a way of misdirecting the attention of voters. The question is: Who is in charge and in whose interest? Governments are marked by the inclination to extract as much revenue as they can from their opponents and to redistribute it as liberally as they dare to their friends. Much of this redistribution today, as implemented (usually, not invariably) by conservative governments, we call 'privatisation'. And government has inevitably been more active than ever in promoting and policing it. Where they set up arms'-length, so-called independent regulators of monopolistic utilities, they go out of their way to ensure that these regulators are sympathetic to government views and are fenced in by appropriate laws and guidelines. Governments, in short, are not in the business of going out of business. To cut off one limb, another must spring up to oversee the amputation. If governments create choice, they do so by denying choice. There is always choice, and always married to denial of choice. The question therefore is not whether government has chosen, but whether it has chosen rightly; not whether it has created choice, but whether it has created the *right* choice.

The emphasis upon increase of choice as such is an especially foolish piece of misdirection. Imagine a kidnapped child, confused and frightened by denial of access to its parents. Imagine the kidnappers, in an attempt at pacification, ceaselessly proliferating offers: 30 different toys, 40 different sweets, adult television, late nights, undeviating attention, piggy-back rides, chess, tric-trac, backgammon and twenty-one, video games and virtual reality, lessons in the dissection of earthworms, white magic and astrology, in rational choice theory and in liberal ethics. The choices reach into the hundreds. And the kidnappers believe themselves to be in the right precisely because they provide such an array of choice – ethically overwhelming the one choice they do not allow, the only choice the child wants, which is that of going home again.

Both good and evil depend upon choice. Evil is not less evil because it is chosen. Choice in the abstract is a *ground* of morality. It cannot be the *object* of morality. A choice is desirable or praiseworthy, not because it belongs to the category of 'choice', but because it is a specific choice of a specific sort and not some other. My sallow choice not to feed the starving child is not made morally robust because in denying the child help, I *choose* to do so. Your choice to feed the starving child is good, equally, not because you make a *choice*, but because *this choice* – to help – is the specific choice you make. I, like you, am always choosing. As long as I am alive and competent, how can it be otherwise? I am no more to be praised for choosing than for being alive and alert. Choosing is simply a part of what it means to be alive, to be conscious and self-conscious. To perceive is itself to decide, to judge. Judgement –choice–decision: these enter into the very meaning of agency. In this context, choice as such (individual or collective) is not eliminable from agency; only concrete, specific choices can be added to or taken away. There is nothing moral about choice in the abstract. There is no use praising or blaming what can only be escaped in conditions of perfect constraint, as ultimately in death.

Even when I choose not to choose, I am still, inescapably, choosing. When my state chooses not to prosecute plainly criminal cases, just as when it chooses maliciously to prosecute cases that are not criminal at all, it exercises choice. When my state chooses not to intervene in Kampuchea or Bosnia or Rwanda, its neutrality remains a choice and has some effect on outcomes in these places. Since I cannot avoid choice – since the condition of enjoying agency forces me to choose – I am not entitled to be praised just because I choose. Since my government cannot avoid choice, it is not to be praised just because it chooses. For my government to be P(ro) or C(ontra), or N(eutral), is all one – as far as choice itself is concerned. For whatever it does it cannot escape being one of these – P or C or N. Whether my government aligns itself or sits on the fence, it can in no way as such avoid *choice*. My government may avoid the specific choice of P *or* of C *or* of N. What it cannot avoid is choosing from P *and* C *and* N. So it is not to be praised or blamed for having to choose, since choice, given agency, is inescapable. It is to be praised or blamed, not in *that* it chooses, but for *what* it chooses. In parallel, it is not to be praised or blamed for allowing me choice, for as long as I have agency, I always have (and have to have) choice. It is only to be praised or blamed for the specific choices that it allows or kills.

No individual government can create or extend choice as such. A government may offer choice of a particular kind, or extend choice into a certain area. But it does not create choice as such, nor destroy it as such. Where a government talks about creating or extending choice, it must be understood either to be engaged in a piece of rhetoric, or to be tacitly referring to some specific choice or area of choice, possibly to both – but certainly not to choice *per se*. My government – with the best will in the world – can only increase the stock of choice in the world by also, simultaneously, depleting it. For example, a government which reduces income tax, and makes up the shortfall by increasing taxes on goods at point of sale (sales tax or VAT), does not create or extend choice *per se*. Rather, it increases the range of economic choice open to the better off by reducing the choice open to those who are worse off.

It is well-known that an income tax characteristically takes proportionately more from the rich and proportionately less from the poor. It is equally a commonplace that a tax on wholesale or retail sales (goods and/or services) takes proportionately more from the poor and less from the rich. So to shift from taxing income to taxing sales has nothing to do with enhancing the scope of choice of citizens. It has to do with shifting the burden of tax from richer to poorer citizens. And this means enhancing the choices of one set of folk by constricting those of another. There may conceivably be some good reason for doing this – but that reason will not be that one has thereby created or enhanced *choice* as such. The relevant question is whether this *specific* choice is or is not morally or otherwise tenable. Governments may prove very successful at selling 'choice'. For their constituents may prove all too content to have unpleasant truths disguised. Americans voted overwhelmingly for Mr Reagan on the improbable grounds that he would both lower taxes and maintain government expenditure.

The fetish of ever-enhanced choice proves clearly attractive. It is similar in many points to the fetish (the ideology) of order. It reflects a category mistake. Just as (some) order is always with you, so (some) choice is always with you. The claim to create choice, or to create order, either presupposes some concrete type of choice or order (which excludes other types), or it merely confuses the general category of choice or order with some specific instances of it. The neo-Thatcherites and the neo-Reaganites who pretend to make an idol of 'choice', just as they do of 'order', cannot see that they are confusing the justification of specific choices and order with 'choice' and 'order' as such.

A government may classically pretend that it enhances my choice as such by returning to me taxes it has taken from me. The more disposable income I have, the greater the range of choice I may be assumed to enjoy. But this apparent relationship between greater disposable income and greater range of choice is deceptive. If the government, by reducing taxes, directly reduces or eliminates funding for various public services – the police, army, public service broadcasting, national health service, libraries, museums, schools, swimming pools and so on – then greater disposable income for me may actually diminish my choice in areas that really count, not only in general, but also *for me* in particular – which is not necessarily to say that I properly appreciate the connection.

There will always be room both for individual resourcefulness and for collective provision. Presumably collective provision should be invoked in circumstances where the goods or services involved are of crucial importance and where, if left entirely to individual action, they will probably fail to be secured adequately, or predictably, or at all. The range of individual choice does not shrink as state activity expands, nor does it expand as state activity shrinks. State activity is often itself a crucial condition for meaningful individual choice. If, for example, education and health are not adequately secured by the community as a whole then the consequence for many citizens, and not only for children, will be that their prospects for productive self-fulfilment are destroyed.

The individual who has more disposable income, in consequence of lower income tax, may now have to forgo library and other facilities; or may require to avoid public water or beaches (since these are polluted by virtue of insufficient state funding to clean them up); or be frightened away from public parks and streets that have become 'no-go' areas (given a public order problem exasperated by the economic abandonment of the inner cities, the poor being surrendered to the kindly attention of undermanned police forces); or be in need of vicious dogs, of houses that are fortresses, of private alarm systems and security firms; or be forced to buy in privately any and all interesting or educational speakers, plays, dancers, documentaries (since a lack of funds for public service broadcasting reduces all radio and television to raw, least-common-denominator commercialism).

Markedly greater choice for some is not only often attended by diminished choice for others. Even those who enjoy enhanced choice do not acquire it without loss. Every choice acquired by any agent is always bought at the cost of some other missed possibility. One, for example, who chooses to be master by the same token shuts off the option of being a friend. One who greedily votes to claw back every penny in his pound or pfennig in his mark or dime in his dollar, by the same motion tears at the fabric of mutual helpfulness and common decency – from which he, as much as any other, expects to benefit. It does not follow that all choices are morally equal; the point is precisely that they are not. It does not follow that the future can be no better than the past; the point is that when it is, it is because it accommodates better and apter choice, not choice *per se*, nor more and more choice of whatever kind.

In summary, there is a three-part difficulty about choice. First, it is always circumscribed. Second, a new choice never just increases the overall volume of choice; a new choice always itself circumscribes further choice; so that choice as such cannot be enhanced. Third, whatever and however much choice is excluded, it is impossible to demonstrate that some total store of disposable choice is or can be reduced. These points are closely connected.

To take the first: choice is always circumscribed. I am never able to do just anything I might wish. I cannot see the film and attend the concert, when they are taking place at the same time in different places. My government, however big its budget, always has limited resources, and should it spend more on guns it must spend less on butter. To do one excludes the other. There will always be things which I and my government imagine we can do which we can't do, and things we can do which we imagine we can't. But there remain limits, whatever we imagine. The Greeks called this Tragedy. Many Christians have called it Original Sin. Contemporary economists speak of it as the principle of scarcity.

To take the second point: choice is not just circumscribed; choice *itself* kills choice. A government which chooses to increase interest rates to stifle inflation also chooses to check growth and delay recovery. A firm which chooses to rationalise its operations to increase profits also chooses to shake out its labour force and heighten un-employment. The robber who chooses to take your money does so precisely by denying you the choice of keeping it. You cannot choose both p and not-p; to choose p is incompatible with not-p; the one simultaneously excludes the other. To go for the new is to lose some of the old. To innovate in whatever degree is to relinquish some part of tradition. Every gain is also a loss. The question is not whether one is losing but what one is losing. The problem is not quantitative but qualitative. If every new choice also kills choice, it is difficult to see how new choices may supply net additions to choice *per se*. The fabulous gains of development are starkly off-set by attendant environmental destruction. (We may read too much Hegel and too little Schopenhauer.)

Finally, the third point: to deny choice also generates choice (short of eliminating agency). We know that there are many things which we simply cannot do. We know that we are circumscribed in infinitely different ways. Yet constraints do not merely deny choice. They also focus choice, occasion choice and, more than that, are a logical condition for it. To choose is not only to say 'I pick this'; it is also to say 'I reject that'. The decision *not* to go to the concert is a necessary facet of the decision to take in the cinema. Rejection is a necessary part of the process of selection. Rejection (denial of choice) in the past is a necessary contribution to selection (exercise of choice) in the present. We therefore have no basis for claiming that the exclusion of choice, which is always with us, does no more than exclude, nor that exclusions ever diminish the total stock of choice as such.

This last point conventionally meets with resistance, hence my excuse for labouring it. None of us is aware of being able to do just anything we wish. We are all of us aware of life as a system hedged by constraints – whether we are government or opposition, student or teacher, M. Monroe or Joe Doe. And yet we are aware that everyone, short of a circumstance like sustained torture, which destroys agency, is constantly executing acts of choice – as in the case of anyone now reading this. For example, we know that imprisonment imposes constraints. But it still cannot be said that imprisonment does not occasion or inspire choice. Adversity, defeat, confinement do not only defeat choice, they also provoke choice – at least up to the limit of the destruction of agency.

Assassinations kill the dream; but they also invent martyrdom and give hope to dreamers. Concentration camps bar escape; they also provoke and excite hopes of rescue or evasion. Prisons confine and regiment; but rather than destroy or diminish choice as such, they only bar some of the paths that choice otherwise might follow. To be imprisoned is not to be deprived of choice, but of a specific choice and of such others as hang on it. Imprisonment specifically excludes the choice of quitting prison. Imprisonment is awful and demeaning. But even it, as destructive as it may prove, is incapable of destroying choice. A person locked away commonly discovers other (not necessarily narrower) ways of concentrating and exercising volition: in reading, writing, drawing; bending, breathing, pacing; plotting, praying, reflecting. This is the story of figures like Gramsci, Papillon, Malcolm X, the 'Bird Man' of Alcatraz, of Mandela ... Given agency, choice is always and at work – even in the army, public school and nunnery; under the slave, share-cropping or communist regime; among Seventh Day Adventists, Mormons and Sufis; both in the drudgery of work and in the release of play. However much reduced our stock of choice may be, what is left still has an infinitely extensive character short of the destruction of agency itself. Choice and power are not the same. The fact that A has more power than B need not mean that A has more choice than B.

It is extremely difficult to see how we could possibly count the total plenum of choices available to us – as opposed to merely noting this choice or that that is opened up or closed off. We know that each new choice puts an end to some other. But apart from that, we simply cannot say what the total run of choices are that remain or have become available to us. If there is such a total, and if we could tabulate such a total, then at least we should be in a position to say what our net gains and losses were. But we do not even know that there is such a total. Certainly we do not know how to tabulate it. And thus we are not, and cannot be, terribly well placed to hold forth on the enhancement of choice as such.

Competition over monopoly?

States are conventionally presented as in some sense opposed to markets, and markets to states. Yet it is clear that, without state protection, markets cannot properly operate, while the reverse does not hold. To allow or to protect or to create markets is an option in principle open to any state. 'Markets', however, are often taken to be the equivalent of 'individuals'. And this is way off the mark. In general, it seems reasonable to allow space for the action of individuals, and also space for the actions of collections of individuals – which we might call 'communities' or 'collectives'. Markets include individuals without reducing to individuals; they encompass (a) exclusively individual activity (at the one end) and (b) the most complex and sophisticated collectives and communities (at the other). The overwhelming bulk of market activity, taking the measure in money terms, is accounted for by (b), not (a). Following the 1994 UNCTAD World Investment Report, the 37,000 parent companies comprising the global network of transnational firms account for annual sales in the order of $4,800 billion – 'the productive core of the globalising world economy'. The top 100 of these transnational companies control about one-third of the world stock of foreign direct investment. Taking account of the global market, it is the large, private collectives that are overwhelmingly dominant – not private individuals.

The market then is overwhelmingly composed of collectives – of families, domestic corporations, transnationals, trades unions. To protect the market accordingly is not, first and foremost, to protect individuals. It is to protect private collectives, and especially the largest of these. The individuals that are in the market form only the smallest part of it. If the market promotes or protects individuals, it mostly promotes and protects them as members of collective and communal entities. In parallel, to protect the state is not, first and foremost, a matter of protecting individuals, unless again it is as members (citizens/subjects) of the state. Private collectives (the most important of which, bizarrely, are often called 'public' corporations), like the public collective that is the state, may either support or override the needs of individuals. Private collectives – whether business corporations or trades unions – need protecting and regulating just as do public collectives.

The great corporations that roam the markets, though they may be inspired more than occasionally by the desire to reduce or abolish *government*, could never succeed in reducing or abolishing *governance*. If the United States or France seeks to reduce the power of the UN by withholding their dues, this only means that they will seek to achieve diplomatic results more by bilateral than multilateral means (whether well or badly). If business corporations seek to reduce the taxes they pay towards the arts or road-building or schools, then they are more likely themselves to sponsor various arts, or to pay directly for tolls and rail haulage, or to the subvention of their own in-house apprenticeship schemes. If no public agency attends to the needs/desires of corporations for diplomatic cover or security or intelligence, then these collectives will deploy, within the limits of their means, their own high-level negotiators or guards or industrial spies. Where private collectives diminish the power of public collectives – government in general – the effect essentially is to expand directly their own power and field of action, whether for better or worse.

The market being dominated by collectives, and the government itself being a collective, the distinction between market and government is not reliably that between individual and collective. A conventional but still important distinction between market and government is that between entities where membership is voluntary and involuntary. All the same, having got well beyond hunter-gathering, we are in no position these days to freely opt in and out of work, nor in and out of the collectives that organise it. Work is essential; in modern conditions it is more specialised; control of it is more centralised; and it becomes increasingly difficult both to change one's special type of work and also to shift from one employer to another. Modern workers tend, therefore, to be increasingly dependent upon the collectives, public or private, which employ them. For example, the miners who were discharged in their tens of thousands in the UK over 1993–4 did not *elect* to be discharged, and were characteristically little able to move on to alternative employers once their jobs had been 'rationalised'.

A conventional but more important distinction between market and government is that between entities that do and that do not seek profit. This distinction is fairly impressive. Public or state television is not overwhelmingly obsessed with profits; private or 'independent' television is. Leaked minutes from the private UK TV company, Anglia, show that over a period of several days in mid-January 1994, when exploring takeover bids from rivals, the only subjects the board of the company discussed were prospective impact on profits, share price, turnover – nothing relating to welfare of staff, pension arrangements, quality of programmes, even future prosperity of the company under new management. This then speaks to the distinctive ends that different collectives may adopt. Some of these ends, like those reflected in the Anglia minutes, may be very narrow; for other collectives, like state television, the ends embraced might prove far more complex.

But in general the distinction between market and government is dodgy, because both will tend to be collectives and both can be overwhelmingly motivated by profit. Some of the private collectives like Shell or Ford or General Motors are hugely more powerful than most of the public sort like Bangladesh, Burma, or Gabon. Some private collectives, moreover, like Sony Corp., may be rather paternalistic, while many public collectives, like Indonesia, are infected by a virulent strain of greed – and even genocidal cruelty in the management of captive dependencies like East Timor and Irianjaya.

The fact that a collective is a government or is called 'governmental' in no way ensures that it will adopt more comprehensive goals than will collectives called, for example, 'public corporations'. Indeed, since states began to emerge as much as nine to ten thousand years ago, they have been typically marked by the simple pursuit of gain –

through war, plunder, slavery, conquest and the sustained exploitation of subjects. It is not as though this profiteering proclivity is in any way absent from the present scene. In 1994, states like Zaire, Myanmar (Burma) and Brazil were not unfairly labelled 'kleptocracies', and most such (Burma aside) survive with the assistance of powerful Western allies like France and the USA.

It may be that our problem is not really to distinguish between markets and states, for a private collective may expand to take on the role of a public collective. And the latter may narrow its concerns to match those of any business – as in the case of the creation and brutal management by Belgium's King Leopold II of what was ironically styled the Congo Free State (1876–1908). Perhaps the two most important considerations to note are the relations of sovereign to non-sovereign collectives (in this case the formal subordination of business to government), and the fact that different collectives may set themselves very different objectives. The question: what should be left to the state, and what should be relinquished to the market? may be a trifle misleading. The more acute question may be: in regard to what functions should a collective seek a monopoly?

It is clear, for a start, that monopoly is not universally regarded as a bad thing. Were it so there would be no justification for any form of government. If a war is being fought, one of the deepest fears of commanders is that 'the left hand does not know what the right hand is doing', so soldiers seek to avoid division of command. Diplomats, negotiating treaties, are assisted by a clear pyramid of authority, so that the deals that may be cut by an ambassador cannot be undercut by the play of consular staff or security agencies or, perhaps, the leader of the opposition. Competition, competing authorities: these are not always seen to be, nor are they always in fact, good things.

Goverment is itself a form of monopoly. To opt for it is to oppose, for example, do-it-yourself justice, the vengeance of Prosper Mérimée's Colomba, of lynch-mob self-expressionism. This is not to claim that government always works. Too obviously, it often fails. But it is to claim, on balance, that a state monopoly in such matters as criminal prosecution is better than the private initiatives of offended individuals in securing justice by their own lights. No one seeks, for any given state, two distinct air forces, or corps of diplomats, or parliaments, or patent offices, or judicial systems. In regard to some functions – here we often if not altogether happily speak generically of 'government' – we seek some form of concentration: monopoly. To plead for some form of separation-of-powers may appear to cut against the grain. But the concern is not necessarily inconsistent with monopoly of the kind discussed, on condition that distinct bodies (prosecutors, judges etc.) are not assigned the self-same duties. For were the same duties assigned to distinct bodies, the outcome must be either (a) immobilism (in consequence of perfect balance) or (b) perfect voluntary accord. Government is defeated by (a), while (b) obviates any need for government. So an ultimate monopoly is not inconsistent with decentralisation and checks and balances. And where we conclude that (some) monopoly is desirable – as in many of the conventional tasks assigned to government – then so do we conclude that (some) competition is desirable.

Monopoly, however, involving exclusive control of a function, is in its nature dangerous. Significant power concentrations inescapably threaten those upon whom they may act. Fear of monopoly, paradoxically, inspires defence both of competition and its converse. On the Right, competition is recommended as an antidote to monopoly (by government) for competing entities are seen to check the supremacy of any one of their number. On the Left, however, monopoly (by government) is recommended as an antidote to competition. For competition, unimpeded, is seen itself to eliminate competition, and in this to strip from ordinary working people minimum and reasonable standards of living and conditions of work. The logic of the position is that competition, left to its own devices, eliminates less efficient individuals and collectives, and removes by the same token distinct centres of power, which all either merge naturally into one simple hierarchy of production/administration, or by contrast agree to act in concert, on a non-competitive basis, leading to price-fixing among economic cartels (oligopoly) or to power-fixing among warlords, princes, great powers or minority parties (oligarchy, balance-of-power, coalition rule).

The Left has.conventionally argued for some significant degree of state control of the economy. This argument has followed three basic steps, thus: (a) competition in the market tends naturally towards monopoly; (b) monopolistic (or oligopolistic) control of economic goods by private agents cannot be in the public good; (c) nationalisation of key economic goods ensures that the public interest is served.

The trouble with this argument lies in the transition from (b) to (c). It may well be right to secure state control of the economy, if, first, such control does not of itself damage the economy, and if, second, it does not result in the simple concentration of overwhelming power at the centre. Putting the first consideration (the economy) to one side, it will be obvious that the Left has not paid sufficient attention to the second problem – of riveting states to a firm democratic and constitutional framework which is strengthened and not weakened by state domination of the economy. This is the key constitutional problem which Marxists have supposed will take care of itself, and which social democrats have calmly assumed to be settled by merely saluting the flag of democracy. State power has drawbacks which it is crucial never to take lightly, even when we have every good reason to make use of it. There is the fact of the compulsory and bureaucratic side of the state, and the fact – however representative government can be made – that it always remains in some degree the discretionary preserve of a few, in fee to their interests.

The core problem, perhaps predictably confirmed by the east European, Chinese and other cases, is that a state which enjoys an economic monopoly, not moderated by appropriate political and constitutional constraints, makes transparency all but impossible. A state which exercises simple monopoly control is likely to have that control appropriated by a few – a New Class (following Djilas), a dominant caste of *apparatchiki*. Such an élite, being comparatively small, enjoying good internal lines of communication and confronted with no political, social or economic counterweight outside itself, can easily shut down counter-argument. This exclusion can range from imposing silence upon potential oppositions to filling all public space with outrageous governmental propaganda. The homogenisation of the media cum poodle ensures non-debate, demonisation, sensationalism, ringing phrases, and suppression of the real agenda.

In such circumstances it is impossible even to attempt to locate local, national or global interests openly and rationally. The language and procedures will be majoritarian, but the narrow options that result purely reflect the interests of the élite. It is no use saying that such an élite governs in the interest of workers, of the majority, of distressed minorities, and so on, for the élite, by definition, are none of these things. An all-powerful élite cannot be expected to allow open and secure airing of the interests and grievances of those whom it makes worst off. Mindlessly concentrated power must rob public debate of its vibrancy and salience, putting efficiency at risk as well. The unanswerability of government has always to be fought against – at the very top, of course, but also at the lower level of the petty, imperious bureaucrat, who need have neither smile nor sympathy for, for example, the troubled pensioner or unemployed claimant.

The Right have conventionally argued for no significant state control of the economy. The argument has tended to be that the economy is by its nature unequal, and even undemocratic, responding best to self-interest, not to moral imperatives. The great mass of people, some have argued, are always at a disadvantage – 'the poor are always with you' – and may always be tempted to suppose that they will benefit from empowering government to tamper with the economy, either by taking it over (perhaps in the way that Henry VIII appropriated monasteries) or by permanently redistributing surpluses from those with more to those with less. The Right do not necessarily argue that the inequality of the market is in itself a good thing, only that (a) state involvement does not necessarily make for more equality, since dominance is only shifted from financiers to politicians, and that (b) state involvement is economically inefficient because control over production is removed from those who know how (the business class) to those who don't (the political class), the result being an absolute decline in production with fewer redistributable resources. Both of these points contain a kernel of common sense and it would be foolish to overlook the concerns they register. The state is no more magical a problem-solver than is the market. The retention of local initiative, both in government (hence decentralisation) and in civil society (hence entrepreneurial and other forms of self-activation) is crucial.

The trouble, however, is that this conservative fear of power – fear of government – is more a rhetorical device than not. It tends to assume in any event (and self-deceptively) that the economy is somehow pristine, untouched, independent, fixed, governed by quite autonomous laws. Unfortunately, it is none of these things. The economy is not, never was, never can be immune to government. If there is a government, then it is inevitably one of the most important sources of demand. If it does anything for its citizens/subjects – health, housing, education, welfare, security, defence – then it is also an extremely significant source of supply. Government is inevitably a part of the market, and itself constitutes the framework for market exchange. The economy persists and changes in response to the actions of the agents active in and impinging on it – these agents inescapably including the state, today on an increasing scale.

The motto of Right in this matter is still surprisingly 'laissez faire'. But we can only leave alone what already stands apart, and cannot be reached, cannot be changed – perhaps God and the laws of physics. If the economy can be affected and altered by the state – as it can – then to insist that it be 'left alone' is an exercise in misdirection, since that is not at all what is being sought. The object is not to leave it alone, but rather actively to protect and preserve it in some particular form, perhaps that in which we now find it, or perhaps in the form we imagine for it one hundred years ago, or in time to come – in any event in some form that we chance to desire. Economy itself, of course, roughly speaking, in some form or other, is always with us. Whether we find ourselves in Silicon Valley or among Druids and Pygmies or with Uncle Tom in his cabin, so shall we have economy: supply and demand, production and exchange, these persist. It is another matter as to whether the economy of a particular era is one that the agent is happy or not to embrace.

The economy persists; equally it is always changing, in response to and as part of the activity of all those agents impinging on it. The share market is affected, not just when dealers buy and sell, but equally when they decline to buy or sell. Our action may generate inflation, our inaction deflation, but the effect is still there. Government affects employment whether it increases interest rates or leaves them alone, whether it maintains a large standing army or slashes it to the bone. It is impossible for government in this general sense to 'leave alone'. The impact of Leviathan when aroused is of course real; the mistake is to suppose that government somehow loses weight or otherwise becomes less tangible because comatose or dead asleep.

What the economy is not is autonomous. It hasn't any pristine, objective, rock-solid or inert form. There can be command, slave, peasant, wage, barter, industrial, service, and infinitely many other types of economy. To advise the state to *laissez faire* when the economy is of the slave type or the market type, is not at all to advise it to do nothing, but to require it to defend a particular system. If 'the' economy were inert, were it possible for it to exist preternaturally, without 'interference', there should be no need to ring it round with 'Keep out!' notices. There can be no point in advising enactment of the superfluous. The state, along with other exogenous forces, would not be able to intrude. The Market – like Plasticman, Batman, Superman, Bananaman, and all other peerless, infantile heroes of our century – through its own boundless resourcefulness, would be perfectly adept at defending itself. Except that it isn't. Governments are warp and woof of market systems. The market is not outside and alien to, but crucially encrusted in and dependent upon, government. It is a point the Right is not disposed to admit and which its own rhetoric does not properly allow it to see.

The Right is not out of place in warning of the prospective dangers of state monopoly. It *is* out of place in pretending that *laissez faire* and competition in the market are as such a defence against monopoly. The Right point to the East – Communist Rumania, East Germany, etc. – as the *reductio ad absurdum* of state control of the economy: we are rightly reminded of the Gulag Archipelago, political oppression, security obsession, and economic crisis. But the Right miss the point that, by this measure, all of those oppressive market dictatorships – the Somoza regime in Nicaragua, Marcos in the Philippines, Mobutu in Zaire, the generals in Argentina and Brazil (the still earlier generals in Spain and Greece, omitting altogether the signally repulsive case of Hitlerian Germany), in every case either supported by or being a Western, market state – must become in turn the *reductio ad absurdum* of all liberal, market regimes. Most modern systems are of the market type, and the overwhelming majority of these are not democratic. Mexico is a distressing example of a market regime, rigged up in democratic form, the content of whose body politic is merely dictatorial presidentialism. A single party (the PR) has been in power for more than 60 years and in 1994 fraudulently took yet another election, marked by continuing assassinations (Colosio and militants on the left), peasant revolt (the Zapatistas in Chiapas state), and endemic corruption.

It will be conceded that Rightist regimes can be as oppressive as Leftist regimes. In both cases the oppression will often be associated with excessive concentrations of power at the centre. Is it the case, however, that only some regimes on the Right are oppressive, as opposed to all regimes on the Left? The difficulty with this view is that any market regime, leaning to the right, bereft of appropriate types of intervention and direction, can veer off into Hitlerian, Francoist, or Salazarist types of authoritarianism, up to and inclusive of systematic genocide. These are the sorts of outcome to which 'the market', left alone, can lead. Market systems that do not go this far, do not do so essentially because they are, in various ways, held in check. Perverse outcomes are not the exception, they are the rule. A pure capitalism, in unadulterated pursuit of profit, is perfectly compatible with slavery and every other imaginable excess.

States are not necessarily democratic. And markets are not necessarily benign. It is open to states to become more like markets and markets more like states. If states are sovereign, and markets are sub-sovereign, then the latter are always dependent upon the former. That apart, they may be driven by much the same motives. If markets remain competitive, that is in part because the state framework is devised to secure this outcome. In this sense, the market is not to be portrayed as autonomous *vis-à-vis* the state, since its character and limits depend upon the type of state by which it is framed. Just as the state must be checked, adjusted, doctored, disciplined, so must markets be. What after all would a hypothetically 'pure' market system resemble? It would be a system in which it was authoritatively urged upon all subjects/citizens that profit was the only acceptable object governing exchanges. And were we to allow this principle to triumph, we should also allow unfettered child labour, sweatshops, environmental degradation and an infinity of similar moral foolishness – all of course sustained at the limit by state authority.

Markets can as easily lead into dictatorial as into other paths. They can even be created. The Pinochet dictatorship in Chile was not a function of spontaneous generation. It resulted from a military coup deliberately fomented by American security agencies with the precise object of creating an unpopular, non-democratic market regime. By contrast, tremendous political energy was invested by the occupying powers in turning post-war Germany and Japan, not into 'pure' market economies, but into constitutionally restrained types of market economy. A part of what these countries are today is a function of such political cosseting. They are not market systems *per se*, nor could any state be. Economy and state are intertwined. It is not easy simply to separate regime from economy, or economy from regime. The question is not whether the state *is* engaged, but the way in which it *ought* to be engaged, in the market.

The Right has its own idealised view of the market, a vision which it seeks to reify. It espouses consumerism, global market relations, private accumulation, self-interest, and those types of individualism that reinforce these tendencies. The Right has girded itself to pay the hidden costs of this vision – unemployment, widening gap between rich and poor, spread of economic insecurity, poorer education, addictive drug-use, greater criminality, heavier policing, collapse of community, etc. In arguing with the Left, the Right pretends that defence of its own vision overleaps any significant recourse to the power of government. The Right thus formally opposes government and wishes to diminish its hold in every sphere. Paradoxically, the

Right does not stint in its own recourse to the state. Seeking to realise its preferred conception of 'the' market, it righteously calls down the power of government to support its initiatives – breaking unions, wiping out university tenure, concentrating private ownership, imposing poll taxes, increasing exactions generally from those worse off, watering down constraints on employers, reducing the independence of the media, etc. The Right portrays such deployment of power as benign; it is not 'intervention'. But where opponents equally seek to deploy the power of government to restrain or alter or block the Right's preferred arrangements, then this power (at least this *use* of it) is no longer innocent or natural; it smacks rather of 'statism', even communism.

What thus obtains here, on the Right, is the compulsive pathology of colouring the state indiscriminately evil, the evil plainly visible only when the Right dislikes what the state does, and becomes suddenly and conveniently invisible – 'the hidden hand' – when the state protects those arrangements the Right regards with favour. The Right is right: the state is in danger. The Left is right: to use the state in support of the untempered operations of the market is more dangerous still. But the point is not really that either Left or Right is right: it is that the play of state power, for whatever objective, is not an avoidable option. Whatever the state does or doesn't do will have an effect. Since it cannot be left out of the equation, there is no use pronouncing so as to suggest it can. The question is not how to eliminate, but what sort of policy to hold it to.

What is to be done about unemployment? Leave it to the hidden hand? That is an option, but it is not passive, nor will it lack in effect. Unemployment, for example, might be affected, on the one hand, by placing industry on a shorter working week, subsidising public works and child-care centres, etc., or on the other hand by pressing on with new management methods, labour-market de-regulation, diffusion of new technology and the spread of global markets. Government is and will be involved either way. Neither set of options is passive. The Right, especially, is caught up in a piece of rhetorical misdirection in pretending that the case can be otherwise. And that may be how it excuses to itself such frequent and sustained use of police and security agencies, at home and abroad, in pursuit of its market objectives. As the Right has a naive conception of its objectives as 'natural', it cannot *see* how far it may strain the resources of the state to secure them.

The state represents a form of monopoly, and it is not without its dangers. At the same time, as intimated earlier, it is not always a bad thing on balance, which is to say that it is not always by any means to be avoided. The Right, in any event, and contrary to its rhetoric, no more avoids it than does the Left. It only camouflages its use of the state to have it appear as something other than what it is. When the Right taxes, as in the case of national insurance, it will do so on the pretence either that this is not a tax or is the minimum needed. When it coldly slaughters dozens of rioting prisoners (as with Governor Rockefeller at Attica) it is only because law and order requires no less. When it engages in costly militaristic forays abroad, as in the Falklands, Lebanon, Panama, Grenada, or the Gulf, these measures are always excused, first as efficient, even 'surgical', and if not that, at least as essential to the 'defence of democracy'. The Right deploys the power of government all the time, not least in the engineering of public opinion, which they are driven to do covertly, in part because of their own anti-statist rhetoric – as with CIA support for The Congress for Cultural Freedom, The American Society for African Culture, manipulation of American universities, 'born-again' churches, and Islamic fundamentalists (as in Egypt and Afghanistan), etc. The Right, in short, is as good as any other faction in ill-judged and callous use of the state.

The modified market regimes in the West have been modified precisely because of pressures from the Left, in and out of government, sustained over generations. The Left is not outside or alien to the political constraints that today mark advanced industrial systems; on the contrary, it is an essential part of the reason for these constraints being in place at all. If modern social democracy is fuzzy, then how much more so is 'liberalism', let alone 'conservatism'. If socialism, taken as the complete ownership of the means of production, is discredited, then capitalism, taken as the unregulated concentration of production in the hands of a few, is no less so. We know no 'pure' capitalism in the advanced industrial systems, for the reason that progressive movements have had the effect of trimming its claws.

Government, any government, is inevitably involved in the market, if there is a market – the principal question being how, not whether, government is and should be involved. Governments always have economic aspects and economies always require some form of management. We are entitled accordingly to move away from *laissez faire* as a piece of incoherence. It is not that governments of the Right are always and necessarily wrong in what they do, but that their anti-statist rhetoric systematically misconstrues what they are actually up to. Government involves some element of monopoly and to the degree that we accept government we equally accept that monopoly is not irretrievably evil. Individuals by themselves have little weight. It is as members of collectives that their presence can be felt. Collectives, public or private, are systematically more powerful than individuals. While collectives help, they are equally well placed to hurt, individuals. So the question of collective organisation – especially of its openness or transparency – is crucial. The problem is less that of the danger to the market from government, but the danger to individuals from both public and private collectives.

Monopolies being both helpful and dangerous, the problem is to determine when we should and should not allow them. Monopoly bereft of any sort of regulation would have to be a bad thing. We accept that a ship must be subject to command. But what happens and who is to say when Captain Queeg or Captain Bligh goes mad or has seriously exceeded his authority? The question is perennial, remorseless: *quis custodiet custodes*? Who controls the controllers? A ship is not to be run competitively. And yet it would make no sense to argue that Captain Queeg is necessarily right, and that there is no place, in some form, for regulation. Regulation (monitoring) may be secured by oversight or by competition. Oversight is monitoring by a superior. Competition is monitoring by struggle among equals. Competition is appropriate between sailors aboard ship, or between defence and prosecution in court, but not between sailor and captain, not between prosecutor and judge. And yet captains and judges cannot be a law unto themselves.

Any person or body conceded authority is only entitled to exercise it within the bounds of fairness or justice. Justice is the most difficult term to apprehend, and yet it is essential that justice be seen to be done. Oversight can be just or not, as competition can be fair or not. Hence the crucial importance in the one case of transparency and in the other of 'a level playing field'. In a democracy, the theory is that administration is overseen – perhaps underseen – by the people, and that government is turfed out where it is perceived to fail. In a market, the theory is that cost is constrained by competing suppliers, and that prices fall when competition is vibrant. We might be tempted to describe oversight as a form of monitoring appropriate to states, and competition as a form of monitoring appropriate to markets – were the distinction between state and market so clear, which it is not.

The state is a monopoly, it is not a competitive body, even when it encourages competition. Competition is not self-sustaining, since it requires protecting – paradoxically through the monopoly that is government. When is it best to accept that a single collective should dominate a sector (monopoly), and when to accept that it should not (competition)? When should a collective be directed by some such principle as 'order' or 'fraternity' and when by some such goal as 'profit' or 'the survival of the fittest'? Clearly it is no use trying to answer by abstractly signalling the 'state', in the one case, and 'the market', in the other. For the goals of collectives, whether the latter are public or private, are readily interchangeable. Collectives are, however, no matter what their goals, morally constrained by the commitment to justice and fairness. So what should be done and what should be allowed are always properly subject to these concerns. What seems perfectly useless is maintaining absolutely either that business is no business of the state, or that the destiny of the state is to own all business. Whether or how or how much is taken over by the state must henceforth be viewed as more an empirical than a philosophical question.

Take the case of whether prisons should be run as private rather than public collectives – by profit-seekers or by civil servants. Prisons we normally concede to be the distinct preserve of the state. Personally, I should prefer to keep it that way. There is something deeply unsettling about shutting folk away, on remand or conviction, to be managed under a compulsory regime, privately owned, whose direct object is to generate a profit for the managers. Nonetheless, if we accept that the state, in requiring children to be educated, may allow them to be educated in private schools, is it reasonable to contend, in regard to prisoners, that the requirement that they must be jailed *necessarily* cannot be met by confinement to private prisons? It is not entirely obvious that prison life must be more abusive, neglectful or costly under private than under public ownership/management.

Prison officers hired for life under a state regime may be better placed to deal helpfully with those in their care. On the other hand, they may have little incentive properly to attend to prisoners, being well placed to keep their jobs however many riots and suicides their indifference or malevolence may provoke. Warders hired by the state may be optimally conscientious and cost-effective; on the other hand, they may be very lax and given to the most extraordinary feather-bedding. Privately owned or managed prisoners might well prove insecure; yet it is possible that they might turn out, over time, to be more secure. Private owners might garner profits from poorer standards and reduced staff; but they might equally do so from more efficient and innovative organisation. Private owners might of course be more cruel; but assuming appropriate types and standards of independent review and inspection, and assuming that profitability depended on a co-operative clientele, private sector warders might prove kinder. In any event, the compulsory regime of the prison remains a compulsory regime, whether owned privately or not. The practical question in all this is whether the normal prison regime can be maintained at lower cost by resorting to privately managed schemes. Across the board, I do not think so. But the relevant consideration is that this is best attended to as a practical matter, to be decided empirically rather than philosophically.

As with prisons, then so with many other sectors. Whether we manage by monopoly or by competition should be determined by empirical considerations. For the state to allow or to encourage competition is only another way of redrawing, not demolishing, its power. Much Right-wing divestment is inspired by greed, and by a concern with decentralisation. The latter concern at least is legitimate. The only question is whether and when privatisation is an apt response to it. In any event, privatisation does not and cannot get rid of the state, as opposed to redesigning it. Monopoly is dangerous – like airplanes and electricity – but also in part desirable. In any event, even if we seek to eliminate monopoly, unregulated competition remains the most reliable means of bringing it back.

Common ownership?

Socialism, we may say with Arblaster, is one (or more) projected means of achieving the common good. This may be understood as community. But socialism cannot meaningfully be construed as an attack upon individuality. If individuality and community are consistent with one another and with the common good, then socialism will prove consistent with both. There must always be variable means of achieving any projected common good. Socialism will represent some particular vision of the sort of end to be achieved, and perhaps of the means of achieving it. Conventionally, socialism has been concerned with the achievement of solidarity and justice by means of some form of economic community – which is fairly captured by the expression 'collectivism'. Solidarity, however, is a form of loyalty (as to family, class, nation), and justice is a principle of right (irrespective of specific loyalties or attachments) – so that although we may speak of being 'loyal' to justice, such usage is misplaced, and justice ultimately trumps loyalty, and therefore solidarity. This then allows us to say that the end of socialism is justice and that the commonest means projected of achieving it is collectivism.

But what does 'collectivism' mean? It has usually been associated in some way with common ownership of the means of production. 'Common ownership', however, is a much under-analysed notion. For a start, the state, on a Hobbesian understanding, is already and implicitly the ultimate owner of all that is accessible and 'owned' by subjects/citizens. This is betrayed by the fact that, if collective decision pronounces on balance that my land is required for public purposes – for example, road and rail construction, crises relating to defence or health and so on – then such property may be compulsorily acquired. If, further, I die intestate, and without heirs recognised in law, then my property 'reverts' to the state. Wilderness, moreover, title to which is not legally assigned to individuals, is assumed already to be held by the state. If, finally, the state is entitled in any event to tax my earnings and property at highly varied rates – which may run in different communities from 10 per cent to 90 per cent, then the implication must be that I can have no *predetermined* right to any proportion of what I normally refer to as 'my' property.

The fiction of ultimate title being held by the community is not a recommendation to the effect that the state directly manage all property within its confines. The fiction of ultimate community title merely reminds us that, at the limit, in conditions adjudged sufficiently serious by collective decision, what is called private property may always be recalled to direct public control. In short, on a residual basis, some species of 'common ownership' can already by hypothesised for sovereign communities. Having said as much, it would obviously be foolish for states to recall property to direct common control on a basis that is haphazard or unfair. For a state to attempt itself directly to manage *all* properties within its confines would be both foolish and impossible. One might call this 'common ownership' but it would amount to nothing more than common despotism.

Now if we conceive of the sovereign community as enjoying ultimate title to all property that is held within it, then what we call 'private property' must be viewed as goods held either with the permission, or

with the protection, of the state. If private property can be held
without condition, then this must mean that the so-called sovereign
community neither has title to it nor means of defending it nor capacity
to expropriate. And this would be absurd. The fact that a sovereign
community reserves to itself ultimate title does not mean that it does
or should attempt direct management. 'Private' property as such is
not to be viewed as antipathetic to the interests of the community. If
we hypothesise a genuinely democratic sovereign community, then all
property held by particulars, individual or corporate, is held with that
community's express or tacit assent, and on the grounds that private
holdings are either consistent, or not inconsistent, with the sovereign
community's overarching interests. Observers may contend either
minimally, that private property does not harm the common interest,
or maximally, that private acquisition is the only means of enhancing
the public good. But both of these positions are consistent with the
notion that substantial decentralised control is acceptable or desirable.
Since private ownership in the modern world nowhere significantly
equates with a complete right of use and abuse, the *terms* of ownership will be far more important than the *fact* of ownership. Bernard
Mandeville's upsetting way of putting this was:

> So Vice is beneficial found,
> When it's by Justice lopt and bound.

We may view state ownership as either direct or reserved, being the
former only sometimes and the latter always. Direct ownership may
be enjoyed by the sovereign community itself, or by sub-sovereign
entities within it. While ownership of goods and services may be
vested in public or private entities, title will not guarantee that
management of either is fair or foul, astute or cack-handed, decentralised or centralised. Ownership is a matter of formal title. In itself it
hasn't anything necessarily to do with the efficiency or morality of
control. Industries whose direct ownership is lodged in the public
sphere may be managed both peremptorily and inefficiently. Industries
in the private sphere may be managed both efficiently and fairly. If we
hypothesise that the state already holds title in reserve, this ceases to
be a matter of importance. Where the state holds title directly, the test
must be: what advantage does this bring? The agents of the state have
limited time and resources. In the course of doing whatever they do,
they must prioritise. In some emergency they may find it essential to

help bring in the harvest, fight locusts, defend against flood. But it cannot routinely be their priority to collect the rubbish or to manufacture pyjamas and bicycles. Decentralisation and devolution are not only political but also economic.

Public ownership as such guarantees little. For though the public – the people – may own an industry, they are not collectively in a position to manage it. Who then will? Those whom Parliament or government appoint. In China and Indonesia, the generals are commonly given these jobs. The problem then becomes that of securing that managers of state corporations are simply not feathering their own nests covertly, as distinct from those in private corporations who do so overtly. The problem is not that business is business and politics not. The problem rather is that an elected government, itself quite small in relation to the population as a whole, has not the capacity to execute all its other business, while directly managing all, or only the more important, sectors of the economy. Common ownership is implicit. Direct ownership is often self-defeating. The problem is not with ownership, but with management, and the two are too often confused.

It may be useful then to inspect ownership and management together. We shall take it that direct ownership may be by public or private agents. We may take it too that what is owned is nothing unless managed, and that management, in two of its more important aspects, is centralist and decentralist. If we devise matrices from ownership and management, each in the two forms proposed, we observe four outcomes, as in the table below.

Management

		centralist	decentralist
	public	CPuO [1]	DPuO [2]
Ownership			
	private	MPrO [4]	CoPrO [3]

These outcomes are (1) Centralised Public Ownership (CPuO), (2) Decentralised Public Ownership (DPuO), (3) Competitive Private Ownership (CoPrO) and (4) Monopolistic Private Ownership (MPrO). Socialists have been conventionally identified as firmly for (1) and against (4). This, as it happens, is equally conventionally a mistake. Many socialists have been firmly opposed to (1), perhaps P.-J. Proudhon most notoriously among them. There is in fact only one unarguable common commitment among socialists – and that is *against* (4). As regards principle, this (and only this) opposition to Monopolistic Private Ownership is bedrock. To enact it, there must of course be some choice of one or more of the other three strategies. But to oppose (4) implies no necessary or principled or exclusive commitment to (1). If, therefore, a commitment to *direct* Centralised Public Ownership is in order, it is entirely derivative, being validated or not by experience. If this conclusion hints at a proximity between social democrats and modern liberals, it is only because, doctrinally, the proximity exists. There may, however, be too much of an inclination to attempt to identify the relevance and meaning of socialism entirely in terms of doctrine or principle. I shall argue, on the contrary, for attending first and foremost to constituency, and then to the principles appropriate to it.

If the object is to achieve the common good, two practical political and economic questions arise. The first is whether there is any necessary relationship between promoting the common good and encouraging particular types of ownership, as by private persons or public utilities. Generally, socialists have been disposed to encourage state ownership. Liberals (and conservatives) have been generally disposed to encourage private ownership. Clearly, who owns a business can strongly correlate with who benefits from it, who actually manages it, and how. But the larger and more complex the affair, the more awkward is the correlation. It will be clear, to begin, that legal ownership does not guarantee control or accountability – whether the owner is a simple individual or the state itself. If a private individual owns the Ford Motor Company, as Lee Iacocca remarked of his boss, he may know nothing of how the business is managed or defended. If, by contrast, the state wholly or partly owns the economy, in the name of the people, this may really be nothing more than a figleaf for, for example, the Soviet *nomenclatura*, or for Djilas's 'New Class' – which is to say for managers who are not only selfish, but inefficient.

The second question is whether there is any necessary relationship between promoting the common good and utilising a particular style of management to do so, perhaps in the form of monopoly, or possibly in the form of diffused (competitive) control. Just as ownership does not guarantee control and accountability, neither does monopolistic management necessarily secure efficiency or public benefit. Where socialists favour monopolies, they tend to prefer them to be public. Where liberals (and conservatives) favour monopolies, they tend to prefer them to be private. But these are tendencies, not iron laws. The socialist, Proudhon, was obsessed with decentralised management. The conservative, Bismarck, was happy to promote government monopoly in the management of particular industries. Are monopolistic public ownership and centralised management specifically and characteristically socialist? These are questions that hang over the history of the movement.

The words 'socialism' and 'communism' were first used in France and England in the first decades of the nineteenth century to cover many different ideas and programmes. The exclusive concern of Macfarlane is with common ownership. He reminds us that the idea is not new and usefully hints at the historical and conceptual complexity of the subject. Macfarlane traces its appearance through such sources as Aristophanes, Plato, the Bible, Chrysostom, Augustine, Aquinas, Marsilius, Wyclif, the Anabaptists, the Diggers, Locke, Rousseau, Paine and others, up to the present.

First, common ownership may be urged upon only a particular class or estate in society, as distinct from all subjects/citizens inclusively. Macfarlane takes us back to Plato's *Republic*, where common ownership is restricted to the class of Guardians. Francis of Assisi believed that individual friars should not possess property. Francis's aversion would be consistent with the position that friars should own no property either individually or collectively, *and with the position* that friars should own property only collectively and not individually. As with Plato, this second position would not extend common ownership to the entire membership of society, but restricts its exercise to some particular caste, class or estate within it.

Second, much radical redistribution has nothing to do with common ownership. For example, the concern to compensate Maoris or Aborigines or African Americans for historic injustices may be projected in the form of simple redistribution of land or goods or tax revenues (as in the case of reparations) to individual members of the communities affected. The classic agrarian concern to take land from the rich and give it to the poor – as in cases like Bolivia, Chile, Zimbabwe or South Africa – has nothing to do with altering the structure of individual ownership, but only with expanding the range of agents admitted to ownership. Macfarlane instances Tom Paine as one who sought redistribution from the rich to the poor, as distinct from commmon ownership among them.

Third, common ownership might in principle extend to all

production – to all industries and services – or be restricted only to some. Common ownership may be severely limited to 'natural monopolies', such as gas, water, or railways, without prejudice to whether any given monopoly is in fact 'natural' or not. Modern social democrats have usually expressed a restrictive interest in ownership and control of 'the commanding heights of the economy'. More generally, common ownership, where sought, will tend to be targeted on those goods or services that are viewed as crucial. To some, what is crucial will be religion and doctrine; these the state may fence off as a zone exclusive to itself; hence such a dictum as *eius regio, eius religio*, privileging a single profession of faith; and possibly too such institutions as may accompany this: exclusive state publishing or state broadcasting companies. Key goods and services may be designated by others as policing and defence; or health and education; or railways and aviation; or steel and nuclear energy; or chip technology and interstellar travel. As history moves, so the list of key goods and services will change. Whatever the list, the cash value of common ownership characteristic-ally reduces to control by limited élites, as distinct from the community as a whole. Common ownership of course may also express, however rarely, a truly representative and inclusive process – as in the occasional tennis club, friendly society or artists' commune.

Fourth, common ownership may be designed to serve many different purposes, not all of them mutually compatible. Karl Schumacher, notes Macfarlane, saw common ownership as crucial to the achieve-ment of democracy. The Diggers saw it as a way to impose strict equality upon everyone. Most liberals and some socialists view the object of common ownership to be the removal of constraints on the emergence of individual excellence. Many conservatives see some degree of common ownership as essential to the strengthening of existing social hierarchies by making the state more popular and the economy more efficient. (This last was the aim sourly attributed by Bebel, Bernstein and a majority of the SPD in the 1880s to Bismarck's programme of state nationalisation, as of the rail system.) At some point or other, common ownership has been seen as crucial to the realisation of a variety of ideals – such as solidarity, consensus and equality, not excluding freedom of choice.

If socialism is understood as committed to the ideals of equality and solidarity, then common ownership, conceived as the technical device of 'wholesale nationalisation', cannot (following Anthony Crosland) be an indispensable means to the realisation of these ideals. 'Common ownership', after all, might mean little more, in any given historical context, than the expropriation by some of all the rest – in which procedure little is to be found that is either egalitarian or solidaristic. More importantly, the notion of 'wholesale' nationalisation is egregiously comprehensive. 'Common ownership' might imply it; but it might equally imply retail nationalisation, a pick-and-choose procedure: *à la carte*. If virtually nobody accepts 'all or nothing at all', then the only true socialist is one who knows to choose rightly or fashionably on the occasion. But this seems a highly subjective principle.

For socialism to be committed to the principle of common ownership is, in any event, not even distinctive. Indeed there can be scarcely any Conservative who opposes *all* common ownership – the army, navy, health, education, the safety net and what the former Tory premier, Macmillan, referred to summarily as the 'family silver'. The idea of common ownership cannot today be exclusive to socialists. This is not really what divides the parties. In so far as common ownership is peculiar to socialists, in the sense that they may mistakenly view themselves as nothing without it, the question is obviously vexed. For socialists must then decide how far common ownership should extend and where it should end. If not all industries are to be nationalised or collectivised, then which are to be targeted and which, by contrast, will you *laissez faire*? The problem beneath the problem is to disengage the principle which aptly shows us where to go in and where to stay out, distinguishing between how much is too little and how much is not enough. It remains to be seen whether any policy issue as philosophically tricky and brutishly concrete as this should be embraced by any party as a matter of self-definition.

There is a hint in Macfarlane that socialism may abandon its distinctiveness in abandoning common ownership. If there can be no socialism without common ownership, then the latter is of the essence of socialism and constitutes its *end*. If there can be socialism without common ownership, then the latter is justified or not by changing historical circumstances, and is accordingly instrumental, a *means*. What makes either answer difficult – common ownership *qua* end or common ownership *qua* means – is the complexity of the subject, a complexity too often overlooked. Common ownership normally means state ownership, and, as earlier observed, state ownership can be either centralised or decentralised. Even socialists who firmly support state ownership do not necessarily support it in its centralised form. If we take an issue like local government, we can see that the orientation of many socialists is in no way distinguishable from that of legions of conservatives: they seek to deny any entrenchment of local authority, and to assimilate all localities to the uniform diktat of the centre. But other socialists are energetically supportive of various forms of local entrenchment, on the grounds that to eviscerate democracy in the regions, counties, cities and boroughs is to make a mockery of the democratic residue kept on ice in the national Parliament or assembly, as Martin Hollis argues.

So state ownership can be centralised or decentralised. To buy into it as such does not assist in determining whether its centralist or decentralist form is the more apt option, either for all time or just on some suitable occasion. Morever, private ownership can be monopolistic or competitive (and diffused). Though socialists are perfectly capable of opposing private ownership as such, they have characteristically attacked it where it is monopolistic or oligopolistic. They have not made a fetish of attacking private ownership where it is genuinely competitive. A competitive private sector is characteristically opposed only where competition there seems perverse. It is difficult to sustain the case for competition in the supply of basic services like water, electricity, hospitals and trams. It seems equally difficult to inveigh against it in the supply of such items as soft drinks, clothing and entertainment (at least in peacetime).

In sum, since just about every party accepts some state ownership, mere acceptance of this is no longer distinctive. Further, to accept state ownership is not to say how much of it one accepts – and the question of how much and where is today the only important consideration. There is in addition the divorce between ownership and management. In complex organisations the location of ownership does not necessarily determine the quality and direction of management. The state may own a business and manage it woefully – with poor service or product and a drain on state revenues. By contrast, the state may not own businesses which are nonetheless managed brilliantly – with good service or product and a boost to state revenues. Ownership, after all, is just an entitlement to use; it may be hemmed in by a range of legitimate constraints. Ownership need not mean that the owner is entitled to do whatever he likes with what is owned. The owner, for example, of farmland may be constrained by easements which allow pedestrians or ramblers right of access. The owner of a factory may be aptly constrained by legislation imposing conditions relating to health, safety, pollution, overtime, minimum wages, child-care, taxation (PAYE) and so on. If the same relevant effect can be achieved without formal title, then it is hard to see why securing title should be made an article of faith. Whatever achieves the object most simply also achieves it best. In short, the question whether to seek direct title or not, either individually or collectively, has every appearance of being an empirical issue, not a matter of principle. Seeking accommodation in London in 1985, it might have been better to buy; doing so in Paris in the same year, it would almost certainly have been better to rent. In the circumstances it would not have been rational to entertain an abstract preference for owning over renting. Neither can there be a rationally abstract preference for owning over managing, and the two remain quite distinct. There is yet a further distinction between managing and regulating. To regulate important sectors of the economy does not necessarily require either direct ownership or direct management.

The persistence of government

Between individual and community there is always, if not conflict, then certainly tension. Between them, equally, there is a necessary degree of mutual supportiveness. It is foolish, first, abstractly to oppose the individual to the community; and second, to invite government to uphold the one as over against the other. Individual and community are symbiotic. But the test – the moral value – of communities is what they do to and for their members, that is for individuals. Communities can be dedicated to the unbridled worship of God, to human sacrifice to allay the wrath of totems, to the suppression of alien nations and races, to the triumph of science, to the supremacy of majorities however secured. And this dedication can be expressed with scant respect for the rights of individuals. But such respect must be the litmus test for the soundness of community endeavour.

Respect for rights cannot be secured if no one has a duty to protect them. Taxpayers, parents, students, and citizens in general ultimately enjoy rights through their mutual obligation to defend them. Ideally, a community is no more opposed to its individual members than duties are opposed to rights. Duties must be imposed as a means of defending rights. Action by the community is necessary as a means of securing optimal outcomes for individuals. The choices open to the individual and to the community are limited. The choices open to the individual are constrained by isolation, on the one side, and by association, on the other. An individual acting alone is constrained by the fact that no help may be secured from fellows; the individual acting in society or state, and thus in association with others, is subject to the constraints imposed by such association. There is an up-side, and a down-side, not only to association but also to isolation.

It is a delusion to think that a community can enhance choice as such, as a whole; the simple fact that it exists, deprives the individual of a certain range of choice. It is equally delusory to suppose that the absence of a community can enhance choice as such; the inability of an individual to associate, to co-operate, to benefit from division of labour, itself limits his choices, inhibits his liberty. It is not possible to measure the total volume of choice available in a community.

Some contend that the end socialists should promote is equality. But few if any socialists are prepared to contend that all rewards should be strictly equal. Some contend that socialists should embrace as their principal end the promotion of liberty. But it is commonly replied that should socialists thus define themselves, they cease to be distinguishable from liberals and conservatives. Some contend that socialism does and ought to concern the promotion of community. Yet socialists are not the only ones to promote community; moreover, the notion 'community' encompasses a whole field of flowers and includes not a few weeds (such as tribalism, racism, nationalism, fascism, communism and a great variety of religious fundamentalisms).

There is a problem about attending to the meaning and relevance of socialism in a mode that is exclusively logical. In this case, after all, we are to do with an historical movement, which displays all of the untidiness of history. In many ways socialism clearly emerges from, and passes beyond, its liberal – whom we are often invited today to denominate as conservative – antecedents. An early liberal like Tocqueville accepted equality as an extension of liberty. He and others like him were fearful of state power because of its absolutist past and clear oppressive potential. Twentieth-century conservatives like Ayn Rand have continued in this tradition. Such figures were and are still mistakenly disposed to think that the promotion of the well-being of individuals crucially depends on diminishing the strength and activity of the state. That these liberals were mistaken in no way means that their fears of statist oppression were unfounded. One of the most obviously crucial defects in Marx's theory is its grotesquely simplistic analysis of the state and its unreflecting acceptance of an underlying liberal ideal: the ultimate 'withering away' of the state. The Bolsheviks who came to power in Russia in 1917 took over the Tzarist state apparatus wholesale, little troubled by the risks of such a move.

Socialist-anarchists like Proudhon and liberal socialists like J.S. Mill shared many of the fundamental fears and ideals of antecedents and contemporaries like Montesquieu and Tocqueville. The difference was that figures like Proudhon, Mill, Sorel, Marx, Bernstein, and Jaurès no longer saw the crucial danger to individual self-fulfilment as lying in statist oppression but equally or mostly or exclusively in the inability of the poorest classes (essentially the industrial workforce) to combine either autonomously or via the state apparatus itself to defend against the most outrageous forms of social oppression. Those troubled by the depredations of the new nineteenth-century capitalism would tend to shift the focus from the state-qua-oppressor to the profit-obsessed owners of capital – whom the night-watchman state was devised to empower and to protect. The new socialisms were more an amendment to, than a repudiation of, the antecedent liberalism.

The trouble with the liberals was their difficulty in appreciating the necessary role of the state in overcoming the unjust and destructive effects of a rampant capitalism. The trouble with some socialists (notably the communists) was their indisposition to recall or recognise the dangers of a state system marked by a virtually complete absence of countervailing powers. Social democrats like the Webbs and G. B. Shaw would seek social justice within the framework of a tamed, constitutional state. Liberal conservatives would still oppose these moderates on the grounds that, were we to succeed in concentrating preponderant productive power directly in the hands of the state, we should just be led back, in Hayek's term, to a form of collective 'serfdom'.

From this perspective, the problem for socialists – certainly for social democrats – became that of making use of the state in the cause of social justice, without allowing it to become anew the major source of social injustice that it always was in the past. The challenge was to allow the state a grander role than that of nightwatchman, without allowing it re-entry as *duce* or *führer*. Because of the grasping insensitivity of so many liberals and conservatives to the plight of the poor and disadvantaged, it was easy for socialists mistakenly to attribute to their competitors totally distinct *ends*. The real problem for socialists, however, was to do with inventing new *means* – of achieving older and largely shared ends of liberty and equality. Any socialist movement that could do this would inevitably attract not only most liberals but also many erstwhile conservatives. This task of inventing the new has become all the more acute, in view of the political and economic collapse of the Soviets and the political bankruptcy of state socialism in China as signalled by the 1989 slaughter of students in Peking's Tiananmen Square.

Contemporary conservatism is little more than a throwback to the last century's formal obsession with excluding government from the management of civil society. Conservatives are disposed formally to assume that less state ownership by definition means greater individual liberty. The formal position is mistaken. Without the police, army and judiciary fairly to protect me, without schools, health care and welfare decently to form me, without safe roads, drinking water and enforced standards of factory production, then my formal liberty is a sodden, paper pennant. The conservative position is mistaken – but also deceptive. For the reality behind it is an unspoken concern firmly to deploy government agencies, directly and indirectly, in the management of civil society, as long as this attracts no excess of public attention.

Conservatives are consistently supportive of the security agencies precisely because they can and do operate in secret. And the interests they generally serve are those of profit, which is best prosecuted in the shadows. Everyone is aware of the CIA. But very few are aware, for example, of the DIA. This is the US Defense Intelligence Agency, located in Virginia and Washington, reporting directly to the Joint Chiefs of Staff, operating globally, with no congressional oversight, and a budget five times the size of the CIA's. It was involved along with the DEA in the destruction of Pan Am 103 over Lockerbie in December 1988, and in the later government-sponsored cover-up that put the blame for this on the Libyans – all in order to obscure cowboy government complicity in the murder of 270 people.

The UK Scott inquiry revealed the duplicity of government and security agencies in stoking Saddam Hussein's military ambitions and their preparedness to see ordinary businessmen jailed who could otherwise connect the UK government with the feverish supply of arms to Iraq. The Irangate scandal, at the centre of which operated Lt. Col. Oliver North, revealed the complicity of the Reagan administration in the supply of money to the Iranian mullahs (to covertly buy the release of US hostages in Lebanon) and the illegal supply of arms to the Right-wing Contras in Nicaragua (to bring down a legitimate Left-wing government there). The Watergate scandal and CREEP revealed the complicity of the Nixon government and friendly, paid CIA operatives in undermining the Democratic alternative to conservative administrations in the United States.

Conservatives are quick to talk about liberty and the dangers to it from government. But they are equally quick to make sustained and duplicitous use of government agencies when and as it serves their purposes. Contemporary conservatives genuflect with notorious automaticity to the manna of privatisation (just as socialists used to bow to the dogma of nationalisation). But in this they largely use government as a means of hiving off public assets into private hands. The latter are characteristically few in number, and they reciprocate government old-boyism and good-old-boyism with heart-warmingly liberal donations to conservative causes – electoral and otherwise.

Conservatives have been indifferent to the trivialisation and banalisation of the media. Conservatives have been presiding over an unprecedented pyramiding of private power in the press, in publishing and in television. The concentration of media power, allowed and encouraged in the case of figures like Conrad Black and Rupert Murdoch, attests to a consistent conservative disposition to seek to massage and homogenise the public mind. Conservatives and their think-tanks and talking societies – like the Rand Corporation, the Adam Smith Institute, The Liberty Fund, together with all their born-again hangers-on and acolytes and fellow-travellers – are autonomically disposed to celebrate what is variably and repeatedly referred to as perhaps 'the end of ideology' or as 'the end of history' but which only amounts to an extraordinary effort to terminate any significant opposition to conservative ideas.

The simple triumph of money is what conservatives have sponsored. As a part of this, conservatives have (usually, not always) been markedly indifferent to greater unemployment and the tremendous insecurity which this breeds. They talk efficiency and profitability, not self-restraint, common decency and fellow feeling. Their policies have made doctors, teachers, journalists and workers in general insecure – the object being to induce quiet and ease of control. Conservatives talk liberty. But they appear blind as to what this means for ordinary men and women. This is because the liberty that exercises them is principally to do with their access to power, their freedom to dominate. And it is important to see the ways in which they make use of government and its agencies, of power central and devolved, of force and of indirection, to promote their objectives.

Socialists have nothing to be ashamed of in their profession of communitarian ideals. At least in this there is honesty. Older conservatives may profess these ideals too. But their progeny see little profit in it, save perhaps in the area of health. So conservatives who profess a love for liberty mostly speak from the tips of their lips: their hearts are elsewhere. What seems to interest them is privilege (new or old), cheap labour, a submissive workforce, comfortable nuclear families, respect for 'leadership' in short: 'order' – of a kind that serves the well-to-do. It is all very fine to talk up liberty. Senator Barry Goldwater remarked that 'extremism in the service of liberty is no vice'. What he managed to overlook was that 'liberty for the pike is death for the minnow'. The problem is not really to do with liberty. In as far as it is, it is no more a problem for the socialist than for the conservative. The conservative is perhaps more interested in some people *retaining* their liberty, while the socialist may be more interested in other folk *gaining* theirs. But that is a difference of constituencies, not of ideals. The problem for the socialist (again and again) is to keep the gains of nineteenth-century liberalism – hence firm respect for a constitutional state – and to marry these with state protection and promotion of the rights of individuals, both formal and substantive.

Historically, socialists have certainly been very much concerned with utilising the resources of the community as a whole in order to empower individuals. In as far as they have customarily sponsored the interests of weaker individuals, they have been concerned to encourage them to combine forces and to fall back upon the device of government where they fairly and effectively can. Social democrats, at least, have been well aware that it is not at all on the cards that the state will disappear. If nuclear energy is not going to be un-invented, it is even less likely that government will be. Like any other invention, it will remain open to the service of all ends, good and evil. That airplanes crash and automobiles pollute is not an argument for vaporising planes and cars; it is an argument rather for making planes safe and cars clean; and this through intelligent government intervention. If the automobile represented choice and liberty as a whole, as such, then there could be little justification for regulating its emissions and movements. But the automobile does not represent liberty and choice as such. Its perfectly free circulation allows one sort of liberty (to quickly visit the country on a Sunday morning), while taking away others (the option among drivers and non-drivers not to suffer rising levels of asthma; the option to avoid reaching Monday morning's work at a speed of 5 mph or less).

It is a customary conservative pastime to pretend that we can lop off the Medusan head of government, or at least shave its serpentine locks. This pretence is more than disingenuous, it is dangerous. For it disguises and obscures the persistent and continuing effects of a form of organisation which has shown little inclination to shrink, let alone to disappear. Government may be quiescent or interventionist. But government as such does not go away. Vacuums will be filled. If 'the' government collapses in Rwanda, then the movement of hundreds of thousands of refugees into neighbouring Tanzania and Zaire ensures that the governing responsibilities of these and other states plus auxiliary organisations like The Red Cross automatically expand. The USSR dissolved; but the CIS sprang up in its place. There was the expectation of a peace dividend; but from the ashes of Soviet collapse have risen (a) a ruthless Russian mafia and (b) a virulent slavophile nationalism led by Vladimir Zhirinovsky, the one being policed in London and New York while the thirst of the other is slaked by an infusion of billions of dollars courtesy of the G7 states via World Bank and other facilities.

The question is not how to reduce government to its most skeletal self. Rather, the problem is to establish the right sort of balance between use of government directly, in the form of collective state action, and use of it indirectly, by allowing and empowering private individuals and firms to perform. No social democratic government wishes to see collective action entirely displace individual engagement. No conservative government wishes to see individual engagement entirely displace collective action. This again underscores the difficulty of establishing a perfectly clear boundary of principle between liberals and socialists. Obviously, philosophical approximations can, shall and should be made. But the moral too is that there can be no safe reliance on abstract principle alone to secure a reliable understanding. Constituency is not everything and it would be politically dangerous if it were. But it is not irrelevant or of secondary importance that, in the UK, the Labour Party receives £2.5m per annum in grants from trade unions, while the Conservative Party relies for the bulk of its funding (its 1994 balance was £20m) upon gifts from business interests, national and international. The danger is, that should socialist parties carry too far their policy of capturing conservative constituencies, they may be abandoned by erstwhile socialist constituencies, which may miserably withdraw from politics altogether, or become vulnerable to the allure of religious otherworldliness, fundamentalism, neo-nazism or the far Right.

Labouring for a constituency

Socialism is as much or more a social movement than it is a philosophical doctrine or a scientific project. It is natural that we should propose to define it, but over-ambitious perhaps to expect too much of our definitions. It is easy enough to establish conventionally what we mean by 'water' or 'quadruped' or 'excluded middle'. The same cannot quite hold for 'socialism' or 'conservatism' or 'liberalism'. It is clear that we have need of definitions. But it also clear that, in the end, they are circular, amounting to nothing more than tautologies. It is easy, often useful, even inevitable for us to claim that 'socialism = such and such'. But the claim must always prove inadequate. The 'such and such' of socialism could be taken to mean something like 'equality' or 'liberty' or 'equal liberty' or 'ownership of the means of production', etc. The definitional claim (whatever it is) may be read too rigidly, so that it fails to accommodate changing circumstance: the tree that does not bend breaks. If, by contrast, the definitional claim is interpreted too loosely, it may be made to fit any circumstance at all: and the emblem of the chameleon is the badge of a loser.

I suspect this fuzziness of definition arises because we are less to do with flat description than with hope and ambition, not of one or a few but of very many people, caught up in an ethical movement which goes back two centuries, and (on some readings) back to the beginnings of Christianity itself. Adherents have confronted marginally different problems, which they have sought to resolve in marginally different ways. Usually, they have had to negotiate compromises of various sorts to take them forward, in intimate seminars and vast conferences. Any definition of socialism which purports to say what all socialists were and are about will not fail to be contested. Not all socialists know what they are about; not all agree on what they know. The reason is not down to avoidable confusion.

All important social movements are protean, hydra-headed, evolving. About them it is less easy to concur than might scientists in plotting the aptest path to Mars, or in recognising a new species of orchid from Fiji. To supply a definition of what we think socialism objectively *means* will have some use. But we must see it as the preserve of the external observer, even if the latter is an 'insider'. The external observer purports to freeze the action and to take it in as a whole. But each individual actor's view is partial. And he who purports to speak for a movement as a whole, when his perspective can be no more than a part, is bound in part to speak a lie. We thus should place no great stress upon objective definitions of socialism, since this may obscure the actual range of claims among those who act as moral agents within the movement(s) over time.

Every social philosophy or social movement must incorporate some concept of justice. Any movement which prioritises liberty or equality (or whatever) thinks, in this, to locate a valid principle of justice. So it is right to incorporate into the meaning of socialism some concern with social justice, while accepting that this is not enough. No social movement is plausibly to be distinguished from any other on the grounds that it and it alone is for justice. No more than any one individual is to be distinguished from all the rest on the grounds that he or she is committed to the truth and the rest to falsity. Liberals, conservatives and socialists all promote themselves as adherents of justice, despite markedly different decency quotients among members, as well as markedly different notions about what decency and justice require.

There are at least five different ways in which distinctions between social movements can be made. (a) The first concerns the motives, or the sincerity with which these are held, by proponents (the *ad hominem* question). (b) The difference between the principles invoked (perhaps liberty rather than equality), and the difference in the way principles are ranked (perhaps equality over liberty) by different parties. (c) The way in which abstract mediating principles (say liberty/equality) are linked to lower level principles (say liberty to private ownership/equality to public ownership). (d) The identity of the specific constituency being promoted or defended (perhaps mill owners versus workers or press barons versus salariat). (e) The logical tenability of the principles espoused – although I omit discussion of this here.

(a) An opponent may possibly be attacked, not for principles professed, but on the grounds (*ad hominem*) that these principles are insincerely held. Is there a fair distinction to be made between liberals, conservatives and socialists in this regard? I find no cause for thinking so. Suppose we claim and agree that socialists view exploitation as morally wrong. We cannot possibly expect that conservatives will then conveniently embrace the idea that exploitation is morally right.

Consider that exploitation, as a matter of course, does not just mean taking something from someone, but doing so unfairly or unjustly, without cause or entitlement. The definition of justice lobbed by Cephalus down the front of Plato's *Republic* was that of 'giving each man his due'. To take from persons what is rightly theirs is expropriation, cheating, theft. 'Expropriation' may tend to refer restrictively to property. But 'exploitation' does not; it expands greedily to encompass labour, rent, service. No such concept as exploitation, which has the notion of wrongdoing wedged in its marrow, can be the acknowledged moral prop of any major social movement.

Because socialists do attack exploitation, they will not find themselves distinguished from other movements and parties in this. Conservatives will not concede, nor will it be true, that they are all or most of them insincere in their espousal of justice. They cannot and will not accept that what they propose and do is somehow in principle wrong and unfair. Not even fascists and nazis would tumble into that crevasse. Thus it is difficult to imagine that there can be any effective or reliable way of distinguishing between major social movements on the basis of sincere, as opposed to insincere, adherence to the notion of justice as such.

(b) Justice, taken as the master principle, has to fall back upon mediating or underlabourer principles in order to constitute itself in some concrete way. I mean by mediating principles, notions like liberty, equality, fraternity, tolerance, etc. Parties may distinguish themselves by including or excluding certain of these principles. Alternatively, parties may salute the same principles, but distinguish themselves by ranking principles in mutually exclusive ways. Can we then distinguish between the major social movements, and the political parties representing them, on the basis of clearly distinct and mutually opposed principles, or on the basis of divergent ways of ranking these principles? Is it tenable to claim that the chief mediating principle of socialism is, for example, equality, or of conservatism liberty, or of liberalism some form of liberal equality?

This is not the occasion to deal with such a question in the detail it requires. My conclusion is simply that today's major social movements tend to employ exactly the same run of general mediating principles, and that, though they do tend to accord these principles different priority rankings, they do not hold to these distinct rankings in a highly stable and reliable way. Let us say for the sake of argument that conservatives support liberty. This becomes an interesting – that is, distinguishing – claim if it means that socialists oppose liberty. But socialists do not. If we take one of the more important meanings of 'liberty' to be 'support for such rights as free expression, assembly and political representation', then obviously social democrats are firmly committed to these forms of liberty.

Let us now take a parallel claim, and say that socialists support equality. Again, such a claim becomes interesting – that is, distinguishing – if it means that conservatives oppose equality. But one of the meanings of 'equality' is some form of 'equality of opportunity' or 'a level playing field' or the equal status, for example, of old and new money. In these and certain other respects, conservatives of the centre and Left are plainly committed at the least to equality *qua* 'equality of opportunity'.

Let us move on to liberals, and say that they support liberal equality, or perhaps equal liberty. This might be taken to mean that liberal principles are somehow neatly lodged between those of socialists and conservatives. It is a plausible claim. Liberalism puts the principle of liberty first. But liberals recognise such liberty to be abortive where it empowers the one or few and demands subjection and servility from the rest. Thus the liberal is led from liberty to equality, demanding more of the second in order to have more of the first. The problem is – from the perspective of establishing differences between major parties and movements – that exactly the same sort of claims can and have been made by both conservatives and socialists.

One argument among socialists is that equality on its own or as such is inadequate. Equality is important, but relates to different objects, and the value of equality will depend upon the objects to which it relates. There can be equality in liberty, but also in slavery. There may be equality in dignified free expression, or in fearful, glum silence; in trial by jury, or by Star Chamber; in decent education, or in distressing ignorance; in excellent health care, but also in widespread illness. In short, only some, not all, kinds of equality are worth having.

From the conservative ranks, it can and has been hinted that liberty as such means nothing. Liberty, after all, only mirrors the object brought before it: proud prince or tatty toad. The despot too has liberty, to dominate, to repress, to revel in what only he has got. Indeed, the despot can be said to be 'taking a liberty'; and there is nothing in this for the constitutional conservative to admire.

Reflective conservatives are no more consistently for an unconditional liberty than are reflective socialists for a mindless equality. In the end, it becomes difficult to distinguish these parties in perfectly clear philosophical terms – either on the basis that one deploys mediating principles of justice which the other simply rejects, or on the basis that each ranks the same philosophical principles in indisputably different ways. One reason for the philosophical proximity between all major parties in advanced industrial states is that they all tend, first and foremost, to be committed to the processes of constitutional democracy, to which the divergencies in their party platforms become secondary. Philosophically, at least, conservatives and socialists, together with liberals, are all muddlers. A much more careful case can and should be made, but this is not the occasion for it.

(c) Can a distinction be made between conservatism and, for example, liberalism in relation to lower level principles? For example, conservative support for the broad principle of liberty is often viewed as a justification for the promotion of private property. Similarly, socialist espousal of the broad principle of equality is often seen as a justification for the promotion of public ownership. Surely much more of case can be made at this lower level than at the higher level, as Brian Barry's argument for collectivism shows. Clause 4 of the Labour Party constitution, for example, famously claims that the party is committed to 'common ownership of the means of production, distribution and exchange'. Common or national or public or collective ownership has been a key element in socialist programmes; and, at this lower level of principle, it has served to distinguish them, if not perfectly, then at least as a matter of emphasis, from parties of the Right. There is much, however, that is imprecise in our understanding of common ownership, as argued earlier.

(d) In how far can major parties and social movements be distinguished from one another in relation to the different constituencies they represent? Constituency is rarely mentioned in close analysis of the ideas underpinning ideological movements. But I suspect that it is at the least as important as any of the factors earlier discussed relating to (a) sincerity of commitment to justice, (b) types and ranking of mediating principles, and (c) the lower level, instrumental principles deployed – which is not to say that the question of constituency is ever entirely separable from the other three.

A great deal of debate has turned round the question of what socialism 'is', and how a socialist party like Labour in the UK might be distinguished from rival parties. It has been suggested, for example, that the key to the differential character of Labour is located in Clause 4 of the party's constitution and that, should this finger in the dike be pulled, the formerly distinctive character of the party would be flooded. There is difficulty with this position. If it is right, then it must mean that the identity of socialism is entirely derived from a lower-lying instrumental principle. It is perhaps like saying that childbirth means exiting the womb *via* the vagina, so that an exit secured *via* caesarean section could not count as birth. In this, the end is reduced to one possible means of achieving it.

Clearly, the object of direct common ownership is to supply a solution to a problem. Even if a proposed solution like common ownership were to fail in every respect, which is very far from the case, we should still have no grounds for inferring that the problem giving rise to it had itself gone away. In illness, it is best to give priority to the diagnosis, not the cure; in hunting, to target before firing; in travel, to allow destination to dictate type of transport. In general, it seems wise to stipulate the problem before supplying the solution. However, even anterior to the problem, it is essential, in any social context, to understand *who* it is that has the problem. To locate the 'body' of a mass political party or movement is no more than to identify its constituency.

In making sense of significant mass movements, we seem disposed to start back to front. We tend to ask, in the case of a party, 'what are its low-level, operational principles?' (Nationalisation? Privatisation?). Before or after, we are disposed to enquire, 'what are the grand ends or overarching problems of the movement?' These enquiries require much more time and energy. In consequence, we often never get around to the question with which we should have begun: Who are the people either that constitute the movement or who cause or occasion its initiation? Mass parties are reliably, and certainly initially, more to do with particular classes of people, and with the gross problems or designs of these people, than with what we take to be their abstract ends or their concrete, lower-level policies.

Important political movements are always associated with powerful, underlying social needs or forces. The traditional support of conservatives has tended to be from business, siphoning off a third and more of working people to the cause of 'capital'. The traditional rod and staff of the socialists have tended to be working people, poorer people, minority and disadvantaged folk, siphoning off from middle and upper income categories a small but significant percentage of sympathy, support and even leadership. In the UK context, the concrete policies of socialists, conservative and liberal parties have undulated up and down over the graph of time, and shall continue so. But what matters most is the relationship between the surface movement of the parties and the submerged social forces which will anchor them, or cast them adrift. What one must fix upon first is constituency, and only after upon the abstract ends and concrete means of guiding it.

First priority must go to securing an understanding of constituency – that body of folk whose just (or unjust) interests are addressed. 'Parties' are called that precisely because they are 'part-ial'. A party without a constituency is not of this earth. A party that seeks to attract support must forge a policy that a sizeable constituency can recognise and own. This is not just a matter of holding a mirror to reality. It is a matter, too, of inventing fair bargains and trade-offs. For there must always be some tension within constituencies, and these differences must be negotiated. A party in power will always clasp to its breast – which is not necessarily to say dishonestly – the 'national interest'. But however fiercely it declares its adoration of the whole, the wise observer will keep an eye on how it defends and promotes its base. In a stable polity, the interests of the better-off are easier to promote than are those of the disadvantaged. And for this reason, the parties of the rich are always more likely to control the state than are those of the poor.

'Conservative' and 'socialist' appear to me to be poor or confusing names for a party. This is so because the first thing these names address is a doctrine, not a constituency. 'Labour' is a singularly apt name for a party just because it omits to succumb to such misdirection. It is open to a party of labour to speak to this constituency in all its forms: to majority labour, minority labour; to women's labour, men's labour; manual labour, scholarly labour; actual labour, prospective labour; to those who are waged, to those on the dole. To be concerned with labour has nothing to do with denigrating business. At the heart of business is production. But of course it is labour that produces. Business and labour may be seen as contrary forces. But their contrariness turns round the proclivity of business to see its purpose as autonomous: in pursuit of profit, whatever the effect of this on either producers or consumers. What labour has to teach business is not enmity, but that this autonomy of profit is both illusory and cruel. Labour's purpose is not to throttle business, which cannot be done without throttling labour. Labour's purpose rather is to channel business: to harness it to a common good, to encompassingly humane ends which business *qua* business cannot know.

The danger to the labour movement is that it may cease to see itself as sufficiently distinct from the instrument which it exists to tame. Too often, the ultimate aspirations of the movement run in tandem with those of the crass business ethic which the movement exists to oppose. Even those most sympathetic to the miners or dockworkers or railwaymen or dustmen, characteristically have no wish themselves to mine, unload cargo, run trains or collect rubbish. Work, from the beginnings of large states and empires, came to be glossed as *the* punishment for sin. To expel Adam and Eve from the Garden was a metaphor for sentencing humankind to a life of travail. We have changed little of this fundamental perspective: on work as a miserable condition to be endured, not as the key mould in which we shape and animate life. There is rather more to work than desperate hopes of escape from it – whether into lottery leisure or the drylands of the unemployment cheque. If labour, itself, can see no further than profit, sees a necessary evil but no opportunity in work, then the ultimate constituencies of labour and business become indistinguishable. The differences that persist become positional: labour seeking to grow into the great tree of wealth and power that business, confining labour to its shadow, already is.

If labour shares the same accumulationist ethic as its opponents, then how can it not be carping, envious, and negative in the way that these opponents claim? There is nothing intrinsically attractive about the less-well-off either being or wanting to become like the rich – fatter, slicker, self-absorbed, turned-off and humanly irrelevant. The labour movement cannot afford to theorise its character in terms of an obsession with 'surplus value', with reclaiming every jot and tittle of its share of the spoils, with an unbridled, devil-take-the-hindmost, unecological 'consumerism'. It cannot afford to concern itself merely with redistributing the tinned sweets of an increasingly febrile industrial and post-industrial system. At least labour has ceased to be abstractly distracted by nationalisation as some species of panacea. What it cannot afford is to be misled by the mirage of unending and comprehensive leisure. Too many people have to work. Too many, even if they have it, despise it. So many more, victims of a lottery mentality, fantasise escape. The stress associated both with the contemporary deformation of work, and with the perverse lack of work, is leading into elaborate forms of escapism and dependency: as upon amphetamines, acid, designer drugs, heroin, cocaine, crack, etc.

In the end, it is crucial that labour repudiate the repudiation of labour – which is to say of work – itself. When the socialist movement finds itself in trouble over its policies, it can be no bad idea to reflect anew on its constituency. If it values that constituency, then it must embrace more warmly the idea of work itself as a value. One can theorise the embrace as a duty. But it makes far more sense to seek work as a way of life. If the socialist movement is not to change its base, then it must attend to it more imaginatively. Labour is under assault. Jobs are entered into later in life. They are held more briefly. They are held less securely, on a shared and part-time and low-wage basis. There may be more opportunities for those with technical training and skill. But there are fewer opportunities for those who are young or middle-aged and whose skills are manual. Management seeks savings by shaking out labour. And this shaking means the breaking of lives. Even those who have work are made insecure in it and increasingly subservient for fear of redundancy. No one much wants to work any more, essentially because, in it, they must endure subservience and *angst*. Nor does anyone much want to hire workers because they find them fractious and without commitment. Both labour and the managers of labour require critical adjusting. Any party of labour needs imaginatively to support and generate work, to respect its dignity and creativity, its utility and indispensability.

The problem with work is not the expenditure of energy it entails. Rather, it is the failure to consult and the indifferent, cold, oppressive and manipulative styles stereotypically imposed by managers. Our media and culture are saturated with untiring talk about liberty. But at work, where some spend a third or more of their lives, it is precisely this liberty that is eroded more and more and respected less and less. Teachers cease to wish to teach, doctors to heal, railwaymen to do what they know best, because those who manage increasingly believe themselves entitled to overthrow the stable expectations, autonomy and dignity of those whom they manage. And so it must be, in large part because of the accelerating decouplement of reward from work.

After the 1989 privatisation and dismantlement of electricity production in the UK, the chairmen (or chief executives) of the 12 regional companies all received dubious increases in salary which, by 1994, ranged from £203,000 to £325,000. Union leaders expressed fears that a third of their members might be made redundant, given managerial concern to keep dividends up and dodgy payouts to bosses high. The process was and remains a general one. Managerial salaries climb, security of work erodes. The gains of the bosses flow directly from their own ruthless disembowelling of employees' jobs. In consequence, the manager-worker relationship becomes taut, unstable, distrustful, adversarial. Managers cannot convincingly or meaningfully display respect or goodwill to labour, since the best personal gain of the one accrues from overwhelming loss to the other. Nor can labour have a very high opinion of itself.

We require, in a creative way, to breathe life into the principle of the dignity and value of labour. We have all gone too far – management, society at large, labour itself – in encouraging folk to assume that Nirvana consists in a simple escape from work. When managers render labour redundant, they praise their handiwork – despite their selfish benefit – as eliminating 'waste', 'efficiency' gains. This is not just because they wish to disguise selfish benefit, but because they, like most of us, have allowed themselves to think that 'labour-saving' innovations are worth virtually any human damage that may result. The managers of such monopolistic utilities as gas, electricity, water and telecommunications will conventionally defend their comfortable surpluses and their destructive approach to labour on the grounds that their priority must be to keep the company profitable, not to protect employees against the dole. The principles of land, labour and capital used to be the staples of classical economics. Land may have been overturned by capital. But capital has certainly not been overturned by labour. What we used to speak of as capital, we more commonly refer to now as 'profitability', the profit principle, or indeed as 'market principles'.

This destructive sway of the market principle is associated with our inclination to overlook and even repudiate the significance of *homo laborans* and, more precisely, of *homo faber*. All that we seem to be able to think to do, whether as conservatives or socialists, liberals or Marxists, is to save labour-time, ultimately and cumulatively with the effect of voiding labour of value. Virtually no plumber or carpenter, policeman or solicitor, property developer or tertiary don, seems able any longer to respect his work, to attend to it properly, to extract any genuine satisfaction from it, to avoid costly corner-cutting – so pressed is *l'homme pressé* always to get away from the very engagement that structures most of his life and gives it meaning. Contemporary socialist parties may have paid too little attention to constituency, and to the underlying forces that anchor it. There is a powerful case to be made for honouring labour. There is a case for promoting a minimum of socially valuable work as a universally appropriate lifestyle for all – of benefit to the individual, the environment, family relationships, the community at large. What markets directly prioritise is capital, profit – not labour. Since markets cannot be expected, in this particular, to correct themselves, one sees a clear role in this for Labour.

Part Two:
Collectivism and Markets

4

Does society exist?
The case for socialism

BRIAN BARRY

The problem

Long after the deeds and misdeeds of Margaret Thatcher have been
forgotten, she may well be remembered for saying 'There is no such
thing as society'. As socialists we believe in society, but what exactly
are we committed to believing in?

It is tempting to say that individualism is the enemy, so we should
oppose individualism in all its guises. To do so would be, I believe, to
fall into a trap. We should not put off potential adherents by suggesting
that to be a socialist you have to accept extravagant and implausible
philosophical assumptions. The Fabian Society has taken as its mascot
the tortoise, no doubt because (like Fabius Maximus) it is patient and
persevering. But we can learn more from the tortoise than those virtues.
It also has the good sense never to stick its neck out further than is
necessary for getting to its destination.

Individualism takes a number of forms and in what follows I shall
look at three of them. In each case I shall ask whether socialists should
adopt the individualist line or the opposite. The first contrast I shall
draw is between individualism and holism. Here the individualist
position denies the very existence of social entities or their ability to
explain anything. I shall argue that the question of existence is trivial
but that the question of explanation is very important, and I shall
illustrate this by showing in some detail how an individualist approach
can usefully be brought to bear on the reform of the National Health
Service.

The second contrast is between individualism and solidarism. The
issue here is between alternative accounts of the genesis of obligations

The original version of this chapter was published by the Fabian Society (pamphlet 536, 1989).

to others. On the individualist account these arise from voluntary acts: the standard form of obligation is a contractual obligation. On the alternative solidaristic account, obligations arise directly from our membership in a society. I shall argue that neither of these alternatives should be accepted and that an account different from either of them is more satisfactory. I shall, however, show that the conclusion sought by the solidarists – the existence of obligations of mutual aid – stands up equally well on my account, but is more securely based.

The third and last contrast I shall draw is between individualism and collectivism, and here I come down unequivocally on the side of collectivism, understood as an emphasis on the importance of collective provision. Indeed, socialism is, I shall argue, best understood as the union of two ideas: social justice and collectivism.

I conclude with a discussion of the implications for the Labour Party.

Should socialists be holists?

Let me begin by dismissing the relevance of one interpretation of the claim that there is no such thing as society. The claim might be taken literally to mean that there simply does not exist anything corresponding to the word 'society'. In the same vein, somebody might say that there are no such things as forests, only trees.

As it happens, we can be fairly sure that Mrs Thatcher did not want to deny that society exists in this literal sense. For she went on to say that 'there are only individuals and families'. This, taken as a claim about what exists, would be like saying that there are no such things as forests, only trees and coppices. It would be hard to take that notion very seriously.

I said earlier that socialists should not automatically join the anti-individualist camp, and I do not think that any argument for socialism requires the existence of social wholes. But neither does any argument for it rest on the denial of their existence. In fact, my suggestion is that socialists need not take a stand on either side of the issue because nothing turns on it.

So, why does anybody think that it matters? The reason is that there is a genuinely significant issue of individualism versus holism, and it is mistakenly supposed that the position one takes on this is determined by one's position on the question of the existence of society. The issue that does matter involves the explanation of social phenomena.

The usual name for this dispute is 'methodological individualism versus methodological holism'. In this context, 'methodological' means simply that we are concerned with how to explain rather than with what exists. The question involved may at first sight appear extremely abstract and remote from any practical question that need concern socialists. I hope, however, to show that this is far from the truth.

The most plausible statement of methodological individualism, which also makes the least sweeping claims, runs as follows: all satisfactory explanations of social phenomena must be capable, in principle, of being couched in terms of individuals' actions.

Before going any further, let me dispel one common misunderstanding. There is no claim here that every social phenomenon must have been brought about by the deliberate efforts of individuals to bring about just that phenomenon. On the contrary, very often an explanation couched in methodological individualist terms will appeal to the unintended consequences of a mass of individual actions.

Thus, orthodox contemporary economics, which adheres self-consciously to the tenets of methodological individualism, does not suppose that phenomena such as inflations or stock market crashes come about because individuals act to bring them about. What it does insist is that we should try to understand how a whole series of individual decisions (for example, to buy and sell) eventually add up to a social phenomenon recognisable as an inflation or a stock market crash. An explanation of a social phenomenon in terms of methodological holism would, in contrast, invoke something like 'the functional needs of capital', while resisting the suggestion that such a statement should be capable of being translated into one about the actions of individual capitalists.

There is a vast and often arcane literature addressed to the truth or falsity of methodological individualism. I shall bypass this by arguing that, even if it is not completely true (though I suspect it is), there are three reasons why socialists would do well to adopt methodological individualism as a working hypothesis.

First, I appeal to the tortoise principle. Methodological individualism is at the very least a plausible and attractive idea. If people are told that to be good socialists they have to subscribe to methodological holism, a lot of potential supporters will be gratuitously put off. They will conclude that there must be something wrong with a doctrine that rests on such questionable foundations.

Second, the explanatory and predictive record of the best-known theory embodying methodological holism, Marxism, has been thoroughly wretched: it has not come to terms with (let alone predicted) any of the major developments of the twentieth century. There are many reasons for this, but I suggest that the habit of ascribing motive power to entities such as capital ought to be high up on the list of the failings of Marxism.

The third attraction of methodological individualism is that it forces us to ask hard questions about the operation of a socialist society's institutions. If we propose that in future things ought to be organised in a certain way, methodological individualism bids us to press the question: how are individual men and women to be motivated to act in the manner that these institutions require? It is highly salutary that such questions should be asked in advance of any attempt to introduce new social arrangements. For otherwise the most likely result of attempting to introduce them will be disillusionment and, following upon this, the discrediting of socialism.

It should be noticed that, as defined so far, there is nothing built into the idea of methodological individualism that sets limits to the kinds of motivation that might be ascribed to people. Thus, you could, quite consistently with the tenets of methodological individualism, say that in a socialist society payment could be entirely divorced from work effort because people would work out of love of humanity or enthusiasm for building a socialist commonwealth. All that methodological individualism insists on is the necessity of confronting the problem of individual motivation and providing an answer to it. Others may then judge the plausibility of the answer and draw appropriate conclusions.

I have emphasised the complete generality of methodological individualism with respect to kinds of motive because it is often tarred with the same brush as a much narrower and, from a socialist point of view, much more sinister doctrine, the idea that people are invariably motivated by self-interest. There is no doubt that applied across the board this doctrine is inimical to socialism. But at the same time I can see absolutely no reason for accepting it.

I can best illustrate what is at stake here by showing the two ideas at work in analysing a particular institution – the National Health Service – which I take to be (in its general principles if not its detailed operation) an exemplary socialist institution in that it replaces profit with service as the rationale of its activities.

No doubt that was enough in itself to make the NHS highly distasteful to Mrs Thatcher and her more ideologically-driven colleagues. But it would be too simple to suppose that the only explanation for the government's revamping of the NHS was the desire to destroy a stronghold of values alien to those of the market. A complementary explanation is that the denizens of the think-tanks whose advice the government listens to really cannot imagine that an organisation can possibly work effectively unless incentives are rigged so that decision makers find it in their interest to do whatever they ought to do. They are so besotted by the rational-choice paradigm in this form that they just deduce from first principles what a health service driven by self-interest would be like and put that forward without feeling any necessity for looking in detail at the strengths and weaknesses of the existing system.

The existing organisation of the NHS does not in general connect decisions about the choice of treatment with the incomes of doctors or of organisations such as hospitals. This creates a certain ethos that both patients and providers find valuable, and for good reason. In the American health care system, by contrast, patients are aware that physicians have a financial interest in either overtreating them or undertreating them, depending on their financial arrangements. If an insurance company picks up the bill, there is an incentive to carry out unnecessary procedures in order to increase income, and there is in fact much evidence that surgery for which there is no medical justification is often carried out. If, however, the patient belongs to a so-called Health Maintenance Organisation (the model for the government's proposals for financing general practitioners in Britain) there is an incentive to spend as little as possible on treatment, since the patient pays a fixed annual fee and the prosperity of the practice depends on keeping down outgoings. Thus, either system gives rise to perverse incentives for the physicians and creates a wholly justifiable mistrust of their motives in recommending courses of treatment.

Fortunately, the American health care delivery system, for all its grievous faults, does not work out as badly in practice as one might expect from that description of its incentive structure. But the reason for this is precisely that physicians tend not to abuse their virtual monopoly of information *vis-à-vis* their patients by recommending treatment in accordance with the economic incentives facing them. This, however, is to say that the system works as well as it does only because most medical professionals are not profit maximisers but are to a large extent motivated by the desire to do well by their patients.

I am not suggesting that American physicians are not deeply interested in the amount that they get paid – but then so are those who work in the NHS. The point is simply that, although no doubt a lot of wombs and tonsils fall victim to the profit motive, the great mass of individual decisions about treatment are taken on legitimate medical grounds.

The lesson to be drawn is that the introduction of commercial calculations into micro-level decisions within the NHS is not the way to go. If we have qualms about the way in which decisions on treatment are taken – that considerations of cost-effectiveness are not given sufficient weight, for example – what we need to do is find out exactly how decisions are taken now and then try to see what might be done to modify this, perhaps by supplying better and more usable information. The object should be to build on, and indeed reinforce, the motive of benefiting patients, rather than seeking to introduce the extraneous motive of material advantage into decision making.

Old-fashioned socialist thinking used to run along the following lines: if we, as a society, want to get something done, the best way of getting it done is to set up an organisation and tell the people running that organisation to get on with it. The history of the public corporations set up by the 1945 Labour government shows what is wrong with this idea. If we want a public enterprise to offer a cheap, safe and reliable service, to provide safe working conditions, to combat racial and gender discrimination and to be sensitive to environmental considerations, we cannot afford to turn over decision making to some obsessively secretive board and sit back.

The virtue of methodological individualism here is to remind us that appropriate motivation cannot be taken for granted. There is no sovereign remedy, but identifying the problem encourages the search for ways of pressing decision making in the right directions. Three devices which international experience suggests are always useful here are: more openness, so that the basis for decisions can be subjected to public scrutiny; more power to those directly affected (for example, workers' representatives with respect to safety); and the creating of jobs within the organisation whose holders are specifically charged with promoting certain objectives such as minority hiring or reducing pollution.

The triumph of the New Right consists not merely in spreading the conviction that what I have called the old-fashioned socialist approach is simple-minded but in making it seem axiomatic that the only alternative is to arrange things so that somebody can make a profit out of doing whatever it is we want to have done. This idea is actually a good deal more simple-minded than the one it displaced, since anyone who gets past the first chapter of an economics textbook will soon realise how restrictive are the conditions under which there is any reason for expecting people pursuing a profit to bring about a socially desirable outcome. (They are grotesquely far from being met by telephones, water and electricity or, for different reasons, health care delivery.) Long live the competing entrepreneurs selling fruit and vegetables to Londoners from their barrows in Berwick Street – but the further we get away from them the more dubious the profit motive becomes.

Methodological individualism, rightly understood, presses us to ask the questions that ought to be asked about the organisation of public enterprises, both local and national. We do not have to make the crass assumption that each person must find it in his or her direct personal interest to follow the right course of action. However, I would suggest this much of a bow to the forces of economic self-interest: it is a bad idea to set things up so that there is a financial incentive to do wrong.

Here is a deliberately simple illustration of the distinction. We pay firemen a fixed amount for doing their job, which means that when deciding exactly what to do in fighting a fire they must be motivated by something other than an individual cost-benefit calculus. We could in theory switch to a system of payment by results, so that a fireman got a bonus of (say) £100 for each person rescued from a burning building. It is, however, highly doubtful that we should feel safer knowing that a fireman, in deciding whether to enter a burning building, was trying to determine on a basis of self-interest whether the risk involved was worth taking in return for an additional pre-tax £100. It is not merely nicer but actually more efficacious to pay people to be firemen and then rely on norms of professionalism and public service to motivate them to accept discomfort and danger in the course of discharging their duties.

There is, then, no financial incentive here for doing more than the minimum necessary to avoid dismissal, but equally there is no financial disincentive. To illustrate a perverse financial incentive, imagine that each team of firemen had their pay reduced according to the amount of water they used. This would obviously mean that they would no longer be motivated solely by their professional judgement in deciding how much water to use but would have a personal financial incentive to minimise the amount. I am suggesting that we should not put people in a situation where doing their job well actually costs them money.

The example I have just given is fanciful (I hope). But the American health care system, as I have pointed out, provides a real life example of perverse financial incentives. For another, we need look no further than the way in which in Britain it is possible (and indeed common) for a consultant under contract to the NHS to work also in the private health care sector. As the leading Canadian medical economist Robert Evans has observed, this arrangement (which is prohibited in Canada) opens up perverse incentives, since

> the British private consultant can use his dual role to select and steer patients according to their resources and the nature of their problem. He can even use his position within the NHS to manipulate waiting lists and other aspects of access so as to ensure that private health care will be preferable to those who can afford it. The Canadian physician who chooses to go private must go all the way. He cannot use a strategic position within the public system to cream off only the profitable patients for his private services (Robert G. Evans, 'We'll Take Care Of It For You: Health Care in the Canadian Community', *Daedalus*, 17, Fall 1988).

This is the kind of case in which the *a priori* approach beloved by the so-called rational-choice theorists comes into its own. We need not, in other words, establish just how frequently abuses of the kind depicted by Robert Evans actually occur. It is enough to condemn the existing system that it sets up perverse incentives. The implication is, obviously, that working in the private health care sector should be incompatible with working in the NHS.

Although more could be said, I hope I have done enough to suggest that a moderate form of methodological individualism, so far from being inimical to socialism, is a useful tool in that it forces us to ask hard questions about the institutions that we propose. And the example just given illustrates that, deployed where it is appropriate, even the self-interest postulate can form part of the arsenal of socialism.

Should socialists be solidarists?

Let us return to the assertion that there is no such thing as society. This is not plausibly regarded as a claim about what exists. Mrs Thatcher need not, therefore, deny that the United Kingdom forms a society whose members are defined by common social, economic and political institutions. But there is a further claim that could be rejected by saying that there is no such thing as society.

This is the claim that the existence of a society (in the sense discussed so far) constitutes a ground for a general obligation to provide for the well-being of the members of the society. 'Society' now carries normative implications: a society is defined by common institutions *and* mutual obligations of care. I shall call this conception of society 'solidarism', because it bases obligations upon social solidarity.

I can best give some substance to the doctrine of solidarism by citing a line of argument that is not uncommonly made in support of various kinds of collective provision. This runs as follows. We think of it as natural and proper for the members of a family to accept some responsibility for one another. A family that had the collective resources to care for all its members but let some of them go without food, shelter, clothing, medical care or education would rightly be condemned. In exactly the same way, the members of a society should accept responsibility for one another. And a society that had the resources to care for all its members but neglected some should be condemned. According to this line of argument, a society is a family writ large. The obligations that are generated by membership of a society are not identical with those generated by membership of a family, but they arise naturally in the same manner out of existing relationships.

The etymology of the word 'society' derives from the Latin 'socius', meaning a friend or comrade. If we take friendship and comradeship to have built into them certain obligations of mutual aid, then we can say that solidarism is a conception of 'society' that seeks to give more than nominal force to its connections with friendship and comradeship. For those who see a society as constituted by common institutions – above all by a uniform set of laws applying to all equally – it is quite understandable that the mode of salutation should be 'Citizen'. By the same token, to the solidaristic conception of society corresponds the salutation 'Comrade'. This does not, of course, entail that solidarists should actually go around calling one another 'Comrade'; but, then, outside the French Revolution (or maybe films about it) people have not gone around calling one another 'Citizen' either. I am merely pointing out that each of these modes of address has a foundation in a conception of society.

Family and social obligations do indeed have a common source. The conclusion of the argument I cited is therefore sound. At the same time, however, I want to say that the premise of the argument – the doctrine of solidarism – is mistaken. But I do not propose that we should, this time, embrace the individualist alternative. Rather, we should reject both. The kinds of conclusion that socialists want to get from solidarism can be better defended through an approach that cuts across the conflict between solidarism and individualism.

If solidarism is the idea that obligations arise naturally out of social relationships, individualism in its pure form is the idea that obligations arise only artificially from some voluntary act. The model of obligation is contractual obligation: people consent to obligations in return for the benefits that they expect to obtain as a result of others likewise accepting obligations.

Individualists are not very often completely pure. Thomas Hobbes is the only major figure in the history of social contract theorising who has followed through the individualist programme with ruthless consistency and sought to ground even obligations within families on contractual relations. John Locke is more typical in fudging the issue of families, and simply insisting that families are in no way a model for societies, which are based on contract. Mrs Thatcher, in excluding families from her anathema on society, thus showed herself to be, whether she knows it or not, an adherent of the Lockean version of individualism. (For a much more detailed discussion of a complex story see Carole Pateman, *The Sexual Contract*, Polity Press, 1988.)

Solidarism and the form of individualism that constitutes its antithesis share a common assumption: that either obligations arise naturally from actual relationships or they arise artificially as the result of the voluntary actions of morally independent individuals. This is seventeenth-century sociology, and I think we should get away from it.

Let us start again in a different place. Suppose that in Britain (but not necessarily anywhere else) a group of people go into a pub and somebody buys a round of drinks. There is then a general expectation that the other members of the group will buy a round in turn. Where does this expectation come from? Not from explicit agreement, so the voluntaristic theory of obligation cannot serve. But invoking a natural obligation scarcely seems any better. The obvious answer is that what is at work here is a convention.

But to leave it there would fail to explain why if someone skips out without standing a round after accepting drinks from others this is regarded as unfair. What this reaction shows is that the convention taps into a moral norm, the norm of fair play. This is a general principle, common to every society, that one should play one's part in co-operative arrangements from which one benefits or stands to benefit. The variable part, which is provided by a convention, is the part that establishes what kinds of co-operative arrangements there are and what constitutes benefiting or standing to benefit.

It is my suggestion that all social arrangements can be analysed in the same way as that rather trivial case. We can always find, in other words, an element that varies from society to society and underlying it a general moral principle that gives it whatever moral force it has. This is not to deny that there are natural inclinations; and no doubt the more durable conventions will be found to be those that go with the grain of inclination rather than against it. But the range of variation in conventions between societies is too great for us to say more than that.

Families illustrate this as well as any other social institution. Doubtless there is some biological basis underlying care of parents for children. The survival of the human race would otherwise have been pretty insecure. But we also have to take cognisance of the enormous variety of kin relationships that within different societies are taken to constitute membership in a single family, and the equally enormous variety of obligations that family membership is taken to entail.

When we reflect on these kinds of variation we are led to reject the idea that we have a fixed set of relations – family relations – and that obligations arise naturally out of these. At the same time, however, we are not in the least tempted to believe that these obligations within families arise out of voluntary agreement among their members.

In place of either of these notions, what I am suggesting is that the constitution of a family and the obligations among its members are both social constructs. They are, in the terms of my analysis, conventions. But it should be borne in mind that, within the usage I am adopting, to say that an institution is conventional is not to say that it is arbitrary or that it could easily be changed. The obligations are real enough. But, as with the convention of standing rounds in a pub, the moral force of the convention arises from the morally relevant general considerations that can be advanced in its support.

My analysis amounts to the proposal that social obligations should be interpreted on the model of legal obligations. A law creates legal obligations as a matter of legal logic, but the moral force of the law derives from whatever value is created by obedience to it. Some laws may be so bad that they are better disobeyed if this can be done without detection, or if the risk of detection is worth accepting. (A perfect example would be a law prohibiting homosexual acts between consenting adults.) But for the most part life goes better if laws are widely obeyed, even if it is possible in many cases to see how they could be improved. Jeremy Bentham's prescription – 'To obey promptly; to censure freely' – is a generally sound rule, and I suggest that the same should be said of the obligations that arise not from legal enactment but from social convention.

Where does this leave the argument that took the social obligations of family members as a model for those of members of a society towards one another? I said earlier that I applauded its putting familial and social obligations on the same footing. But I must lay rough hands on the form of the argument itself, even while endorsing its conclusion in favour of the welfare state.

From the perspective I am putting forward, the family as an institution in Britain today consists of a core of legal obligations reinforced and extended by social obligations. For example, a man has a legal duty to support his family, and can be put in prison for wilfully failing to do so, though this sanction is rarely invoked since he certainly cannot support his family while in prison. But the expectations that arise from shared social norms about what family members owe one another extend far beyond anything captured in legal enactments.

Both the legal and the social norms derive whatever moral force they have from the same source: the valuable results that follow from adherence to them. But when we look at the contribution that families make to the realisation of human welfare, we soon see that they have severe inadequacies. The case for the welfare state is the same as the case for family obligations in that they are complementary means of serving the same ends.

The full development of these ideas would require a lot of space, but, at the inevitable risk that brevity will make for crudity, let me give a few illustrations. A family is, among other things, an economic unit. In societies where extended families are the norm, families offer some real protection against adversity: one adult who cannot find employment or is incapable of work can be supported by the work of several others. The nuclear family, in contrast, offers a very weak defence against loss of earnings, and this establishes the case for a programme of income replacement based on individual earnings.

Similarly, within an extended family the cost of rearing children can be spread over a number of adults. The nuclear family cannot provide this kind of limited collectivisation of the cost of child-rearing, and the high rate at which marriages break up means that many children are raised in one-parent families. We can easily see here how to make out the case for collectivising the cost of child-raising across a whole society, so that every child attracts a grant corresponding to the full cost of food, clothing, shelter and recreation in (say) an average working-class household.

In the same vein, we can observe that, in the four decades since Michael Young and Peter Willmott did their fieldwork in Bethnal Green, families with grandparents and other relatives living next door or just around the corner have become a much rarer phenomenon (*Family and Kinship in East London*, Routledge & Kegan Paul, 1949). The need for provision of creches and nursery schools thus becomes more pressing as the alternative of child-minding within an extended family declines in importance.

The line of argument just presented eschews any appeal to the idea that social relationships are somehow pregnant with social obligations which may or may not be actually incorporated in practice. Instead it takes a positivist view of both legal and social norms: they have a verifiable existence, though the process of verification is quite complex. But we must then ask whether, as they stand, they are well adapted to achieving the outcomes that we regard as morally important.

As we have seen, where families fall down on the job, we are led to turn to societies to step in to do what is needed. In the nature of the case, the element of legally-mandated provision will be higher for burdens carried at the societal level, though we should also be looking for changes in social norms to accommodate social changes.

The same analysis must, however, be pursued beyond the level of societies. Just as a family is too small a unit to be an unconditionally self-sustaining economic entity, so is a society. At least half the world's population lives in countries which could not, however well they organised their internal distribution of income, give all of their members a decent standard of living. The case for transfers from rich countries to poor ones is exactly of the same kind as the case for transfers within countries.

Needless to say, the entirely different institutional setting of international transfers means that the arrangements will have to be quite different. But the point to be made here is that there are no conceptual problems in making the case. At the minimum all we need to do is acknowledge that malnutrition, disease, ignorance and poverty generally are evils and that it is possible to alleviate them. This is quite enough to ground a case for transfers.

In contrast, the solidarist approach has a great difficulty in generating international obligations that are not based on the mutual self-interest of states. Either supporters of this approach admit that obligations stop at the boundaries of countries or they are forced to invoke a 'world society' in which to ground international obligations. But whatever solidarity there is among the world's inhabitants is scarcely enough to generate much in the way of obligations.

I have been arguing that solidarism is an ill-conceived moral theory. However, reflection on the case of international transfers may well suggest that it still has a valid place as an explanatory theory. That is to say, it seems pretty clear that as a matter of fact human beings are much more likely to accept sacrifices to benefit those with whom they interact or share common institutions than they are to accept sacrifices to benefit other people to whom they are not related in these ways. The implication of this is plain: that if moral considerations lead us to the conclusion that the existing amount of transfer is inadequate, we should favour anything that increases a sense of solidarity.

This should be qualified. The Second World War was an excellent creator of a sense of solidarity, since everyone shared in the danger of defeat, and the blitz created a genuinely common hazard. And generally natural disasters of all kinds have been found to have a stimulating effect on mutual aid, at any rate up to the point at which a sentiment of *sauve qui peut* takes over. But this should hardly lead us to welcome an increase of solidarity created by war or natural disaster. We must therefore fall back on shared institutions.

Socialists are right to think that public transport is more than a device for moving people around: it also throws people from different social classes and areas of the country together and creates a common interest in the efficient running of the system. Conversely, driving a car creates a spirit of competition with other road users in which those who are prepared to be anti-social (for example, by pulling into an intersection or not letting pedestrians cross the road) gain at the expense of others. It is a common observation that, as traffic congestion gets worse in London, standards of civility and considerate behaviour decline. Is it likely that the aggression and rudeness displayed on the road are completely left behind when the car is parked?

The socialist case against the car in city centres is not just that it creates mutual frustration but also that it makes people worse. Across the board – education and medical care are two other obvious examples – collective provision on a universal basis fosters attitudes of co-operation and concern while private provision is divisive and conducive to selfishness.

Should socialists be collectivists?

Although I have talked about socialism a good deal, I have not so far offered a formal definition of it. I have, however, presupposed that socialists share certain objectives, including the preservation of the National Health Service from market forces and the defence and expansion of the welfare state. Any satisfactory conception of socialism would, I take it, have to lead to the implication that these are socialist measures. But the time has come to put all this on a more systematic footing. I propose, then, the following concise definition: socialism = social justice + collectivism.

It is significant that both 'socialism' and 'social justice' seem to have originated at about the same time, around the 1830s in France and Britain, in response to the perceived evils of the emergent form of industrial civilisation. And the two ideas have run in tandem ever since, with 'social justice' to be found on the lips of socialists, while anti-socialists have tended to disparage the very notion of social justice.

The claim underlying social justice is that all the major institutions of a society can and should be subjected to the test of conformity with principles of justice. This includes the methods of political decision making, the legal system, the educational system, the way in which work is organised and paid for and the system of taxes and transfers.

What, then, are these principles of justice against which institutions are to be assessed? The most basic principle, which underlies all post-Enlightenment ideas of justice, is one of the fundamental equality of human beings. We start from a rejection of any claims to special treatment based upon any alleged fundamental superiority whether grounded naturally or supernaturally. Racism, the privileges of an hereditary aristocracy, and any system of thought such as the Hindu *varna* system are thus ruled out.

What follows from this is that all inequalities in rights and access to scarce resources have to be justified in terms that can be accepted by everyone, including those who stand to finish up with less than others in the way of rights and access. There are only two candidates with any plausibility: desert – those who deserve more should get more; and common advantage – if everyone stands to gain from some social arrangement that sets up or generates an inequality, we have at any rate a *prima facie* good reason for everyone to accept the inequality.

The big problems arise not in stating the criteria but in trying to determine what concrete implications they have. Thus, although there is unquestionably a logical connection between justice and desert, this leaves a good deal of room for disagreement about what kinds of activities create desert. Some socialists, from Robert Owen onward, have argued that in the economic sphere the conditions required for differential desert do not obtain, since anybody with superior productive abilities owes them to some combination of fortunate genetic endowment and fortunate environment. Others have followed John Stuart Mill in suggesting that effort should be rewarded but not, for example, skill – except in as far as this is itself the result of previous effort. Other socialists have a more relaxed attitude to desert, and are prepared to countenance as a basis of extra reward productive capacity not traceable to current or previous effort, so long as the educational and training system has not provided some with unfair advantages over others. (Since this proviso is unlikely to be met, the last version may not differ in actual consequences from the other two as much as might appear at first sight.) I shall not attempt to adjudicate the issues here. For whatever its precise scope, the criterion of desert constrains severely the kind of thing that can be said in defence of inequalities.

Common advantage, even more than desert, clearly leaves open a range of disagreements about its practical implications. Thus, in the economic sphere, familiar arguments about allocative efficiency and incentives enter in as justification for unequal rewards. If we think (as I believe we should) that among the equal rights that people should have is the free choice of occupation, thus ruling out the direction of labour, we are committed to some degree of material inequality unless we are extraordinarily optimistic about the potential of moral incentives. However, a lot of the arguments put forward for the efficacy of inequality are made in bad faith. There is, no doubt, some room for dispute about the degree of inequality that can be justified by invoking common advantage. But the example of Sweden shows that a country can be highly prosperous while greatly compressing lifetime post-tax earnings, so that only a minority of workers in full-time employment are more than twice as well off as those on the minimum full-time wage.

Thus we can again say that the criterion of common advantage, while leaving room for some disagreement as to its implications, sets severe constraints on what kinds of inequality can be defended. To see that the two criteria set real limits to inequality, we have only to observe that inherited wealth can be justified only to a quite small extent (and then only by looking at it from the point of view of the testator rather than the beneficiary) and that the inheritance of wealth that was itself inherited cannot be defended.

By defining socialism as social justice plus collectivism, I thus depart in two ways from the idea that 'socialism is about equality': by substituting 'social justice' for 'equality' and by adding collectivism. Equality is an inaccurate representation of a distinctly socialist goal. If taken as fundamental equality – the equal claim to consideration of all human beings – it does not distinguish socialism from liberalism or indeed from most (non-racist) forms of modern conservatism. If taken as material equality, it is also inaccurate since very few socialists have ever been or are now in favour of complete material equality. What is true is that social justice entails far greater equality than now exists in Britain. But if social justice is the goal and relative equality a theorem derivable from an adequate account of social justice, we should say that.

Those who argued for dropping collectivism made things much too easy for themselves by showing that it was inadequate as the entire specification of socialism. They should have recognised that the alternative to dropping it was adding to it. It is an undeniable objection to the identification of socialism with collectivism that the two biggest monsters of the twentieth century, Stalin and Hitler, were both collectivists. And, of course, while Stalin maintained that he was building 'real existing socialism', Hitler led the National Socialists. But their claims would collapse under my definition because both Stalin's Russia and Hitler's Germany were so far from satisfying the criteria of social justice.

A second argument was that the definition of socialism should concern itself with ends and that collectivism is a mere means. The fallacy here lies in supposing that collective and individual provision are no more than alternative ways of achieving a certain distributive goal which would be equally valuable achieved in either way.

What has united socialists historically – and this is a statement that would include Marx, the Webbs, and everybody in between – is a belief in collectivism. If this is dropped from the definition of socialism there is no way of distinguishing socialists from adherents of social justice who favour dividing everything up so that each person gets his or her fair share and then leaving them to pursue their ends independently. 'Socialism' as a term, then, would no longer be distinguishable from the Leftist branch of liberal individualism.

I have not so far given an explicit account of the contrast between collectivism and individualism, though I think that in broad terms it should have been fairly clear what I had in mind. The issue between them is the desirability of collective action to bring about ends that cannot be achieved by individual action. Individualism in its classic form is the idea that the state should create a framework for individual action by prohibiting injury to others and enforcing contracts. The Left liberal version that I mentioned stipulates that income should be redistributed through some general system of taxes and transfers. In other respects it follows the same line. Collectivism is simply the rejection of individualism in either its classical or its Left liberal form.

It is individualism as anti-collectivism that has flourished in the past fifteen years. Although it would not naturally be expressed by saying that there is no such thing as society, it does systematically downplay the significance of the aspirations that people have as members of a society and exalts those that they have as individuals.

The case for collectivism is twofold. The first is the one outlined at the end of the previous section: the more that the members of a society are associated in common institutions the more likely they are to see themselves as being all in the same boat and to accept redistributive measures. An extension of this is simply that the human quality of a society in which people concern themselves with the fate of others is higher, quite apart from any difference it may make to policy outputs.

The second argument is that there are many things we want which can be achieved only by collective action. This is worth some more attention because the cliché that the Left 'has been losing intellectual ground' seems to be very largely based on the idea that some powerful new argument in favour of individualism has been discovered recently. This idea is that it is better to have a choice than not to have one. To the intellectual standard-bearers of the New Right, 'choice' has become a shibboleth. That some state of affairs arose as a result of a set of individual choices is supposed to put it beyond criticism.

This celebration of choice as such, regardless of its object and context, is quite witless. Stated baldly, the proposition that a choice is always better than no choice is false. Stated with qualifications it is of no interest since, if more choice is only sometimes better than less, we have to proceed on a case by case basis, and we then need some other criteria for assessing the value of choice in particular contexts.

Thus, it is extremely easy to see that a certain person having a choice may be worse for other people than that person not having a choice. Suppose that in the 1980s you had a choice between putting leaded and unleaded petrol in your car. According to the free-market paradigm, you are better off having the choice. You may well decide that the ambient lead level will be so slightly raised by your using leaded petrol that you are, all things considered, better off using the cheaper leaded fuel. But the rest of us are made a little bit worse off as a result of your having the choice. We would prefer it if you had no option but to use unleaded fuel.

Moreover, it may well be that all of us would prefer a rule prohibiting the use of leaded petrol to one permitting it, when we take account of the increased cost of lead-free fuel and compare it to the reduction of the amount of lead in the environment. Thus, we may all lose from our all having a choice, because we would prefer the outcome that occurs when we are all prevented from doing what we would choose when given the choice.

Can it be worse for the person concerned to have a choice? Clearly it can: everything turns on the precise terms of the choice. Consider the following question: Is it better to be offered a choice between your money and your life than to be killed outright without the option? Obviously, it is better to have the choice. But is it better to have to choose between your money and your life than not to have to make that choice at all? Equally obviously, it is better not to be placed in a situation where you have to make the choice. So we must conclude that, given the situation, you prefer having the choice. But you would prefer not to be in that situation in the first place. For you would be better off if you could keep both your money and your life.

It may be said that this does not show that an extension of options can make things worse for the person concerned. But there is no difficulty in suggesting cases where someone would be better off if a certain option were withdrawn. The disappearance of the option of fighting a duel saved many people from a violent death. Similarly, the option of being paid below some statutory minimum wage or borrowing money at a usurious rate of interest is not necessarily an advantage to the person with the option, for his or her bargaining position may be stronger if excessively disadvantageous options are ruled out.

The case of hospital consultants, mentioned earlier, illustrates the same point very well. The choice offered by a consultant between private and public treatment is, literally, the choice between your money and your life – if not your actual existence then your freedom from pain and discomfort and your ability to function normally. The existence of the choice does nothing to add to the resources of the NHS. The waiting lists are just as long, and all that happens is that there is an option of jumping the queue by paying for the privilege.

From the point of view of the collective interest of users of the NHS, there is nothing to be said for this state of affairs. Choice is worse than no choice. We cannot draw any conclusions from the fact that when the choice is offered some choose life over money. It is equally true that most people confronted with a mugger prefer to hand over their wallets.

The school system offers another example of the way in which choice can make things worse. To make the point as simply as possible, let us contrast two kinds of set-up. In one, children are allocated to schools so that each school will be representative of the social and ethnic mix of the district – say the area of the local authority. In the other, parents either have educational vouchers which can be used at any school or have the right to apply for their children's admission to any school in the appropriate age range run by the local authority. The schools in turn can select children from among the applicants.

Looking at the operation of the second system, the decisions by parents and schools will result in some pattern of allocation which nobody chose and perhaps nobody wants. Typically, it will be one in which there is a pecking order of schools. Even if all the schools in an area have equally good facilities and equally good teachers, all that is needed to create a hierarchy is a preference by parents for schools with more rather than fewer children of high academic attainment and selection by schools among applicants based on academic attainment.

From a consumer's point of view, this may be a quite unattractive outcome. If there are five schools and most parents rank them in the same order, most of the parents are going to be disappointed. Freedom of choice is really no more than freedom to apply: the only school that can be chosen unconditionally is the one at the bottom of the heap – precisely because so few have chosen it. There is no way in which it can be shown *a priori* that parents or children will be more satisfied on average with such a system of so-called parental choice than with one in which each child is allocated to a school whose composition is similar to that of the others in the area.

Suppose, however, that parents were happy enough to have their children educated in schools that were relatively homogeneous with respect to social class and ethnicity. The system of parental choice could then count as a success from the consumer point of view. But from the point of view of the citizens – those with children currently in the school system and those without – it should be looked on with misgivings.

We all have a legitimate interest in the harmony and stability of our society, and a legitimate concern – derived from considerations of social justice – that all children have equal opportunities at school. We all therefore have good reason for fearing the legacy of socially and racially separate schools, and for objecting to a system of sex-segregated Muslim schools designed to restrict the occupational opportunities and aspirations of girls emerging from them.

Socialism and the Labour Party

This essay was first published in 1989, the centenary of the *Fabian Essays*. This provided me with an occasion for quoting from Sidney Webb's contribution, and to build on it an analysis that seems to me to have stood up well and indeed to have been ever more strongly supported in the six years since then. What Webb wrote, in line with his belief in 'the inevitability of gradualness', was that collectivism was already well advanced (he particularly drew attention to the then current vogue for taking water supply into municipal ownership), and that all this had 'been done by practical men ... [who] in their every act ... worked to bring about the very Socialism they despised; and to destroy the Individualist faith which they still professed'.

Webb's claim was well founded. Interference in the market and its outright replacement occurred during the hundred years beginning around 1880 as a response to the manifest failure of markets to provide the conditions of civilised existence. Most obviously, it has always been true that in a market society those who live by their labour must fall into penury whenever their capacity to earn ceases for whatever reason. Beyond this, however, it became clear as capitalism matured that market wages would in many cases be insufficient to provide every family with decent housing at an affordable cost, with an education that gave opportunities to all children, or with good quality medical care for everyone who needed it.

Over time, it became equally clear that the workings of the market have no tendency to eliminate the deep-seated inequity between the pay of men and women, or to prevent racial discrimination in the job or the housing markets. It should be said that there is indeed an argument, popularised by the American economist Thomas Sowell, which purports to refute the last proposition. But the most that it shows is that discriminating may cost the discriminator something in that it may entail turning down the highest bidder for his house or the lowest bidder for the job on offer. But the price of discriminating will not generally be very high and, almost by definition, in a racist society very many people will be willing to pay that cost. Sowell's argument tells us that if people were 'rational' – that is, had no racist preferences – the market would work satisfactorily. But if hardly anyone had racist preferences there would be no problem in the first place.

Again, common sense suggested and common experience verified the conclusion that 'natural monopolies' are most appropriately publicly owned, whether municipally or nationally, because the private monopolist has no incentive for providing a cheap and efficient service on standard terms to all. 'Gas and water socialism' was introduced in the cities by Liberals such as Joseph Chamberlain for precisely that reason. Similarly, it was found highly unsatisfactory to have public services in London run by a patchwork quilt of more than 300 single-purpose authorities for sewerage, paving, etc. They were swept away in 1855 and replaced by a more coherent system, which in turn was replaced by the directly-elected London County Council in 1886.

Mrs Thatcher, like the mad scientist in a horror movie, subjected the British body politic to an experiment which succeeded only in proving the collectivist case. The government's lack of regional policy, its hands-off attitude to the housing market, and its draconian restrictions on the activities of local authorities have meant more ill-housed and homeless people. Everyone sees that the privatisation of 'natural monopolies' results in higher cost. The abolition of the GLC has had the result that there is no body with the authority deriving from direct election to take the hard decisions that the management of the capital's problems requires.

It is apparent that traffic congestion in London is getting worse and has now reached the point at which it only requires the closure of one of the Thames bridges to create paralysis. Strong measures to encourage the use of public transport and discourage the use of the private car are needed, but nobody except the central government now has the power to act. The various 'residuary bodies' created to take over the functions of the GLC have no authority to take a broad view of their duties that would fit particular policies into an overall strategy.

The most important lesson to be learned from the Thatcher episode is the power of an idea – even a bad one. Does the Labour Party have an alternative idea? Six years ago, I suggested that the Labour front bench did a good enough job of capitalising on the unpopularity of particular government measures but failed to tie together these criticisms so as to present them as 'elements in a coherent alternative to the marketeers' vision'. As a result, I argued, a Labour lead in the polls reflected 'dissatisfaction with the government rather than reflecting enthusiasm for a completely different set of ideas'. I added that the Conservatives might be 'obliging enough to lose the next election without Labour having to win it', in which case, I said, 'there may be some electoral merit in the present strategy of eliminating everything from the Party's programme that might offend anyone and then sitting tight.' But I cautioned that this could not be counted on, since 'Conservative governments have a way of pulling something out of the bag when it is needed – a well-timed boom or a foreign adventure, for example.'

In the event, of course, the Conservatives succeeded in winning without either of these customary aids. All they needed to pull out of the bag, it turned out, was a rather mangy rabbit in the form of John Major, who proceeded to pick up votes by running against the record of the government in which he had played a prominent part. It seems strange to me that, two leaders and a lost election later, the Labour strategy appears to be more of the same: to make itself an even more inconspicuous target and hope that next time around the government really will be so unpopular that Labour will win by default.

Perhaps it will: the government is more unpopular at this stage in the electoral cycle than last time; and the deeply unpleasant human beings who came into Parliament in the wake of Mrs Thatcher can probably be relied upon to keep the pot of scandal simmering until the election. All the same, a strategy that leaves all the initiative in the hands of the other side must surely be inherently vulnerable to the manoeuvres of the increasingly desperate figures who make up the Conservative leadership. At the time of going to press (June 1995) it is uncertain whether or not the Conservatives will try a repetition of the dumping-the-leader trick that worked last time. Whether they do or not, there is still the possibility of attempting to woo back the disenchanted Thatcher voters with an electioneering budget or a synthetic crisis in Europe designed to mobilise their disposition to xenophobia.

Leaving aside electoral considerations, we are bound to ask what the Labour Party is *for*. No doubt any politician finds it personally gratifying to get a ministerial salary and ministerial perks, be deferred to by senior civil servants, and cut a figure internationally. But why should anybody else take an interest in the replacement of one government by another, if that is all it amounts to? I think that, even granting that it would amount to nothing more, it would be very welcome in current circumstances, if only in virtue of the element of truth in the conventional wisdom that Britain relies on alternation of parties in government as a substitute for having a constitution. There is only an element of truth in it because it is a very poor substitute at best, but it is clear that the present government has become corrupt and has in turn corrupted the civil service and the quangos that it has created so profusely.

Taking a more optimistic line, it is at any rate possible that a Labour government would devolve power to a Scottish assembly and increase the powers of local government, dissolving in the process many of the obnoxious quangos. Perhaps it would also bring in a Bill of Rights of some sort. These would not be contemptible accomplishments. Virtually the only lasting achievements of the Wilson governments (Callaghan's, I assume, had only negative achievements) were the liberalisation of the laws on abortion, homosexuality and obscenity. A Blair government might similarly be remembered for its record on the extension of civil and political rights.

Beyond that, the omens are not encouraging. To the extent that it is possible to discern anything about Labour's social and economic plans in the event of its gaining office, it seems clear that they rest on the acceptance of all the main features of Mrs Thatcher's counter-revolution. We can expect a continuation of deflationary macro-economic policy and no significant reversal of the Thatcherite slashing of the higher income tax rates. There will be no substantial increase in the share of public expenditure in the gross national product. Nor can we even look forward to a significant shift in the orientation of public expenditure by cutting the military budget to (at most) the same level as that of our European neighbours and competitors. Privatisation of the public utilities will not be reversed, nor will the undermining of the public service ethos in education and the health service by market-inspired notions of competition. In short, socialism, as defined in this essay, is off the agenda. What is on offer to the voters is a promise of more open, competent and humane administration of the Thatcher legacy. There is no suggestion that Labour stands for an alternative form of society.

If that were all, it would be depressing enough. But I believe that an equally important liability is the way in which in the past ten years open discussion within the Labour Party of alternatives to whatever is the policy (or absence of it) currently favoured by the leaders has been increasingly effectively suppressed. Let me give two illustrations: readers will no doubt be able to supply many more of their own. One is the apparent impossibility of initiating any serious debate about macroeconomic strategy. We have the extraordinary spectacle of a Shadow Chancellor who is, like a latter-day Philip Snowden, more wedded to the Bank of England orthodoxy than his Conservative counterpart. Yet, as Bryan Gould found to his cost, anybody who dares to suggest that a Labour government should be more interested in employment than in meeting monetary or fiscal objectives is simply frozen out.

Now let me mention an example of microeconomic policy: the use of the tax system to bring about environmentally desirable effects – or at least avoid environmentally perverse ones. The official Labour line on the imposition of VAT on heating fuel was an illustration of the unprincipled opportunism that I referred to earlier. Anyone concerned about pollution and the generation of 'greenhouse gases' would have to applaud the extension of VAT as a first step towards the much higher 'carbon taxes' needed to reduce emissions. It was reasonable enough, of course, to insist on adequate compensation for those on low incomes; but the principle of an increase in relative prices should not have been challenged. Despite this, nobody (to the best of my knowledge) on the Labour side in Parliament broke ranks with the official line on environmental grounds. However, my colleague at the London School of Economics, Professor the Lord Desai, was unceremoniously sacked from his position as spokesman on economic affairs in the House of Lords merely for ruminating in public that there could be worse things than extending VAT – such as not raising the money at all and hence not having it to spend on nursery schools or other public purposes.

A party leadership that is incapable of tolerating such mild dissidence is clearly one suffering from paranoia on an almost clinical scale. What fuels this paranoia is an obsessive fear of newspaper headlines about 'Labour Split'. Yet the absence of internal debate has, I believe, grave implications for the Labour Party's electability, even more its re-electability, and more still for its doing anything worthwhile in government if elected. Let me explain why I think this.

What the media regard as interesting, and the television companies count as politically neutral, is the range of policies defined by the positions of the party leaders plus those that are subject to serious debate within one of those parties. For about the last ten years this has meant that most attention has been focused on alternative positions within the Conservative Party. The steady Rightward drift in the terms of public discourse is the inevitable consequence of the dynamic set up by the asymmetry between Left and Right.

By taking up a position close to that of the Conservatives and then colluding with the press in branding all ideas to its Left as 'loony', the Labour leadership has sawn off the branch on which it was sitting. Small wonder if it now finds that it has only a small area on which to perch, and that it has to share that with the Liberal Democrats. It is instructive to contrast the instinctive reaction of Labour leaders from Kinnock onward to ideas coming up from their Left with Mrs Thatcher's attitude to the product of the Right-wing 'think-tanks'. By welcoming their ideas, however extreme, as constructive contributions, she was able to widen the area of legitimate debate on public policy and thus make the subsequent incorporation of these ideas into government policy (perhaps somewhat watered down) seem like the quite reasonable adoption of a proposal that was by this time established within public discourse as one to be taken seriously.

Even if your ambition as Labour leader is no more than to be moderate, it can be achieved only if there are publicly-audible voices to your Left. No position is intrinsically moderate; moderation can be defined only in relation to the range of positions actively present within public discourse. Given the electoral imperatives imposed by the first-past-the-post system, there is room for only one party of the Left. So if ideas to the Left of official Labour policy are to enter the public arena they can do so only from within the Labour Party. In the absence of such ideas, simple logic shows that the political centre of gravity will always be to the Right of the official Labour position – wherever that may be – so long as that position defines the Leftmost end of the range of positions taken seriously by the media.

A major opportunity to extend the range of 'respectable' ideas within the Labour Party was lost when the Commission on Social Justice produced a report that displayed all the passion of an accountant, the panache of a rice pudding and all the coherence of a committee.[1] It sank without leaving a trace on the public consciousness. What doomed it above all was that members of the Commission, instead of having the courage of their convictions, spent all their time looking over their shoulders at what a Labour shadow Cabinet might or might not be prepared to endorse. The report was thus pre-censored to ensure that it did not stray too far from current orthodoxy.

Thus, for example, having made out an impeccable case for universal child benefit as a way of maintaining horizontal equity between those with children and those without (p. 134), the report then turned its back on the principle and suggested that those paying the higher rate of income tax should have their child benefit taxed (p. 317). The only argument for this was that the taxation would produce money that could be used to fund an increase in child benefit! But the same additional sum could obviously be raised by increasing the tax rate of the better off across the board, maintaining equity between higher-income taxpayers with and without children.

It is, indeed, easy enough to imagine a future Labour Chancellor of the Exchequer viewing child benefit as a pot of money to be raided. Perhaps there are circumstances in which political expediency would indicate that the principle of horizontal equity should be sacrificed. The point is, however, that one of the things we pay politicians for is to make squalid compromises with principle of precisely this kind. The job of a Commission on Social Justice should have been to set out the principles as forcefully as possible, not to sell them out in advance of any proven necessity.

Another illustration of the crass short-termism of the Commission was its treatment of the proposal for an income ('basic income' or 'citizens' income') to be paid to every adult without any conditions. Anyone who takes the trouble to plough through the Commission's numerous and complex proposals for tinkering with the existing system of cash benefits will be able to see that they might have been given coherence and purpose by being presented as piecemeal moves towards a basic income guarantee. Instead, the Commission, having acknowledged the attractions of the idea, rejected it primarily on the ground that public opinion was not ready for it: it 'would have to be backed by a broad-based consensus, of which there is, as yet, no sign' (p. 262).[2]

Surely, the whole point of a body like the Commission on Social Justice should have been to give a lead to public opinion, not merely to reflect it. Politicians whose time-horizon is limited to the next general election may well fall in behind public opinion rather than endeavour to shape it. But that makes it all the more essential, if public discussion is not to be completely mindless, for others to refuse to be bound by the same limitations.

F. M. Cornford, in his classic account of academic politics *Microcosmographia Academica* (London: Bowes and Bowes, 1964), catalogued all the arguments commonly advanced for doing nothing. One of those that he enunciated was the 'argument that "the Time is not Ripe". The Principle of Unripe Time is that people should not do at the present moment what they think right at that moment, because the moment at which they think it right has not yet arrived' (p. 24). The Commission on Social Justice carried this principle of inaction to a still higher level, arguing that people should not even advocate what they think to be right because the time at which other people will think it right has not yet arrived.

To sum up: socialism equals collectivism plus social justice. The argument for socialism is a good one, and is capable of being presented attractively. If it is permitted to enter the public arena, there is every reason to hope that this will over time reverse the Rightward trend in the shared assumptions of public discourse.

Since the extension of the suffrage in 1868, the longest continuous period in which the Conservatives have been excluded from office is ten years (1906–16); during the whole century and a quarter, they have been in power for far more of the time than they have been out of it. The Labour Party's current strategy seems to me to ensure that any future government it forms will be no more than a brief detour on the long Conservative march. To bring about a more permanent change of course, the Labour Party will have to challenge the underlying assumptions of Thatcherism, and establish others more favourable to itself. This, if I am right, means preaching socialism.

NOTES

1. *Social Justice: Strategies For National Renewal.* The Report of the Commission on Social Justice ('Borrie Report') (London: Vintage, 1994).
2. This is the first point advanced against it. The rest are mere debating points, of a kind that advocates of basic income could meet. At least one is simply invalid.

Thus, it is suggested that many married women might give up paid employment 'risking future insecurity and poverty' (p. 263). But by detaching income from employment status, basic income would prevent insecurity and poverty following from divorce (which is presumably what, if anything, the author of that sentence had in mind).

5

Is collectivism essential?

DAVID WINTER

Introduction

In chapter four, Brian Barry argues that socialism is social justice plus collectivism. He gives arguments in favour of methodological individualism and against solidarism with which I broadly agree. I also agree with his re-casting of the broad range of egalitarian and fairness objectives, rights and freedoms under the simple but effective phrase, 'social justice'. The controversial and most stimulating part of Barry's tract is the status he believes socialists should grant to collectivism. This is what I want to discuss.

It is hard not to accept that collectivism has traditionally played an important part in traditional socialist thought. And one of Barry's weakest arguments in favour of collectivism, it seems to me, is that because (from Marx to the Webbs, etc.) traditionally socialists have advocated it, so should we. It seems quite possible that traditional socialists may have been simply wrong, or social and economic circumstances may have changed so much that their arguments are no longer relevant.

It is now widely accepted, I hope, that central planning was a most unfortunate way, except under rather special circumstances, of allocating resources in an industrial economy. Yet for a number of years and probably for a majority of socialists (from Kautsky to Benn?) central planning was regarded as an essential feature of a socialist industrial economy. They were wrong, and it will probably take socialism many years to recover from this mistake. It would be a pity, then, to attach collectivism to socialism for sentimental reasons.

A second minor argument which Barry uses is that without collectivism, socialism becomes a form of Left-liberalism. We need collectivism in order to differentiate the product. It becomes necessary to adopt collectivism in order to keep ourselves in business, so to speak. I'm sure this argument is not intended seriously. However as socialist philosophers we should, I think, have the courage of our ideas (if not of our convictions). If our ideas lead us to embrace Paddy Ashdown and democratic liberalism, then we should have the courage to make the effort, however unpleasant this prospect may appear.

Having dealt with these two minor points, I shall turn to my principal argument against Barry's definition. After this I want to discuss in broad outline the recent New Right attack on collectivism. There is a tendency for socialists to belittle the opposition at least in intellectual terms. It may have been absurd for Mrs Thatcher to pronounce that there is 'no such thing as society', yet the ideological background which enabled her to make that remark has not only had considerable political success, but is also based on some powerful ideas which are not entirely false. At the risk of going over familiar territory, I think it is worthwhile considering these again. Finally I turn to consider the appropriate place of collectivism in a concept of socialism.

The trade-off

Brian Barry's definition is quite clear that by adding collectivism to social justice, it is intended that collectivism is a socialist goal in its own right. Collectivism is not being recommended simply because it may, in certain circumstances, be a good way of achieving social justice. However, most of the examples given of the virtues of collectivism are in fact precisely of this kind: the National Health Service, education and road congestion.

In viewing the need for certain kinds of collectivist arrangements as a means of achieving social justice, it may be thought that I am simply extending the scope of social justice in such a way as to absorb collectivism. The precise relationship between the two will, I hope, become clearer below.

For the moment, I will assume that any socialist concept of social justice contains a requirement that everyone's access to health care should be based on need rather than ability to pay. Similarly, equal opportunities should be available in education. Social justice may require that equal education be provided in a 'socially efficient' manner – that is, that everyone receives education up to the point where the marginal returns are equalised (the talented receive more).

Or it may require education to be provided in a socially egalitarian manner, that is, that everyone is educated to the point where their skills are approximately equal (the talented receive less). But this is not a question we need settle here.

Now whether these services are best secured using collectivist or decentralised mechanisms is an empirical question. In some circumstances, under certain economic and social conditions, one method may appear to be better; in others a different method might be preferred. Julian Le Grand has, for instance, argued that a voucher system in education could be organised so as to fulfil the requirements of social justice.

One reason why the NHS provides health care at relatively low cost is its success in keeping down doctors' wages. It is perfectly possible to envisage a set of circumstances where this was not the case. Suppose, for a moment, that under a decentralised market system doctors' wages were relatively low and health care was supplied by a compulsory subsidised insurance scheme in a low-cost and efficient manner which fulfilled all the requirements of social justice. At the same time suppose that a collective system of provision turned out to be relatively expensive, involved long waiting lists and had the additional feature that only those who had personal friends in the NHS had much chance of receiving decent health care. In these circumstances, according to the Barry definition of socialism, socialists would lend at least some support to the high-cost, inequitable collective system, simply because it was collective.

This kind of trade-off seems to me to be very unattractive. First of all it is not clear why socialists should wish to support the collective system at all. In defence of collectivism, it is sometimes argued that, by supporting a collective system which is socially unjust, people may come to prefer collective solutions in the future. This argument has two obvious weaknesses. First, even if such a collectivism did kindle 'positive collective feelings' among its users, who would then support more collective provision in the future, it is unclear why this should be attractive to socialists, unless the intrinsic virtue of collective provision has already been established.

Of course, if collective provision is being advanced as being the best method in the relevant circumstances of achieving social justice, then this becomes an instrumental justification of collectivism. Some extra collectivism now will achieve more social justice in future.

The second reason why this inter-temporal argument is unconvincing is that people will observe that collective provision violates some principle of social justice. They are not then likely to regard collectivism as a more attractive solution to social problems either now or in the future.

Apart from the difficulty in justifying violations of social justice in order to promote collectivism, the idea of a trade-off between the two concepts also presents difficulties. How are these trade-offs to be made? Are those who lose out in terms of social justice going to be compensated by those who gain by collectivism? It may be argued that making difficult trade-offs is the essence of political decision making. The classic example is the well known trade-off between efficiency and equity. Presumably any concept of social justice has embedded in it a theory as to how such a trade-off might be made.

For instance it might be argued that everyone has a right to receive education up to the point where each person has roughly equal productive potential (the egalitarian concept of a socially just education system). Such a system could be expected to have at least some, perhaps a high, cost in terms of efficiency; educational rights here being considered more important than efficient production. Such rights-based arguments, which insist that losses in terms of efficiency can be justified in order to achieve equality of opportunity, have a familiar ring. No doubt there are other ways in which to justify various positions in this kind of trade-off.

However in making the trade-off between collectivism and social justice, I'm not aware of any well-established arguments for taking decisions about particular trade-offs. It is hard to see why anyone should want, let alone validly claim, a right to collective provision.

The New Right attack on collectivism

As we are all aware, the attacks from the New Right on collectivism have had a great deal of influence on the policies of recent Conservative governments. Since the New Right gives very little weight to egalitarian outcomes, the main burden of this attack is that collective provision is inefficient. Collective provision provides either the wrong information or the wrong incentives to suppliers and as a result less is supplied at higher cost.

In the pursuit of efficiency the New Right usually advocates competition over monopoly and as a result favours small decentralised units of production over large ones. There is, in fact, a fairly substantial division on this issue. Ever since Schumpeter defended monopoly capitalism as being more innovative than competition, the New Right has sometimes defended privately owned monopolies for this reason, but not, as far as I know, publicly owned ones. In this context, it would be of interest to know whether, for instance, the record of the NHS on innovation is as good as in decentralised health care systems.

Apart from this little difficulty, the New Right's position is coherent and straightforward. In order to emphasise its position on information it necessarily plays down the importance of externalities. In order to ensure that collective provision always leads to 'rent-seeking' by producers, it confines its analysis of motivation to self-interest.

Any defence of collectivism, even of an instrumental kind, will therefore stress the importance of externalities and other informational deficiencies of decentralisation. All three of Barry's examples – road congestion, education and health – have these features. And it seems to me that the arguments for collective provision in these areas are indeed extremely strong. Indeed they are so strong that in most industrial countries, virtually none of which is usually considered socialist, collectivist arrangements in these areas have been adopted, or are being seriously considered.

There is nothing particularly socialist about realising that an efficient public transport system, or a public education system which attempts to provide all children with equal educational opportunities, can confer substantial positive social benefits.

The New Right's analysis of motivation is more difficult to deal with. This is partly because motivation appears to be rather more difficult to observe, but partly because, in a large number of cases, producers do appear to undermine the possible benefits of collectivism by their own self-interested behaviour.

In order to appreciate the strength of the New Right's position on motivation as opposed to information, it is instructive to look at the traditional debates over the centrally planned economy. The main thrust of the original arguments of Von Mises and Hayek against the possibility of efficient central planning rested on information. Planners would simply not be able to acquire the information to plan properly. Accordingly the socialist response was that that there were indeed methods by which the central planners could acquire the right information.

A full reckoning of the story of the centrally planned economy has yet to be made. But at the moment it certainly looks as though the causes of its downfall were far more closely linked to the incentives problem than to the information problem. A quick trip to any Western economy would have given central planners more than enough information about what consumers would like to buy. Indeed many of the attempts to reform central planning gave emphasis to the need to provide Western-style consumer goods and services. These reforms came to nothing, or at least to very little, mainly because the planners could not provide the incentive structures which would encourage these kinds of goods to be produced.

This is not to say that the axiomatic belief in the primacy of self-interest is entirely correct either. Barry's analysis of the differing incentives in the NHS and US health care systems bears this out. He shows how self-interest can only partially explain observed behaviour. The vast empirical literature on labour supply which has been able to find only weak links between various measures of labour effort and incentives is another indication of how crude the self-interest hypothesis is.

A final and substantial weakness of the New Right's position on motivation concerns the modern corporation, in which private ownership is divided from managerial control. The various attempts to rescue the modern corporation as an 'incentive compatible' institution seem to me to be unconvincing. Indeed one possible way in which to advance a socialist case is to adopt self-interest as the major motivating force and then to argue that the modern corporation fails to provide the necessary incentives for efficient production. Taking this position obviously then concedes the argument on incentives to the New Right.

Most socialists may not be willing to go this far. Nevertheless in the absence of better theory and more empirical evidence, the New Right's position on motivation is, I believe, its strongest argument. Of course socialists always like to believe that people will behave for the better, that the man or woman in Whitehall not only knows best but behaves best as well. But the events of the last few years, particularly in eastern Europe, do suggest that any socialist argument which is based on the assumption that people do not act only in their own self-interest, should provide some very good evidence to support this contention.

Two kinds of socialist collectivism

The argument so far has, I hope, established two points. First, collectivism can only have an instrumental place in any concept of socialism.

Second, the argument for collectivism is strongest where, for one reason or another, decentralisation deprives agents of the correct information on which to base decisions. In these cases it may not make just socialist sense, but almost any kind of sense to suggest a collectivist solution. Collectivism should not be a socialist goal in its own right. Certainly it cannot be claimed that only socialists employ it as a solution to various social problems. As this is so, the question arises as to why collectivism has for so long obsessed socialists.

There are, it seems, two different ways in which 'collective thinking' has been important to socialists. The first I will call communitarianism. This is the belief that a person cannot lead a satisfactory life without a well-defined and important relationship with some social aggregate larger than the family. The community in question may be the village, the region, the state, class, the nation or something even larger. I shall leave discussion of communitarianism largely to others, except to say that the concept of a civil society in which people's relationships with a number of overlapping 'communities' are allowed spontaneously to develop is attractive. But I am not sure whether a psychological or metaphysical preference for communitarianism is more consistent with decentralised than with collective procedures for allocating resources.

The second aspect of collective thinking which socialists have pursued is to stress the importance of the empirical interactions between people. We all, or at least most of us, recognise that when factories produce smoke, this can cause distress to neighbours. But most Right-wing or even liberal thought presupposes that such externalities are the exception rather than the rule. The socialist disagrees. The socialist assumption is that every act has externalities, pleasant or unpleasant, for other people in society. Again there may be exceptions to this rule, but they are of minor importance.

Thus a liberal (or even a Left-liberal) may see nothing wrong with the spread of international chains of food supply. The gains of trade are, after all, a classic liberal benefit. The socialist, while not denying the possible gains from trade, will also want to investigate the role of cheap immigrant labour in reducing labour costs in Californian agri-business (not to mention the huge subsidies such business receives from the Federal government in the form of cheap water supplies). Thus the socialist will be aware, as she enjoys her Californian avocado, that she does so partly as a result of poor educational opportunities in Mexico. At the same time, she will recognise that the existence of an immigrant labour market in California may help to raise wages slightly in Mexico itself, though possibly at the cost of depriving Mexico of some of its more talented workers, etc. As economists know all too well, general equilibrium analysis is very complicated and rarely leads to neat conclusions.

While this portrait of the right-thinking socialist avocado eater may not be immediately attractive, it is I think distinctively socialist not only to recognise these general equilibrium effects as being of importance, but also, as a response to this, to widen the concept of social justice in order to deal with these interactions. If as consumers we benefit from the lack of educational opportunity in Mexico, then it seems odd to base any concept of social justice concerning education on one which excludes Mexicans.

The argument should by now be clear. Collectivism is not a separate socialist goal, but the socialist nevertheless incorporates a maximal view of collectivist interdependence into the concept of social justice itself. This is not based on what I regard as a metaphysical view of the individual's relationship to social aggregates, but to empirically verifiable relationships. The spread of capitalist market relations throughout the world provides the socialist with a transnational concept of social justice.

6

Citizenship, rights and socialism

RAYMOND PLANT

Introduction

Democratic citizenship can provide a unifying framework within which policy can be elaborated and a link to Labour's historical principles maintained. A citizenship approach is not new for Labour. Indeed, the theme was taken up in the party's earliest days, reflecting the impact of social liberalism. This tradition is in urgent need of rethinking and updating much as the modern Conservative Party has rethought the tradition of classical liberalism.

Citizenship and class

The other main strand of opinion in the early years of the Labour Party, reflecting the Marxist tradition, emphasised a class-based strategy. The class-based approach sees the market as inherently capitalist and its relationships as exploitative and dehumanising.

This clashed with the citizenship approach which assumes that there are common values between different groups and classes in society which are genuine (not the product of what Marxists would call false consciousness). These values can provide a basis for political action to secure the rights and resources of citizenship within a mixed economy with some degree of private ownership. The citizenship approach rejects Marx's argument that since class determines political interests there can be no common basis for citizenship while there is some private ownership of the means of production and associated class divisions.

The class approach sees a sense of solidarity and common purpose among members of the class as a necessary prerequisite for the funda- mental transformation of society which alone will end exploitation

The original version of this chapter was published by the Fabian Society (pamphlet 531, 1988).

and bring about socialism. The citizenship approach is much more at home with individualism: it sees citizenship as securing the framework of rights and resources within which individuals can pursue their own conception of the good in their own way; and the communal basis of society is reflected in agreement about the common resources and means of citizenship rather than in terms of common ends.

The difficulties with the class approach are manifold. First, the industrial working class is too small a base from which to gain power. Despite the Marxian prediction, capitalism has not destroyed farmers, merchants, craftsmen and artisans so that in elections socialists could attain an 'immense majority'. On the contrary, the industrial working class has contracted and a minority status combined with democratic politics will condemn a class-based strategy to purist impotence. There has to be a way of breaking out of the numerically narrow bounds of class interest to reach out to other groups in society. A search for a common basis of citizenship would provide one central theme to attract people back to support the party on a wider basis of interest. This is wholly unlikely to happen were the party to retreat into a laager of restricted class interest.

Second, the class-based conception of the good is usually seen in communitarian terms drawing from the forms of solidarity historically found in working-class life at work and in the neighbourhood. There is no doubt that some of these evocations of the socialist vision of the good are immensely beguiling and certainly, as someone who grew up in a very working-class area in Grimsby after the war, I remain moved by them. However, nostalgia is not a good basis for political thinking and particularly for a radical party.

The numbers of people for whom such communitarian visions are good and mean something at the level of their everyday experience are declining, attenuating their moral force. With the decline in the numbers of people for whom these experiences and values are central, the socialist has to be realistic and recognise the individualism of the age. This is itself in large part the result of the decline in community, which in any case was frequently far from the idyll which it may have seemed. Invoking unspecific communitarian values is of very little practical use in trying to determine a way forward in policy terms. This is not to try to devalue the idea of community, only to be sceptical about its precision and to indicate the need to rethink its role in the future of socialism.

Third, socialist thought and practice in Britain in this century makes it abundantly clear that the citizenship approach has played a central role in Labour Party thinking, particularly in the work of Tawney and in practice, for example, in Haldane and Attlee. It has a broader resonance in the labour movement (in the WEA, for example), and in approaches to thinking about the welfare state associated with Titmuss and Marshall. It has also been central to continental socialist parties in France, the Danish Social Democrats, the German SPD (and not as mythology would have it from the Bad Godesburg conference in 1959, but from the Erfurt congress of 1881), and in Sweden. It is obvious why this should be so. Given the failure of Marxist predictions about the shape of class in capitalist society, socialist parties sought an opening to other classes and this has to be on the basis of some common identity such as citizenship.

Hence, a citizenship approach to the Policy Review is not a betrayal of socialism. It is, on the contrary, an attempt to rethink a set of issues which have always had a central place in the life and thought of the Labour Party, and which most continental parties have resolved.

One problem which preoccupied continental parties in relation to a non-class approach was whether votes would be lost among workers if socialist parties turned towards a non-class strategy. This is not so real a danger in Britain. First, the class basis of politics is itself in decline and second, there is no plausible party to the Left to which those disenchanted by a citizenship approach could turn.

Interest groups

An alternative approach to rebuilding Labour support is that of seeing the Labour Party as representing a coalition of interest groups. Indeed, this approach arises quite naturally out of the decline of the class approach. Either politics addresses itself to individuals defined in terms of groups, such as classes or by religious, ethnic, linguistic, sexual, etc., characteristics; or it tries to surpass all of these with a more communal appeal in terms of citizenship. The Conservative Party, in the grip of classical liberal ideas, is attempting to appeal in the economic sphere purely on an individual basis, while in other areas using images of the nation as a way of transcending the individualism of their economic approach. Labour has to abandon a class approach but should it adopt an interest-group strategy?

There are various difficulties in seeing a political party as a coalition of interest groups. The first is that a coherent political programme must have some core ideas and policies which go beyond aggregating the often incompatible demands of sympathetic interest groups. If a party falls prey to interest groups, there are attendant political dangers of arbitrariness and incoherence, a feature of the Labour Party Manifesto in 1983. A secure basis for devising a policy strategy requires a basic underlying benchmark to evaluate the claims of interest groups. A coherent account of democratic citizenship could provide that basis for considering interest-group claims. The Conservatives have benefited by having a set of core ideas at the heart of their strategy in government which has given their programme a high degree of coherence.

Second, interest groups aim to secure some concession or resource which will be to the advantage of members of the group or the interests which the group represents, the costs of which will be borne by citizens generally. The benefits of interest-group membership are highly concentrated, the costs highly dispersed, but the cumulative effect of these costs may well be very high. Without some benchmark defining the general good (such as the common basis of citizenship), interest-group pressures will be very difficult to resist. Unless there are ordered priorities around agreed principles and values, a Labour government concerned with the distribution of resources in the interests of need and social justice will fall victim to the most powerful groups and interests. Instead of a distributive ideal, social justice will become a camouflage for powerful special pleading.

The Conservatives have found it easier to resist interest-group pressure because they have sought to lower expectations about what government can and should do. So the government has tried to restrain its own intervention in the economy and has abandoned the pursuit of social justice. The Labour Party cannot adopt such a strategy: it is rightly committed to intervention in the economy and to social justice. Principles are required to deal with interest groups seeking subsidies and resources if they are not to drive up public expenditure and over-extend government's role. There is a growing belief on the Left that the future of socialism does not lie with big government. However, one of the major causes of the growth of government since the war has been its expansion under interest-group pressure. If the Left is serious about limited government, it must place its approach to interest-group politics on a more principled basis.

The idea of democratic citizenship is the only basis on which Labour can hope to reach a value consensus to determine the broad boundaries of government responsibility and within these to separate legitimate from illegitimate claims. Citizenship embodies a concept of the common good which appeals not to highly specific and sectional goals, but to a set of needs, rights, resources and opportunities which all individuals must have to pursue any goals at all in our sort of society. Such an underlying idea will also indicate the forms of collective and communal provision which are necessary to provide these and the respective roles of the market and the state.

Citizenship and social values

In his Preface to *Democratic Socialist Aims and Values*, Neil Kinnock writes:

> We want a state where the collective contribution of the community is used to advance individual freedom. Not just freedom in name, but freedom that can be exercised in practice (Labour Party, 1988).

Here, government is seen as an enabling power to secure real freedom. This idea contrasts sharply with the Conservatives' view of freedom as absence of coercion from identifiable agents. The Conservative definition requires a limited role for government in terms of liberty, ideally a framework of law within which one individual is prevented from coercing another. There is a clear distinction to be drawn between freedom on the one hand and ability, power and resources on the other. Given this distinction Sir Keith Joseph drew the appropriate conclusion in his book on equality when he argued quite clearly that 'poverty is not unfreedom' (Sir Keith Joseph and J. Sumption, *Equality*, Murray, 1977).

Freedom, power and the market

In the view of Conservatives there is a categorical distinction between being free to do something and being able to do it. (This is central to Hayek's criticisms of socialist conceptions of freedom in *The Constitution of Liberty*, Routledge, 1960.) In the first sense someone is free to do X if no one is deliberately preventing him from doing it. The fact that someone lacks the capacity to do it – perhaps because of a lack of resources – does not in itself limit the freedom to do X.

Clearly if freedom is understood in this sense, then government has a rather limited role in the protection of free and equal citizenship. Its role is to provide equal freedom under the law and collective resources such as police forces and courts to secure this. It is *not* a legitimate function of government to secure for individuals specific resources to enable them to do what they are free to do. No one is able to do all that they are free to do, and this indicates that there is a distinction to be drawn between freedom on the one hand and capacities, resources and opportunities on the other. If this were not so then I am unfree whenever I am unable to fulfil my desires. If government had the role of securing resources for liberty in this positive sense, then its task would be endless.

But there is a stronger reason why Conservatives wish to separate freedom and resources, identified by Hayek. If freedom and ability along with associated resources are seen as the same thing, then resources should be redistributed in the interests of more equal liberty. The sharp distinction which they draw between freedom and resources effectively blocks this argument and makes it impossible to argue for a collective redistribution of resources in the interests of individual freedom.

Excluding government as far as possible from the allocation of resources is reinforced by the New Right's belief that markets are the correct mechanism for allocation between individuals, because they cannot infringe freedom.

Markets are complex institutions within which millions of people buy and sell goods and services and no doubt do so deliberately and intentionally. These complex interactions produce a distribution of income and wealth and other resources, which is an unintended consequence of all this buying and selling. If the outcomes of free markets are unintended then markets cannot limit freedom because freedom under the neo-liberal definition can only be limited by intentional or deliberate coercion.

Hence, the New Right argues, there can again be no case for collective action to preserve the liberty of individuals in the face of markets.

Liberty and citizenship

There is no reason to dissent from the neo-liberal definition of freedom and what it enjoins in terms of government in itself. But it should still be rejected as a full characterisation of the nature of liberty.

It is true that freedom is limited by coercion whether it is by individuals or government and the Labour Party accept this part of the definition of freedom and what follows from it, namely a concern with law and order and the protection of people from coercion, as well as a limitation on the arbitrary power of the executive. Labour should accept that government itself is a coercive power and that this power should only be used in a principled and justified way.

Indeed, the definition of liberty as the absence of coercion is vital because it is a necessary condition of the exercise of liberty in the broader sense which Neil Kinnock, Roy Hattersley, Bryan Gould and others have argued for, namely that freedom has to do with being able to do things. But we need to establish the link between freedom and ability and to show that markets do infringe freedom in terms of their outcomes before we can go on to argue for a broader conception of citizenship which will involve collective provision for liberty in the sense of increasing abilities, opportunities and resources for emancipation.

The central argument against the neo-liberal's distinction between freedom and ability is to ask what is freedom in the sense of the absence of coercion valuable for? The most obvious answer to this question would be that if I am free from deliberate interference then I am free to do what I want, to live a life shaped by my own values and purposes. Freedom is valuable because it is a necessary condition of autonomy. But if this is why freedom is valuable, it cannot be separated from ability, resources and opportunities. I can do what I want, lead a life shaped by my own values, only if I have the capacity to fulfil my desires. (For further discussion of this point, see K. Hoover and R. Plant, *Conservative Capitalism in Britain and the USA: A Critical Appraisal*, Routledge, 1988.)

The neo-liberal will reject this account. If people who lack the resources to do what they desire to do are unfree, then equal liberty is an unattainable ideal. There are always going to be limits on people's abilities and they will differ from one another.

There are two answers to this charge. The first is to recognise that only some forms of inability or incapacity can be changed by collective action – natural inabilities will always remain and they lie beyond the scope of political remedy. So it is perfectly true that we cannot finally equalise abilities, but that should not rule out action towards achieving a fairer distribution of resources. Most Conservatives regard perfect competition as utopian but it does not stop them regarding a more and more competitive economy as a goal.

Second, it is clearly absurd to believe that to be free one has to have all the resources to fulfil one's wants whatever they are, so that someone who wishes to live a life marked by a desire for expensive tastes will not be free unless he or she has the resources to pursue such tastes. Public provision is concerned to secure access to that range of resources which are necessary conditions of living an autonomous and purposive life – the necessary conditions of agency, not the necessary conditions of pursuing individual preferences. We are concerned with needs rather than wants. The satisfaction of the needs of agency are part of a feasible collective programme for active citizenship, because they are general within our society.

Without education, health care, income, self-respect and a framework of law within which one can live one's own life in one's own way, one cannot be an agent in the sense of having the resources to pursue goals which make freedom worthwhile in human life. But these resources must be provided in ways which do not threaten their overall purpose – the emancipation of individuals and communities.

If these are the basic goods of citizenship there are still questions as to how they are to be distributed and how they are to be resourced.

Needs, poverty and citizenship

The New Right claims that social justice is not possible through government action and that the distribution of resources is best left to the market. It is a central argument of the New Right that needs cannot be identified in an objective and consensual way. If we are committed as a society to meeting the needs of citizens, then just because such needs are open-ended, the resources required to meet them can be bid up. Pressure will come not only from consumer interest groups but also from producer interest groups, that is, those who have an economic interest in seeing a particular set of needs recognised and met in the public sector. The conclusion drawn from this is that the free market is a better mechanism for meeting subjective needs rather than collective or political provision which rests upon the mistaken view that there is an objective, or at least consensual, basis for needs.

Yet strangely, many thinkers on the right utilise a very definite concept of need in attacking the relative view of poverty. They argue that claims about the extent of poverty in Britain are exaggerated when the state provides enough to meet the basic needs for housing and subsistence. On this view the relative approach to poverty is defective because it links poverty to the expenditure of the rich rather than to the needs of the poor.

For example, Sir Keith Joseph argued as follows in *Stranded on the Middle Ground*: 'An absolute standard of means are defined by reference to the actual needs of the poor and not by reference to those who are not poor . . . . A person who enjoys a standard of living equal to that of a medieval baron cannot be described as poor for the sole reason that he has chanced to be born into a society where the great majority can live like medieval kings. By any absolute standard there is very little poverty in Britain today' (Centre for Policy Studies, 1976).

This attempt to distinguish between absolute and relative poverty, or as the New Right would see it, between poverty and inequality, makes it impossible for the New Right to operate without a concept of need. It is this concept which defines the standard of absolute poverty against which other conceptions are to be criticised. They would, of course, argue that there is a consensual view about what an absolute standard of need is, that is to say what is required for subsistence. But this idea of an objective standard of subsistence is a will-o'-the-wisp notion which has bedevilled thinking about social policy. Even the most basic need for food may well mean resources not merely for purchasing food but also the resources to get to distant shops and the related infrastructure of public transport, etc.

The New Right cannot reject a needs-based approach to social justice on the grounds that needs are elusive when they depend upon it to differentiate their own view of poverty from a more socialist conception of relative poverty. The only real debate then is how needs are to be interpreted.

There is no apolitical way of deciding what needs are basic and any level at which the claims to needs are to be met will reflect social values and democratic processes. This is a moral question for political debate, not one which can be derived from a purely administrative approach. But the Left should argue that citizenship requires the opportunity to participate in the normal or expected patterns of individual and family life and in the workplace, and define needs in the light of this.

This approach also allows us to reject the critic's view that needs-based policies will always be open-ended and can be pushed up by interest-group pressures in an unprincipled way. Since the New Right implicitly adopts a needs-based approach their conception of needs is equally vulnerable to bidding up. Once government is in the business of meeting needs then interest groups are bound to arise. It requires some agreement about what is a reasonable range of resources for citizenship, this will make interest-group pressures more manageable.

Distribution

Even if there is a set of basic goods which is central to the exercise of citizenship in a free society, how should they be allocated? The Right argues that it is impossible to find a just way of distributing goods through political means for two main reasons.

The first is that any attempt to intentionally redistribute resources will produce injustice. The market on the other hand redistributes without injustice because its outcomes are unintended. That is why we do not regard the outcomes of earthquakes and famines as injustices; why we do not regard children suffering from genetic handicap or cancer as suffering from injustice. These are forms of bad luck or misfortune, not injustice, precisely because they are not the outcomes of intentional processes.

Second, even if intentional redistribution could be justified we have no way of agreeing about the criteria of distributive justice. There are many possible criteria – need, merit, entitlement and so on. Given the moral divergence of modern society how are we to agree on the appropriate criteria of distribution?

Hence, in the view of the New Right the requirements of citizenship have nothing to do with distributive justice or the fair allocation of resources through political action. On the contrary, the needs of citizenship are best provided in the market rather than through state action. This is to be achieved through the trickle-down effect of the market whereby what the rich consume today will be available to the rest of society including the poor in the long run. This view has been explicitly endorsed by the present government and lay behind the Budget of 1988. There is no need for organised collective action to meet the needs of citizenship because the market will do it for us.

One consequence of this argument is to justify inequality. Only by making the rich richer and thus producing the supply-side effects which such incentives are supposed to bring will the poor be made richer. Hence the solution to this problem of poverty is greater inequality.

A second consequence is to establish the criterion that the position is improving if the poor have more today than they had yesterday. It does not matter that they are consuming a lower percentage of the resources than the rich because such a view is locked into a mistaken relative view of poverty which in fact is a disguise for egalitarianism. The free market theorists' withers remain unwrung by studies which show that the rich are now consuming more resources than they were in 1979. What matters on this view is the absolute standard, not inequality.

Social justice

Even if markets are impersonal forces which are lacking intention, this does not mean that we should ignore their outcomes. Justice and injustice are not only a matter of how a particular state of affairs arose, but also of our response to it. An earthquake or famine is not an injustice *per se* but there is the question of the justice or injustice in our response. If we can compensate the victims at no comparable cost to ourselves then to fail to do so when they bear no responsibility for their condition is where part of the potential injustice lies.

So it is with markets. If we can compensate those who are the victims of this supposed impersonal force at no comparable cost to ourselves as a society then to fail to do so would be an injustice.

However, this characterisation of markets is itself tendentious: the outcomes of markets may not be intended but they are foreseeable. The New Right argues for market solutions to problems because such solutions are likely to bring about what they take to be desirable results. So, for example, they are in favour of the abolition of rent controls because this will lead to an expansion in the supply of rented accommodation. Hence it is central to the whole rationale of the free market theorist that the outcomes of markets are foreseeable even if they do not embody an individual's intention.

If free markets are grafted on to a society with large-scale inequalities in resources then it is foreseeable that those who enter the market with least will leave it with least. We are usually, as individuals, held to be responsible for the foreseeable, even if unintended, consequences of our actions – as, for example, in manslaughter. It could be argued, by analogy, that if we support the introduction of markets and it is foreseeable that those who enter it with fewest resources will leave it with fewest, then we can be held responsible for such outcomes. Thus the question of justice and collective responsibility have purchase once again. It is difficult to overestimate the importance of this issue because the New Right regards social justice as the central value of socialism and argues that it is a concept without moral purchase.

Consensus

If social justice has moral relevance, can it be grounded in consensus given the degree of moral pluralism in society? The first response is rather opportunistic but nevertheless is worth making. The New Right argues for moral diversity and subjectivism when it comes to social justice while, at the very same time, supporting policies which imply a moral consensus over things such as Victorian values, the role of the family, the national curriculum and so on. Moral diversity is invoked only to block social justice.

More important if we accept all the points made about moral subjectivism, we can still derive principles of distribution. A deep philosophical attempt has been made by John Rawls, namely a theory of presumptive equality which moves away from equality being justified because it benefits the worst off members of society. I have defended his views as being relevant to a socialist view of distribution elsewhere (see 'Democratic Socialism and Equality' in D. Lipsey and D. Leonard, *The Socialist Agenda: Crosland's Legacy*, Cape, 1981).

However, such a view can be defended even on the New Right's own subjectivist premises. If we have no way of judging people's needs, merits, deserts and entitlements as the subjectivist position argues, then one response would be that a presumption in favour of equality can be argued since no one can be thought of as having a more just claim than anyone else. Moves away from greater equality would then be justified if inequalities in society worked to the benefit of the worst off. That is to say the basic goods of citizenship which we discussed earlier are to be distributed as equally as possible unless a more unequal distribution would produce more resources for the worst off. The theory would become one of legitimate inequalities. If our concern is with the worst off then it would be irrational to prefer a more equal distribution of resources if a more unequal one would produce more resources for all including the poor.

This is to agree to a central role for the market not as some amoral force but as part of a just society. The socialist approach to the market and its inequalities is that these are tolerable if the market mechanism is working better than any alternative to produce resources for all members of society, but particularly the worst off. As we shall see later, the market has to be constrained in the interest of the community as a whole. Because equality is a rather unspecific idea meaning anything from procedural equality of opportunity to equality of outcome, it might be best either to adopt an expression for legitimate inequalities such as Rawls' term 'democratic equality' or to abandon the expression altogether and talk about fairness.

Trickle down

The final part of the New Right's critique of social justice is the trickle-down theory. We do not need distributive politics with all the interest-group pressures which go along with it: rather the free market will produce the goods which people need even though it will produce inequalities.

Clearly there would be a lot to be said for the market mechanism if it did this in an impersonal way without political intervention and guidance. However, even on their own terms the free market is not working to increase what the Right takes to be the absolute standard of the poor. Whatever the subtleties and controversies of measurement, being eligible for income support (supplementary benefit) and being homeless seem to be self-evident indicators of poverty. On both of these counts the free market has yet to work in the way suggested by its defenders. Between 1978 and 1987 personal disposable income in Britain rose by 14 per cent in real terms, while supplementary benefit levels fell from 61 per cent of disposable income per capita in 1978 to 53 per cent in 1987. Using this criterion the incomes of the poor have not kept up, never mind increased with the development of the free market.

Second, the number of people being drawn into supplementary benefit and hence into the group which is not sustaining its share in total national income increased dramatically from about three million in 1978 to about five million in 1987. Of course, this only indicates the recipients of benefits, not those who are dependent on them. It is estimated that in 1984 about 7,729,000 were dependent on supplementary benefit compared with about 5,750,000 in 1979.

Again homelessness, a clear enough symptom of poverty, has increased alarmingly. In 1970 the figure for homeless people was about 56,000 families; in 1985 the figure had grown to 100,000 and is likely to be far more now. Thus to rely on the market and a residual welfare state which seeks to provide only for an absolute standard of need will not provide adequate resources for democratic citizenship. Social justice is central to securing the basic goods of citizenship not just to some but to all citizens as a right.

Rights and citizenship

If the basic goods of citizenship should be available to all, they should be considered as matters of right and entitlement. This in turn raises questions as to how these rights are to be guaranteed and entitlements made available. Rights can proliferate endlessly with interest groups making claims of one sort or another as basic human rights. It is not in anyone's interests that the range of rights should be so utterly open-ended. It devalues rights and over-extends the role of government so that the powers which it needs to protect expanding rights actually become a major threat to liberty.

Citizenship involves negative rights such as rights to be free from coercion, interference, assault, freedom of expression and association – all in effect traditional civil and political rights. These are usually regarded as negative rights since the corresponding obligation on others is to refrain from assaulting, interfering and coercing. However, as we saw earlier, the goods of citizenship have to go beyond civil and political rights and embrace rights to resources, income, health care, education and welfare. These are usually called positive rights in the sense that they involve a claim on the resources of others through the tax system.

This latter view of rights and entitlement is firmly rejected by the New Right arguing that positive rights are rights to resources which are in themselves scarce and cannot therefore be considered to be objects of rights. Claims to civil and political rights, because they are rights to be free from interferences of various sorts, do not involve direct claims to resources in the way that positive rights do. Indeed, the New Right asserts that only civil and political rights are genuine rights of citizenship whereas economic and social rights are not.

Resources

Of course social and economic rights are asserted against a background of scarce resources, but the contrast between civil and political rights on the one hand and welfare rights on the other is not as clear-cut as is suggested.

Civil and political rights which imply the corresponding duty to abstain from coercive action may appear to be costless. In reality this is not the case since people do not always abstain from such actions: they do assault, coerce and interfere and they have to be prevented from doing so. To protect such rights, therefore, there is a need for police forces, a legal system, and a system of justice. These institutions involve resources.

Likewise, negative rights such as the right to privacy and the right to security imply that other people should abstain from interference. But the institutions which are necessary to ensure that such obligations are satisfied involve costs. For example, what is necessary to secure the right to privacy changes with advances in technology. Before the advent of the computer, the Data Protection Act was not necessary and the costs of enforcement were not incurred. Similarly, in the case of a right to security, various forms of expenditure are necessary such as street lighting and so forth. The degree and amount of street lighting and other security-inducing measures will run up against resource constraints as much as welfare rights.

The critics' arguments can be put in other ways. One is for the Right to argue that in the case of civil and political rights the corresponding obligation is categorical: it is to abstain from action and therefore we know when the right has been fully protected. Welfare rights are based upon needs which are in principle open ended so we can never know when the rights have been fully protected and respected.

The point can be put starkly in relation to different interpretations of something as fundamental as the right to life. To the neo-liberal such a right will be understood in negative terms as the right not to be killed or murdered and the corresponding duty is to abstain from these action. On the Left, the right will be understood partly as that but also as the right to the means of life – to the resources necessary to maintain life. In the latter case it is harder to agree about what will meet the claims falling under the right. But the examples of privacy and security indicate that the difference between the two sorts of rights are not as straightforward as this. The degree to which we collectively provide resources to protect privacy or security is as much a matter of judgement and political negotiation to be undertaken against a background of limited resources as for welfare rights.

The second approach by critics of welfare rights is to argue that because they are open-ended they will become subject to interest-group pressures and political bargaining in a way that the more categorical civil and political rights will not. These rights are thought of as, in a sense, beyond politics and political negotiation; whereas welfare rights are always going to be subject to political pressures. However, this optimistic approach is false for the reasons which we have already discussed. The resources given over to maintaining security and property rights are going to be as much a matter of interest-group pressure as welfare rights.

It follows from all of this that we can not draw a sharp distinction between 'real' rights such as traditional civil and political rights on the one hand and illusory welfare rights on the other. Equally if civil and political rights are genuine, then there can be no case in terms of resource constraints for arguing that welfare rights are not genuine. In the real world all sorts of rights run up against resource constraints and are subject to political negotiation and pressure.

The Right will also argue that since welfare rights imply resources, they must infringe property rights, an illegitimate interference with the property holder's right to use his or her property as he or she pleases. However, all forms of rights including property rights infringe freedom. Taking property rights as given in our society in which there are virtually no unowned resources restricts the freedom of non-property owners to exercise their liberty. Hence, the real question is not about the infringement of liberty. The question is rather whether, for example, the right to the means to life has priority over the unfettered right to property. For the socialist the answer will be clear. However, we should not succumb to the liberal suggestion that this is an undifferentiated infringement of liberty.

Enforcement

I now want to look at the question of enforcement, particularly in relation to welfare rights where the problem is thought to be more troublesome. This is not to say that the ways in which civil and political rights are to be protected are unimportant, far from it given the growth of arbitrary actions by government. However, in this field, the issues such as whether there should be a Bill of Rights are well understood and have been quite extensively discussed. The issue of enforcement in the welfare field, however, is more intractable.

The critic will argue that social and economic rights are not genuine because they are not justiciable, that is, cannot be enforced in law. The example of the recent litigation over young children requiring heart operations in Birmingham would support this view. There the judges argued that they could not interfere with clinical judgement in relation to waiting lists.

However, there are alternatives to this model of enforcement. The first would come closest to the justiciable one and argue that although a judge may not be able to enforce a particular right to a specific form of treatment, he does have a role in determining whether a patient's interests have been fully taken into account and that his or her plight is not the result of negligence or inadvertance. So there could be a place for judicial review in this narrower sense. This is not as novel as it looks and applies to a civil right such as equal protection before the law. While a judge cannot dictate the policing policy in a particular city there have been cases where individuals have taken their grievances about policing to court and the question of whether those individuals' interests have been properly taken into account is one to which a judge can address himself. This is not different from the welfare case: the deployment of scarce resources requires professional judgement, but the professional has an obligation to make sure that all interests are properly weighed.

More generally, welfare rights could be protected by empowering the specific individuals in several different ways. It is possible to define certain rights in terms of cash entitlements which could be protected by law. This could be done through a minimum income policy or through giving a legal guarantee to income support. Indeed, many social security benefits could be treated in this way. Certainly in terms of the liberty of citizens, avoiding stigma and securing a sense of independence, there is a lot to be said for cash rather than in kind or service-based benefits.

In other fields, perhaps particularly health and in terms of care for the elderly, it might be possible to define entitlement in terms of a cash surrogate like a voucher. Such vouchers might empower a patient who needs medical attention to have the operation done in the shortest time outside the local hospital system. If we are to be serious about rights and empowerment in the welfare field we must be prepared to consider such alternatives. As the Policy Review document says: 'Rights without enforcement are a mockery.'

However, enforcement can take on forms other than the judicial, and one way is to put more power by way of strict entitlements into the hands of consumers. A strong commitment to rights in the welfare field is not compatible, for example, with major regional disparities in treatment times. This sort of disparity may not be cured just by the commitment of more resources, important though that is: we have to give consumers more voice to constrain the system reflecting more the choices of professionals and bureaucracies rather than those with the rights which the institutions are to serve.

It will be argued that if choice is entrenched in the welfare field to this degree, those with the least capacity to make informed choices will get the worst service. A more collective, bureaucratic mechanism allocates medical care fairly rather than empowering individuals which will produce poor results for some. This raises an interesting conflict between libertarian and communitarian forms of socialism. The libertarian wants to disperse power more to individuals; communitarians are worried about the overall consequences of individual choice. More resources for welfare without empowerment of consumers within it will not meet the mood of the times.

Providing a basis of entitlement and empowerment in the welfare field means challenging many of the professional producer interest groups in the public sector. Clearly the empowerment of the citizen as consumer will involve a limitation of the power and scope of professional groups such as social workers, doctors, teachers and social security officials. Claims to professional expertise as against the limited knowledge of the consumer have to be challenged if we are to have a real society of active citizens, instead of a society managed by experts. Of course there is expertise in these areas, but it should not be allowed to be a cloak for the assertion of professional power over the lives of citizens in a democratic society.

If rights are to provide a basis for individuals to lead a secure and autonomous life then institutions must themselves enhance this autonomy. Too often the institutions of the welfare state and the growth of professionalism within them have actually led to a reduction in the capacity of individuals for choice and judgement. I doubt whether there is a real way forward in the welfare field without empowering individuals through cash, rights, entitlements and cash surrogates such as vouchers. This is particularly important when the state is effectively the monopoly provider of services in health and welfare for the vast majority of citizens. If they are denied exit either through lack of resources or because the private sector has been removed, then the democratic voice must be increased drastically if we are to be responsive to the idea that citizenship, individual freedom and personal responsibility go together.

Empowerment could also involve the public funding of voluntary agencies in the welfare field. Such initiatives have been crowded out to a degree by the growth of professionalism in welfare. Obviously there is a professional expertise here, but it should not be used to downgrade other forms of provision in some areas where expertise is not so salient and in ways which extend the control of the professional over the nature of the service.

Citizenship and obligations

Some maintain that the rights of citizenship depend upon the performance of obligations. This approach, deployed particularly on the American Right (for example, by Lawrence Med in his book *Beyond Entitlement: The Social Obligations of Citizenship*) raises the question of whether citizenship rights are conditional or absolute. It is also of political importance because the radical Right in Britain has taken it up as a response to the dependency argument in welfare which it would be very foolish to dismiss.

The case for conditional entitlements for the fit and able-bodied is as follows. Suppose the government is committed to securing as far as possible and practicable full employment, decent levels of unemployment benefit, regional policies to spread investment and job opportunities more broadly, and well-resourced and relevant training. It could then be argued that entitlement to benefit by an unemployed person, if not their dependents, should depend upon their willingness to undertake training, or satisfying a stringent available-for-work criterion. There are several possible justifying arguments for this policy.

First, in our society it is widely believed that a right or an entitlement arises either because it has been paid for or out of contract. Rights depend on reciprocity of some sort. If we are in favour of matching rights to resources then given this background of values we shall only be able to make our case convincing if some of the entitlements are linked to fulfilling obligations.

It is difficult to deny the widespread nature of this attitude. On this view the community has no duty to provide the resources for citizenship to those who are capable but refuse to accept the basis of the common obligations of citizenship. It might be argued that such a proposal would increase public support for the government expenditure necessary to provide good training and better unemployment benefits. Certainly, in socialist Sweden those who refuse work or training lose benefits for themselves (though not for their dependents).

It can also be argued that training is in the interest of the unemployed. Detachment from the disciplines of the labour market seems to be one of the major obstacles among the long-term unemployed to getting a job. Training of a decent sort and associated adequate levels of benefit may well be a way out of privation, marginalisation and being demoralised. This is essentially the case for obligation in the context of the dependency argument. Welfare beneficiaries become dependent on welfare; there are no ladders out of being trapped within welfare. One way of creating such a ladder, it is argued, is through making welfare dependent on discharging community obligations to inculcate attitudes which will be important in the labour market.

But there is a much more central socialist argument, namely that within the socialist tradition work has been regarded as essential to human dignity and development. Productive labour also provides the resources for the distributive side of socialism. It is therefore arguable that benefits created by taxation on the community (including the lower paid) should be available, in the case of the able-bodied, only to those who are actually prepared to enter the labour market either by undertaking training or through the operation of a stringent availability-for-work criterion. There is little in the British socialist tradition which sees citizenship wholly in terms of passive entitlement: there has usually been an equal stress on the performance of duties and obligations.

Clearly this issue raises a deep issue again between the libertarian and the communitarian strands of socialism. The ideas above lean much more to the communitarian side of socialism, seeing the community as having a right to insist on obligations as a condition of some benefits of membership, and certainly this idea fits many models of community. The libertarian, however, will see these ideas as intolerably coercive.

Liberty

The libertarian critic will draw upon two arguments. The first is that civil and political rights are not conditional. The right to equality before the law, for example, is not dependent on discharging an obligation so why should welfare rights be any different?

One answer to this would be to claim that there is in fact a sharp distinction between the two sorts of rights, a point discussed earlier but rejected. So this cannot be the basis of the conditionality of welfare rights. A more cogent response would be to claim that civil and political rights in fact secure the independence and self-confidence of individuals whereas the dependency theorists argue that when welfare is seen as an entitlement without condition, then this creates dependency. This is an empirical claim which needs investigating in the British context. If it turned out to be the case then certainly some forms of welfare (which would not include health, education, services for the elderly and the non-able-bodied) could be linked to obligations if they were thought likely to overcome dependency.

The libertarian critic will still argue that, rather than conditional entitlements, it would be better to stimulate self-help among poor communities and families, by the use of community development and social work. The dependency theorist, however, will argue that just because such schemes are voluntary they will not in fact reach those who are most marginalised and dependent and who need skills the most. Again this is an empirical argument about which socialists need to make a judgement.

A more theoretical response from the libertarian would be to claim that a policy of conditional entitlement is coercive in the sense that it is an intentional attempt to get someone to do what they would otherwise do by changing the costs and benefits attached to their particular desires.

This may well be so but the tax system *is* coercive and bears heavily on the lower paid. They have no choice but to pay the tax needed to finance benefits. Should, therefore, those benefits be available as a matter of unconditional right to beneficiaries? Further, what matters is not whether the proposal is coercive but whether it embodies legitimate coercion. Most actions by government are coercive as the tax example shows. What matters is whether the coercion is being exercised towards legitimate ends. At this point all the arguments discussed above come back into play.

This issue is difficult to resolve in a socialist context but given the salience of dependency theories in Britain and the USA it will not go away. It has to be resolved in the context of a socialist theory of citizenship which recognises the centrality of production and supply as well as distribution. Obviously any introduction of conditional entitlements in Britain at the moment would be deeply unjust because the economic prerequisites mentioned earlier – full employment, regional policy, defensible levels of training – are not in place.

Citizenship and the market

There is growing recognition on the Left of the role of the market. I want to look at its strengths and weaknesses to see how it can be used to enhance citizenship. The idea of democratic citizenship is a profoundly anti-capitalist one: it embodies the idea that individuals have a status and a worth to be backed by rights, resources and opportunities which is not determined by their status in the market and their economic value. The underwriting of these rights of citizenship requires collective action and politically guaranteed provision outside the market.

Nevertheless, the economic market is a very useful and indeed central instrument for securing socialist aims. The draft statement of Labour's *Democratic Socialist Aims and Values* and the first Policy Review report *Social Justice and Efficiency* stress the role of the market in distributing many sorts of goods. At the same time, it has to be kept within control and its outcomes have to be subjected to modification. A recognition that the market is central is not necessarily to succumb to capitalist values.

Markets and distribution

Currently the market enables a vast range of goods and services to be produced and distributed in the economy. Some have argued against the Policy Review because it embraces market forces. If the market is essentially capitalist, then intellectual honesty requires that we should be told how goods and services will be produced in a socialist Britain: presumably via some form of either centralised or democratic planning. If, however, critics believe that there should still be a role for a market, then what is the nature of their quarrel with its endorsement in the Review?

The arguments against a centralised economy are overwhelmingly strong in theory and practice. Such economies have not worked in the USSR, in China or in eastern Europe. They have endangered civil liberties and because of the centralised and political nature of the planning they have fallen victim to élite interest-group pressures. Planners and bureaucrats are not always selfless pursuers of the public interest. They have interests of their own which make them responsive to political pressures.

Individual choice and pluralism are essential to citizenship and both are threatened by centralised planning.

In theoretical terms, the work of Menger, Mises and Hayek still stand as a formidable challenge to the economic assumptions of central planning. Their case rests upon the nature of ordinary economic knowledge and the ways in which this cannot be drawn together by central planners. In the economy, knowledge is dispersed among millions of economic agents who use it all the time in their economic transactions out of which prices and distributions emerge. Usually, this knowledge is tacit in the sense that all the knowledge and assumptions which go into making decisions are not explicit: it is a case of 'knowing how' rather than 'knowing that'. This knowledge, dispersed and inexplicit, cannot be drawn together by a planning agency to replicate the ways in which prices are set and demands for commodities occur. The market, however, is able to use this dispersed knowledge just because it is such a highly decentralised institution.

This is the strongest argument against centralised planning and it is an argument of principle not of complexity. The problems which Hayek identifies cannot be solved by more complex computers because the knowledge in question is normally of a non-propositional sort. Only the hubris of centralising politicians who are over-convinced of the capacity of human reason could maintain a strong belief in centralised planning.

If centralised planning is impossible and indeed is a threat to the values of citizenship, are there other decentralised mechanisms for replacing market mechanisms and in particular democratic procedures operating on a decentralised basis? There are some encouraging examples of local planning mechanisms, such as the late GLC and Sheffield, but these do not in any way displace the market. They operate in an economy which is overwhelmingly market-based and signals about price and demand are available from the market sector. The planning that was done was in association with the market, not seeking to replace it. These planning functions were much more ways of trying to intervene in and socialise the market in the sense of making the market responsive to social considerations than an attempt to replace it by a different system of production and distribution.

It is difficult to see how it could have been otherwise. Localised democratic planning can only avoid one part of Hayek's critique: it can cope with the dispersal of knowledge but it cannot cope with its tacit nature. Democratic planning requires propositions and arguments which are hard to distil from the knowledge how which is characteristic of the economy. This of course is not to say that both central government and democratic values have no place in economic life. On the contrary, we have to consider the defects of the market as well as its strengths and how these can be countered in a democratic society.

Reference has already been made to the undesirable outcomes of markets and I argued then that without the redistribution of resources both as a condition of liberty and in terms of social justice, the market would be incompatible with the values of democratic citizenship. However, there are other important defects:

- the free market leads to concentration of wealth and power;
- the market prefers long-term to short-term returns;
- despite embodying individual choices, markets may lead to outcomes which might not have been chosen had they been foreseen;
- the external effects of markets on the environment;
- the ways in which markets undercut any appeal to the public good on which their own operation may well depend.

I conclude with a brief look at these factors.

Concentrations of wealth

On the strict liberal view, what matters about markets is not their outcomes but the fact that in a free market we find the embodiment of free and uncoerced exchange. Justice consists not in outcomes but in non-coercion and in a market we find uncoerced exchanges. From this it follows that all the accumulations of wealth which arise out of individual uncoerced exchanges are morally legitimate and just. (This view is defended by Sir Keith Joseph in *Equality* cited above. It is provided with its deepest philosophical rationale by R. Nozick in *Anarchy, State and Utopia*, Blackwell, 1973.)

However, even if we grant that wealth is accumulated in a non-coercive way in a free and democratic society, the incremental outcomes of free exchange are important. First, accumulations of wealth usually imply power. In a democratic society, we should be concerned with the dispersal rather than the concentration of power. Even when the outcomes of markets are the consequences of free exchange, they may be incompatible with the values of a democratic society.

Central to this approach, therefore, should be an attempt to disperse capital and power more widely. Apart from general progressive and redistributive taxation which was discussed in the context of social justice earlier, there are various ways in which this could be done, particularly individual or group dispersal. Individual dispersal could, for example, involve giving workers shares in companies after a parti-cular length of service. Labour would, therefore, create some property rights in their enterprise instead of being based entirely on capital input (a wholly anti-capitalist idea). It could be done by means of a negative capital tax as once proposed by Professor Atkinson. Capital could also be dispersed by encouraging other forms of ownership, particularly workers' co-operatives and providing for favourable forms of credit on the part of government.

Secondly, people in markets usually take a short-run view of returns. This can lead to underinvestment, a lack of infrastructure, and a lack of commitment to high-quality, long-term training. These things are not themselves antagonistic to markets – indeed on the contrary they will make markets work better. But they will not neces-sarily be provided by markets. It is, therefore, a central and ineradicable role for government to use collective resources to provide these sorts of goods.

The third feature of markets which makes them an instrument of policy rather than a panacea is that they may well embody individual choices, but the incremental effects of such choices may well be unforeseen and may produce consequences which would not have been chosen. So, for example, because individuals choose to shop at a hypermarket outside the neighbourhood, local shops which the very same people found convenient may close. In this way, amenities may well be destroyed by what Fred Hirsch in *The Social Limits To Growth* called the tyranny of small decisions. The dispersed decision procedures of the market are not suitable for every choice that we make. This requires a plurality of institutions which can act as checks on one another.

So, for example, in the case discussed, there would be a need for democratic, participative planning procedures to counterbalance the likely outcomes of dispersed market choices. This is not to say that political or collective procedures are infallible or can foresee things in a way in which people in markets do not. It is only to recognise the fallibility of all institutions including markets and the need for a demo-cratic and collective counterpoint to markets if our own longer-term choices and judgements are to be accorded any weight.

Fourth, markets produce external effects such as pollution of the environment which call for government responsibility and collective action. Some on the New Right argue that such externalities can best be dealt with by strengthening individuals' property rights and then allowing these externalities to be fought in civil courts as a matter of compensation. However, the most obvious answer except to the most blinkered defender of the free market and minimal government is for the state to enforce standards in this field and to prosecute those who fail to abide by them.

Finally, markets operate on the basis of the rational calculation of self-interest. This is of course a fundamental human emotion and motive and it would be difficult to imagine life without it. However, it needs to operate in only a limited framework because the more the market mentality comes to dominate our lives, its associated motives become more and more dominant. Then other values which cannot be captured in terms of self interest and the calculation of advantage will be undermined.

However, such values are not peripheral in human life but play a central role in the complex web of relationships and motives which make us what we are. But more importantly in the present context, motives other than self-interest may be important for markets as well. Markets cannot exist in a moral vacuum: generally they presuppose certain values such as honesty, fair dealing, promise keeping and some orientation towards the common good and civic virtues. The more sophisticated early defenders of the market such as Adam Smith realised this.

The growth of a new type of trader in the City who seems to be emancipated from more traditional values embodied in 'my word is my bond' led to crooked dealing and scandal which in turn necessitated elaborate and costly regulatory mechanisms. The market here worked more efficiently and without regulation when there was a more widely accepted basis of morality and fair dealing. Now it seems that self-interest has displaced such values with all the consequences which we have seen over the past years.

If self-interest is the only motivation which counts, how do you convince a businessman not to seek monopoly, or subsidy or price fixing? All of these have deleterious consequences for the market even though they may be in the individual's own interests. There needs to be some orientation to an idea of the common good or the good of the community to argue against such behaviour. There is no point in saying 'what would it be like if everyone did that?' since the individual knows that everyone is not doing that. This argument is powerless if the only motivating force is that of self-interest.

So the market itself needs a framework of civic responsibility within which to operate just as interest groups and unions do. Unless such a civic vision is articulated and defended, not just as a matter of altruism but as something which is in all our interests, then the political community will fall victim to strong special interests whether in politics or in markets. In its claims about the centrality of citizenship and the sense of belonging, the Labour Party is in a better position to defend the range of values which are essential to human life – including self-interest – in a way that the Conservative Party used to do before the accountants took over.

So the markets have a central role to play within a socialist society. But they must operate within a set of community values where outcomes will not be regarded as impersonal visitations but adjusted within a framework of social justice. As such the market can play a central role in promoting the efficient production of resources without which the ideal of democratic citizenship involving resources, liberties, rights and opportunities will be impossible.

Citizenship and community

The necessity for communal provision for which I have argued presupposes a commitment by the community to all of its members. After years of undermining the case for collective provision this commitment cannot just be assumed, it has to be rebuilt. Polling and survey evidence suggests that there are still communal and mildly egalitarian values within the population and the possibility of rebuilding is there. However, it will have to be a thoughtful rebuilding which learns from the mistakes of the past – which does not mindlessly overextend public policy and the capacity of government; which does not seek only centralised and bureaucratic solutions; which will constrain the power of producer-interest groups and professions; which will allow a variety of ways of meeting needs; which is aware of the power of interest groups.

The final condition is the most important, namely that the whole notion of collective and public provision has to be defended partly on moral grounds and partly on grounds of efficiency. Because of acute political dilemmas, there has been some loss of confidence in politics and the use of political power for allocative purposes. The market benefited from this. Confidence in politics against the market will not be enhanced until some of the lessons of big and centralised government have been learned and a robust attitude to interest groups is taken.

The aims I have suggested are of an enabling kind. In the context of community it is not the function of public policy to try to create a specific form of community for the whole of society whatever conservatives of the Left and Right might think. There are profound totalitarian dangers in that. Our natures are too diverse to fit into a single pattern of life. We should, however, seek to enable people to form and sustain, where they already exist, their own forms of community which meet their needs. To do this we do need some general community spirit to sustain collective provision, but this only needs to be modest. The idea of community is beguiling but as a general idea and as a guide to policy almost wholly indefinite. People wish to create and sustain their own forms of community, not to have them imposed upon them. Given the resources, a society of citizens, rather than individuals or subjects, would be able to form their own communities, as indeed they did in the early years of the socialist movement.

Part Three:
The Poverty of Egoism

7

Friends, Romans and consumers

MARTIN HOLLIS

As eastern Europe buries its Caesars without praising them, and western Europe merges its nations, thoughts are turning to the meaning of citizenship. What is this elusive relation? What was it in a more settled world and what will, could and should it become? To judge from the Western chorus hailing the victory of capitalism over communism, to be a citizen is to be legally protected in the private enjoyment of what one gains in the market place. To judge from the words of the local victors themselves, communism is to be replaced with a neighbourhood socialism of ordinary citizens. Meanwhile, other forces have smouldered on since 1917. They are those of nationhood and, deep in its shadow, anti-Semitism, of bourgeois aspiration of Bürgertum and of religion. So, although slices of the Berlin Wall are for sale in velvet pouches in the shops of New York, there are other portents. Neo-nazis have paraded in Leipzig, Christmas carols have been broadcast in Bucharest, and Islam too is rallying its faithful.

Since the most fragile of these contenders is neighbourhood socialism, persons of liberal instinct are worried. The need to rethink the idea of citizenship in a liberal democracy is urgent. My title picks out three candidates for its key. 'Friends' have a small-scale, personal tie, resistant both to the commands of the state and to cost-benefit calculation. 'Romans' belong to a *civitas*, whose spring is public duty and whose sentiment is republican or nationalist. 'Consumers', striking a modern note in the funeral oration for dead Caesars, are individuals related through contracts made to mutual advantage. I mean to enquire which, if any, of these relationships holds the key to civil society in a world where old ties have lost their magic.

To focus this daunting question, let us start close to home with a

This essay appeared previously in *Ethics* 102 (1991) and in D. Milligan and W. Watts Miller (eds.), *Liberalism, Citizenship and Autonomy* (Aldershot, Avebury, 1992).

current British concern about citizenship. The British Parliament launched a Commission on Citizenship in December 1988, under the patronage of the Speaker of the House of Commons and prompted by a lack of communal enterprise in the enterprise culture. There seemed to many observers, including the then Prime Minister and her Home Secretary, to be a dangerous malaise, taking the form of public apathy among the respectable and a rash of antisocial behaviour among the lower orders. A plausible diagnosis, connecting the two groups, was that enterprise can undermine the very culture which it needs, if it is to flourish. The call to enterprise bids each of us pursue his private good. The famous invisible hand works only if enough of us include a contribution to the quality of communal life in our idea of the good. 'Culture' is one name for the public ethos which reinforces this virtuous habit and thus by restraining self-interest also enables individuals to do better for themselves than they would in a merely selfish society. But what is true for all is not true for each and the dominant logic of the free-rider problem erodes the benefits of co-operation. Although this threat to citizenship has been of concern since the industrial revolution, it has advanced with the revival of libertarian incitements to individual enterprise.

The Commission, in a draft of its report produced in 1989, declared its aim to be 'to consider how best to encourage, develop and recognize Active Citizenship ... provisionally defined as the positive involvement of the individual, group or organisation in the wider community.'[1] The preamble described its approach as seeking 'an enhanced vision of citizenship', thus adding a fourth dimension to our notion of citizenship which currently involves 'political, civil and social entitlements and duties within a framework of law'. This fourth dimension 'would involve the ideal of public good and civic virtue which finds its expression in the largely voluntary contribution to society of citizens acting either as individuals or in association with one another.' The need was deemed to arise for three main reasons: that too great an emphasis on the self-reliant individual acting in competition can undermine social cohesion; that associations are needed to mediate between central government and the individual; and that the delivery of social rights at a level appropriate to a civilised and modern democracy may be threatened by expanding need, slow economic growth and a shortage of skilled wage-earners.

This all sounded like a well-rounded expression of open-minded concern, until one noticed its oddity. The 'fourth dimension', summarised as 'the citizen acting in a voluntary capacity', was presented as an extra and novel dimension. Yet how could any notion of democratic citizenship ever have done without it? In describing our current notion as one of 'entitlements and duties within a framework of abstract law', what did the Commission suppose currently animates citizens? The implicit answer, I think, was that citizens are self-regarding individuals, who are prone to count their entitlements as benefits and their duties as costs. They incur the costs because minimal duties are enforced and there is overall benefit in citizenship, defined by T. H. Marshall, whom the Commission quoted with approval in both draft and final reports, as 'a status bestowed on those who are full members of a community'. In that case, however, individuals, seeking to minimise the cost of their bestowed citizenship, do well to avoid voluntary public activity and it is a wonder that Britain has a public life at all.

In fact, of course, there has long been plenty of activity 'in a voluntary capacity', mediating stoutly between central government and the individual. The Commission overlooked it because it was oddly silent about *local* government. By thinking in terms of government (paid?) and the individual (voluntary?) it underplayed the unpaid activity of many thousands of citizens who contribute to a thriving tradition of local government. Here, for instance, is a public arena where women can and do take part in a proportion to their numbers unknown at Westminster. Here is the basis of Britain's claim to be a plural democracy, in so far as pluralism has to do with sources of authority distinct from that of central government. Even if one tries to insist that local politics do not count as 'voluntary activity', the boundary is importantly fuzzy, with no shortage of individuals who operate on both sides of it and in the overlap. To neglect so plain an aspect of current citizenship is to regard local government either as a mere agency of central government or as an excrescence. Otherwise the 'fourth dimension' described as an addition is simply a necessary component of what already exists.

Consumers

The point suggests that the Commission's view of its task was a symptom of the problem addressed, rather than a step towards its solution. The problem itself is urgent, and I agree that social cohesion has become fragile of late, that mediation between government and individual has become harder, and that the delivery of social rights is under threat. The particular urgency arises because so many citizens are thinking of themselves as the 'Consumers' of my title or, to put it abstractly, in terms which presuppose that the basic political relation among us is contractual and that the political community factors as an association of private individuals whose public contributions are instrumental.

That makes the communal aspect of citizenship a public good, in the economists' sense that its benefits cannot be confined to those who contribute to its costs. The resulting free-rider problem has a standard remedy of state intervention 'not to overrule the judgement of individuals but to give effect to it', as J. S. Mill remarks smoothly in what is perhaps still the best formulation of the difficulty.[2] But this remedy has always had the snag that, although the use of law may secure the grudging payment of contributions, a cheerful public ethos is what is really needed – the original problem over again. Furthermore the recent libertarian revival is hostile to enforcing anything smacking of a moral view of good citizenship, because moral choices should be left to the individual and cannot be made compulsory without robbing them of their moral value and undermining individual responsibility.

There are other attempted remedies, however, notably of late those prescribed by Mrs Thatcher, when Prime Minister, and Douglas Hurd, when her Home Secretary. Mrs Thatcher started from her oft-quoted conviction that 'there is no such thing as society' and corresponding injunction that collective social arrangements are legitimate only in so far as they do not fetter the individual will. Her celebrated address to the General Assembly of the Church of Scotland in May 1988, better known as 'the Sermon on the Mound', set out her general line on freedom and moral responsibility very clearly. Christianity, she said, is about 'spiritual redemption and not social reform'. It tells us to render unto God the things which are God's; for the things which are Caesar's, it commands us simply to obey the law and use our talents to create wealth. Having quoted St Paul ('If a man will not work, he shall not eat'), she remarked that 'abundance rather than poverty has a legitimacy which derives from the nature of Creation'. The wealthy will, one hopes, be spiritually moved to mercy and generosity but that is their (spiritual) business and 'any set of social and economic arrangements which is not founded on the acceptance of individual responsibility will do nothing but harm.'

With her strong sense of original sin, she is not for a moment suggesting that the problem will go away, if it is left to individual voluntary initiative – 'making money and owning things could become selfish activities', she warned. Her line is only that compulsion makes matters worse. Persuasion can be tried, however, and she prescribed a spiritual cocktail of family values, a democratic ethos honouring individual responsibility, education in our Judaeo-Christian tradition, and patriotic celebration of our national identity. She then spun the threads together in the words of the hymn *I Vow to Thee my Country*, noting its mention of a second unseen country of the spirit – 'soul by soul and silently her shining bounds increase'. 'Not group by group or party by party or even church by church', the Prime Minister added, 'but soul by soul, and every one counts.'

The crux here is the divorce between the material and spiritual sides of our lives, thus making us economic individuals for purposes of government and leaving mercy and generosity to our private consciences. The creation of wealth precedes good works; for, as she once pointed out to the House of Commons, no one would have heard of the Good Samaritan, had he not had money. I stress that she is not saying that citizenship, construed as supererogatory contributions to the good of others, will flourish, if left to individuals, but only that this is the best we can do. All the same, it seems to me a very unpromising way to try harnessing self-help to the communal wagon.

In effect it takes citizenship as a status bestowed only on those who are *full* members of the community in that, like the Good Samaritan, they have made a success of their individual responsibilities. Losers, who have not made the grade, are owed nothing. Winners, meanwhile, have made it by helping themselves; and why should they not continue to do so? A straw in the wind was the 1989 Mintel survey of young opinion, *Youth Lifestyle*. It reported 'a new consumption and success ethic among the young', which led 31 per cent of the respondents to list 'money' among the top five ingredients of happiness, whereas only 17 per cent listed 'love' – 'an "I-want-it-now" generation' was Mintel's summing up. Another straw is the failure of income tax cuts for the better off to show up in rising donations to charity. The corner which the wind is blowing from was memorably pin-pointed by a successful builder interviewed lately on television and asked what lesson he drew from the last ten years. His pithy reply was, 'Sod the little man!'

In Chapter XXXI of *Leviathan*, Thomas Hobbes tempers his dour picture of the Natural Condition of Mankind as Concerning their

Felicity, and Misery (Chapter XIII) by observing that for a full knowledge of our civic duties, we must know the laws of God, which enjoin
'equity, justice, mercy, humility, and the rest of the moral virtues'.
But I cannot see why these optional extras should come into play. The
contractarian core of economic individualism says nothing about God
and seems to recommend only such virtues as it pays to practise.
Success in an enterprise culture does not come from mercy and
humility, nor in any obvious way from equity, justice and the rest. So
why will the successful have any reason to reverse the attitude which
gained them success? It may be said, as in recent contractarian theory,
that individuals do best to act as maximisers constrained by a moral
point of view, when dealing with others similarly rational. But, unless
this amounts to more than advising the strong to deal justly with the
strong, it is all too consistent with the strategy summed up as 'Sod the
little man!'

That does not dispose of contractarian ethics, which I shall consider
in a moment, but it will serve to introduce Douglas Hurd's idea of
citizenship, which he has been formulating in a series of articles and
speeches, begun while he was Home Secretary. In that office he was
alarmed by growth in petty crime both among the dispossessed and
among the vandals and lager louts on the lower slopes of the enterprise
culture. Being no more enthused by the growing white collar financial
crime higher up, he set about reviving an older conservatism which he
hoped to marry to the new libertarian variety. 'The government is not
about to adopt Thomas Hobbes as its patron saint', he assured readers
of the *New Statesman* on 27 April 1988.[3] Instead he took his bearings
from Edmund Burke and this quotation from *Reflections on the Revolution in France*:

> No cold relation is a zealous citizen .... To be attracted to the sub-
> division, to love the little platoon we belong to in society, is the first
> principle (the germ as it were) of public affections. It is the first link
> in the series by which we proceed towards the love of our country
> and of mankind.

Here in 'the little platoon' of family and neighbourhood, our
strongest loyalties still reside, Hurd affirms, *en route* to his own similar-
sounding conclusion:

> Those qualities of enterprise and initiative, which are essential for
> the generation of material wealth, are also needed to build a family,

a neighbourhood or a nation, which is able to draw on the respect, loyalty and affection of its members.

Hurd's citizens are not Mrs Thatcher's atomic individuals. 'Men and women are social beings', who find it natural to be sociable and to express 'affection and allegiance for many collective organisations – from a soccer club to a choral society or even a political party.' This temperament shows itself in 'the English tradition of voluntary work' – Justices of the Peace, school governors, neighbourhood watch co-ordinators and 'the thousands of people who give their time freely to the huge and thriving number of British charities'. Witness these examples, the tradition is diverse, plural, innovative and runs counter to the obsession on the Left with 'a society dominated by the relationship between the individual and the state'. It thrives wherever power is kept out of the hands of the corporatist battalions and given to the little voluntary platoons. 'Private property is the natural bulwark of liberty because it ensures that economic power is not concentrated in the hands of the state.'

The obstacle to voluntary activity is thus located in the bureaucratic state and its corporatist battalions, which are 'emphatically not what Burke meant by "the little platoons"'. Unfortunately, however, neither are neighbourhood groups of self-made persons with families. The little platoons of Burke's eighteenth-century England belonged to the battalions and regiments of a hierarchical society and were disbanded, along with this whole rural army, in the industrial revolution. Can they be re-formed through the qualities of initiative and enterprise essential for the generation of material wealth? I doubt it. Our new men seem to me too like those described by Tocqueville in *Democracy in America*:

> Each of them, living apart, is a stranger to the fate of the rest ... his children and his private friends constitute to him the whole of mankind; as for the rest of his fellow citizens, he is close to them, but he sees them not, he touches them, but he feels them not; he exists but in himself and for himself alone; and if his kindred still remain to him, he may be said to have lost his country.

In short the problem remains why the qualities needed for success in an enterprise culture should lead anyone to care about neighbourhood or nation, let alone (as in Burke's chain but not, I notice, in Hurd's) mankind.

The best current philosophical answer is that ideally rational egoists are too long-sighted to cut off their separate noses to spite their collective faces. By idealising the agents, recent contractarians hope to improve on *Leviathan* – the canonical text for an enterprise culture – and Hobbes' contention that the benefits of trust and co-operation can be had only by instituting 'a common power to keep all in awe'. For Hobbes' breed of rational agent it may be true that 'covenants without the sword are but words'. But ideally rational agents appreciate that this kind of common power ensures only the minimum of voluntary input and requires a policing whose costs are a deadweight loss. So perhaps they can be rationally persuaded to adopt a moral point of view and thus comply in full without needing more than an assurance that others are as rational as they.

The moral point of view, for these purposes, is that of an impartial umpire applying universal rules which do the best for all consistent with the basic interests of each. The recent contractarian revival stems from Rawls' hunch that rational egoists, set to draw up a constitution while knowing nothing of their own particular prospects, would hit on and agree to those very same rules. The idea that moral principles are equivalent to the shrewdest all-risks insurance policy for the unborn is sweetened by including welfare clauses which benefit those who turn out to be worst off in a society marked by democratic communal concern. By that token, however, John Rawls' version in *A Theory of Justice*[4] sets an awkward problem of why the better off will rationally comply once they know that they are among the strong and fortunate. Hence the rational citizens of an enterprise culture may be more impressed by David Gauthier's *Morals by Agreement*[5] where people who know their endowments still find that it pays to act morally, at least until they suffer for it. Gauthier's rational agents are not 'Simple Maximisers', who would defect whenever it pays and thus be sunk by the free-rider problem, but 'Constrained Maximisers', who play 'Tit-for-Tat' and defect only when others defect.

But Gauthier's nakedly mutual-back-scratching approach does more than cut out the distributional bias to the worst off, and the strong, if covert, notion of community in Rawls. It thereby invites rational egoists to form cartels. Since there is no point in the strong playing fair with the weak, Tit-for-Tat becomes the best strategy only among those with sharp elbows. Then, even within this group, defections which would be foolish on the part of a single individual can become profitable for sub-groups. An antique-dealers ring, for instance, which practises honour among thieves in order better to exploit outsiders, will be able to cover for each other.[6] Whenever a general benefit of co-operation can be distributed in two ways, each of which is a Nash-equilibrium – for instance, if one gives men more of the surplus than women and the other gives more to women – then the stronger sub-group will rationally organise the share-out accordingly. Members of the weaker sex remain morally in play, in the sense that even a smaller share is better than nothing and cannot be had without moral restraint. But the market-place society involved is no longer one where all share a concern for the interests of losers. The original problem of an enterprise culture is reinstated.

Romans

The last paragraph is not meant to refute Gauthier out of hand, although it may suggest that the impersonal features of the moral point of view can influence the outcome of rational bargaining only if the bargainers are as ignorant of their prospects as Rawls makes them. But it will serve to introduce the 'Romans' of my title. Gauthier's 'Constrained Maximisers' adopt a *disposition* to play fair with those who play fair with them and are willing to presume that other people have this disposition until proved wrong. To that extent they regard themselves as dealing with fellow members of their circle. But they do not regard themselves or others as entering the sort of relationship which, according to Rousseau, produces 'a remarkable change in man' (*The Social Contract*, Book I, Chapter VIII). They remain 'Consumers' first and become citizens only for instrumental reasons. Granted, for the sake of argument, that the compliance problem is insoluble without a deeper change of heart, I shall next try reversing this priority.

By 'Romans' I mean members of political communities whose identity is defined by where they belong. The plural is meant to signal a variety of groups more historically and contingently situated than Burke's 'mankind'. These communities need be political only in the Aristotelian sense that politics concerns '*ta koina*', the public life of a civil society. The variety envisaged ranges from totalitarian states, where all activity is public in principle, to republics, which insist only that public duties are prior to private rights. The common factor is a *conscience collective*, a shared sense of morally binding incorporation in a collective undertaking, which makes Romans self-consciously Romans or Romanians self-consciously Romanians. Witness these examples, however, the abstract terms of incorporation are pretty indefinite, leaving it unclear quite who is to be deemed incorporated and quite what is the unifying bond.

In the abstract, the idea is to extend the boundaries of the self to include relations with other people mediated by shared incorporation in the polity. The problem is to set a limit, so that the self is not swallowed up by an overweening state. By way of illustration, consider those orphans in Ceauşescu's Romania, who were nurtured with the sole aim of producing utterly loyal members of the Securitate. They grew up to become not individuals, nor even, one might say, comrade-citizens, but comrade-soldiers and comrade-officers in a branch of the state which behaved as if it was the soul and will of the state. Something had gone radically wrong in applying an idea of political community, whose unperverted form might be hoped to yield something in the republican tradition. But it is not easy to state the limit which a true idea of community must not overstep.

It might perhaps be done by attempting a liberal reading of Rousseau's *The Social Contract*. There 'The People' embodies a 'General Will', which expresses the desire of each citizen to bring about what is best for the community. While this sovereign body functions perfectly, it makes each citizen 'as free as before' even when forced to conform to wills not his own. For, even when assigned a role as a subordinate, one is still not 'personally dependent' on the will of superiors but is playing one's part in the community and is protected by it from abuse. 'Freedom is obedience to laws which we prescribe to ourselves.'

This balancing trick depends on a positive notion of freedom as the ability to choose what is for the best. It depends also on the brief chapter 8 of Book I, where Rousseau contrasts the natural liberty of a state of nature, populated by narrow, stupid animals, to the moral liberty of a society where, by becoming a citizen, one is transformed into a creature of reason and a man. Such citizens retain a private will as individuals but put their civic duties first. Even if one is tempted to regard one's duty as a burden, and so 'seek to enjoy the rights of a citizen without doing the duties of a subject', the temptation is resisted by truly free and rational persons and the free-rider problem is overcome, as Rousseau supposed it to have been in ancient Sparta or the Roman republic.

Even if a liberal reading can be sustained, it is precarious. As practical advice, it carries an alarmingly high risk of tyranny. The state has but to become a little corrupt and the noble equation between the good of each and the good of all ceases to hold. Since the citizens have laid down all their defences when joining the social contract, they are at once in the chains from which Rousseau hoped to rescue them. Nor is it easy to know when corruption has set in. Formally, what emerges from the process of government is then no longer a 'General Will'. But, practically, since there is no independent way of identifying a 'General Will' except as whatever emerges from a process satisfying the conditions which Rousseau specifies, departures from the ideal will be as undetectable as they are insidious. Disturbances have no inherent tendency to return to the ideal equilibrium, once the ballast of power has shifted.

Rousseau's readiness to let a community prescribe moral imperatives to itself without theoretical limit offends against the liberal conviction that autonomous citizens must be left a personal choice of ends. Yet this conviction cannot be sustained in any pure form, which makes the principles of justice and social organisation purely procedural. (Although I cannot prove this point in short compass, it is instructive that Rawls has lately conceded it and I shall assume it for purposes of argument.) Hence the liberal conviction needs to be that some morally justified limit has to be set to what 'The People' can insist on in the name of a conception of the good. Thus laws which discriminate by race, gender or religion are ruled out not because they offend procedurally but because they are morally offensive. Pluralism is not morally neutral throughout. It relies on a positive, objective notion of autonomy which sets substantive limits to the collective options which a society may choose.

This raises the question of whether citizenship is an identity in some sense stronger than associate membership. Communitarian thinking tends to suggest that it is – witness those explicit versions where the community which demands its members' total loyalty is a nation or a church. Here, if sub-communities are tolerated, it is within limits hierarchically ordered, so that conflicts of loyalty are always settled in favour of the central body. Pluralist versions, however, are ambivalent. On the one hand they recognise and respect differences between, for instance, Muslims and Christians, men and women, blacks and whites, gays and straights. On the other they set limits to dissent, as when confronted with Muslim attitudes to Salman Rushdie or the education of women for subordinate roles. Where the limits lie is obscure. Is a plural community to allow conscientious objection, polygamous marriage and Lesbian parenting, for example? Such questions call for a definition of citizenship which specifies a moral core to the concept, even if as modest a core as it can. That sets a dilemma for those, like Douglas Hurd, who declare that men and women are *social* beings but remain staunchly individualist at heart. What is it that social beings have essentially in common, regardless of sex or gender? If it is merely that they have wants or needs which can be satisfied only by social intercourse, then the earlier destructive atomism resurfaces. If it is that they are ultimately their social selves, then it is unclear why the claims of nation or religion cannot be supreme.

Friends

A 'plural community' thus threatens to be a contradiction in terms, with 'community' demanding that all members subscribe to a single, shared identity and 'plural' refusing this demand. This is a practical problem too, witness the havoc caused by efforts to state and apply the proper recipe for multicultural education, when faced with the claim that ethnicity or creed constitutes identity. Yet I do not despair of a notion of plural community as liberal republic, which can parry the threat of a contradiction in terms. Meanwhile, in search of an escape from the impasse, I turn to the 'Friends' of my title, meaning an attempt to think of 'social selves' in terms of small-scale, fragmented relationships. Burke's image was of links in a series proceeding from 'the little platoon' to 'country' and thence to 'mankind'. Let us try recasting it as one of concentric circles, with the individual as a notional blob in the centre of an inner ring of personal, intimate relations, like family and friends, then an intermediate ring of semi-personal role-relations, like neighbours and colleagues, an outer ring of fellow citizens and an outermost, universal ring for 'mankind'. Might the inner ring, typified by 'friends', hold the key to the rest?

If so, it is because the inner ring contains basic non-contractual relationships, which express the self rather than serve it. I assert this contrary to contractarian theory, which deals wholly in rational egoists, whose primary motivation is instrumental. Certainly intimacy can be treated in this way, as when partners to a prospective marriage start by writing what they hope is a fully contingent contract specifying the division of household labour, child care, career options and, in the event of divorce, records and rugs. For, as Gary Becker strikingly remarks, 'a person decides to marry when the utility expected from marriage exceeds that expected from remaining single or from an additional search for a more suitable mate.'[7] But this perversely imports the contractarian problem of trust among rational egoists into a relationship one of whose charms, when it flourishes, is that it by-passes the problem. Equally friendship can be reduced to commerce but, to be brief, the result is not friendship, for reasons to do with the master-slave dialectic. By 'Friends' I mean to gesture to small-scale, local and intimate relationships which constitute who one is and where one belongs. They are contingent in that they are voluntary in their exercise, even if some of them are not chosen, and historical in that they are governed by social norms which vary through time and place. Without them we would not be social beings.

The image of concentric circles is one of sharp boundaries and so misleading. The self, once tempted out of the vanishing point in the centre, becomes a polypod. Family ties, for instance, can be more constraining than expressive; friendships, like marriages, come and go; some roles are crucial to the shape of a life, whereas others are means to unrelated ends. Concentric circles belie the fluid character of what matters. But they do convey the thought that they can rotate in conflicting directions. The usual idea behind attempts to identify a moral point of view is that the self should be guided by the demands of the outermost ring – the greatest good of the greatest number or the categorical imperative, for example. There is no obvious reason why these demands should be consistent with those of roles and commit-ments, which in turn need not be consistent with each other. The suggestion being made is that citizenship involves normative expecta-tions of a locally variable sort and that, in cases of conflict, our loyalty should be to our own.

Yet, if this means that we should in general put personal ties before others, it cannot be right. Indeed it would be hard to find a neater definition of corruption in public life. Good citizenship is precisely not using one's offices for the benefit of one's friends. It will not do to replace 'Romans', who put duties to the state before all personal duties, with 'Friends' who simply reverse this priority. An active citizen needs to be so located that both pulls are at work, regarding fellow citizens as neighbours but impartial in contributing to the common good. Furthermore, if the retorts to egoism for each local community are not to sum to the original snag on an international scale, some notion of a citizen of the world will need to be included.

The Speaker's Commission thus had a daunting task in defining what it sought to activate in public life. Fortunately it could avoid having to draw up a blueprint for an ideal democracy. Recall the objection to Rousseau that there is no way of identifying the 'General Will' independently of the fragile process of local discourse and decision. The best reply, it seems to me, is to grant the point but blunt it by contending that we can work out some conditions in which discourse and decision will produce something as close to a 'General Will' as is humanly possible. Similarly one can try to work out what sort of active engagement may be trusted to sum to a flourishing public life, without having to delineate the result in advance.

There seems to me nothing amiss with the broad idea that the aim is to animate 'the citizen acting in a voluntary capacity'. My objection is only to regarding this as a novel 'fourth dimension', with 'voluntary' construed as meaning independent of government. As remarked earlier, the scheme of 'entitlement and duties within a framework of law' is doomed without voluntary activities by people whose citizenship, incidentally, is of right rather than 'bestowed' on them. As noted earlier, I take heart from local government. This is the obvious forum where the process of public decision can harness the virtues of neighbourliness and hold the decision-makers accountable by making them live with the outcome. By the same token it offers a practical response to doubts about what is for the best, when abstract theory gives no clear guidance. Local government, with its pragmatic sense that the best is the enemy of the good, settles for defensible choices which the defenders must live with in person.

Citizens in midstream

That is not a final answer to the question 'Who is my neighbour?' Here I am not sure what to conclude about the blending of personal aims and public good. So, to focus discussion, I offer a small allegory about an environmental group campaigning for a clean-up in the area around the Chesapeake Bay in the coastal strip of Virginia and Maryland. It used to be a verdant landscape, where every prospect pleases; but, as usual, man is vile and the campaign is almost too late. Homes have been springing up in the trees, each pleasantly sited when it was built but each new one whittling away a little more of what Nature provided. Gradually there is more waste to dispose of in the shrinking woods or in the darkening rivers, where it joins the profitable fertilisers sluiced off smiling farmlands. The fish grow scarcer as the water carries the silt away and down to the dying Bay. This is a familiar story of the search for positional goods but the campaign slogan is unusually instructive: 'We all live downstream.'

This message is both uplifting and absurd. How uplifting to hear that we are all part one of another, all exposed to one another's evacuations and all with the same interest in cleaning up! How absurd to fancy that those upstream will give it the slightest credence! Yet it is not mere foolishness. Consider those who live in midstream with upstreamers above them and downstreamers below. At present, perhaps, they greet the pollution arriving from higher up with righteous anger but save themselves trouble and expense by adding to the pollution lower down. Since they live halfway down, they might be rationally willing to subscribe to a clean-up. But, since they live half-way up, they have a free-rider's resistance to a categorical maxim that no one shall foul the water. So the campaign organisers have thrown in an incentive designed to appeal even to those living squarely upstream. Everyone already ensconced is vulnerable to a threat of further newcomers. To repel these potential boarders there will have to be planning controls. But that requires the votes of those who currently live downstream and the price of their votes is a genuine clean-up after all. Thus, you see, we do all live downstream.

In this allegory what persuades the advantaged not to enjoy the rights of a citizen without doing the duties of a subject is a common interest in keeping outsiders out. The categorical imperative gets a hypothetical grounding. But there will be trouble presently. Since upstreamers do not truly live downstream, they constitute a potential faction, which will become active once planning controls are in place. The wider alliance, which works while the strong need the votes of the weak, will shrink when the power of the weak can be safely eroded. This is a fair portent for an enterprise culture, which bids each of us move as far upstream as he can get and then reflect that those left downstream have failed through lack of enterprise. If the message is seriously meant to be that we do indeed all live downstream, then it implies the kind of voluntary activity which brings about a remarkable change in man by turning acquaintances into friends and strangers into neighbours.

Citizenship, then, requires an animating sense of the common good which consumers lack. But it cannot embrace the idea that we all live downstream in a global way. Citizens form a sovereign body, whose leaders are accountable to its members and whose members have special duties to one another. This depends on setting a boundary between neighbours within and strangers without. Burke's series, starting with little platoons and progressing to love of country, does not extend to the global love of mankind. Rich nations need not go out of their way to injure poor ones but governments rarely accept much duty to help, even when their way has had this effect. Sovereignty and accountability belong in midstream.

Viewed globally from downstream, sovereignty matters less than it used to. Interdependence is growing, both because commerce laughs at boundaries and, more ambiguously, because we all inhabit the same greenhouse. Sovereignty allows of degrees. Local government can flourish without full control over its activities and supported by budgets dependent on national grants and taxes. So too nations can group into confederations, then into federations and finally into unions. Although it would be rash to suppose that consolidation into blocs tends towards a single world government, autonomy does not demand complete separation.

Accountability is more fragile. Citizenship changes character in the process of turning strangers into neighbours. As it becomes more distant and formal, less personal and friendly, public life takes on a different complexion. Local government is again instructive. The last ten years in Britain have turned it increasingly into an agency of national government by eroding its powers in education, housing and most other areas. The Uniform Business Rate, which transferred the levying of taxes on businesses from local to national control, has snapped a reciprocal link. The Poll Tax put a stop to local policies designed to benefit the worse off. Local councillors, accountable to their local electors, are effectively being replaced by decision-makers in London who are not. But this is not the inevitable result of the parts of Britain becoming more interdependent. It is a conscious denial of pluralism, with its degrees of decentralised authority.

There is a delicate balance here, which, abstracted from current British politics, poses a final dilemma for believers in liberal democracy. On the one hand liberal persons are no doubt delighted when the European Court of Justice settles issues of individual rights by over-riding national directives. Such a higher authority is an attractive way to shed reforming light not only on the practices of governments but also on forces like anti-Semitism which flourish in the dark shadow of nationalism. On the other hand accountability flourishes only in the shade of a local autonomy which, however constrained from above, still lets boroughs, provinces or nations go their own way. The claims of citizenship are not simply those of universal rights.

I urge the virtues of local government not because they are unsullied but because they protect the shade for neighbourliness among citizens. If more global authorities have scope for spreading greater wisdom, they also have scope for greater corruption. So I settle for some midstream mixture of Friends and Romans as an account of citizenship in a Europe which has buried its Caesars. I had hoped to end with a final word from Shakespeare on how best to blend these elements. But Mark Antony is of no further help. When he had finished turning Romans into friends with a promise of seventy-five drachmas per head from Caesar's legacy, he remarked simply

> Mischief, thou art afoot
> Take thou what course thou will

and added most implausibly for today's world

> Fortune is merry
> And in this mood will give us anything.

NOTES

A version of this paper was presented at the Colston Symposium on Political Philosophy held at the University of Bristol in 1990. I am grateful for the many helpful comments received on that occasion. This version was published in *Ethics*, October 1991.

1. The final report, *Encouraging Citizenship: Report of the Commission on Citizenship* (London: HMSO, 1990), defined its purpose more narrowly as 'to propose practical ways in which our participatory arrangements can be strengthened' and muted its broader ambitions, perhaps because of sceptical press comments on the earlier draft. But the draft better represents the spirit and climate in which its task was undertaken.
2. J. S. Mill (1871), *Principles of Political Economy*, seventh edition, London, Book V, Ch. 11, especially section 12.
3. The quotations which follow are taken from this article. More recent writings have continued in the same vein, for instance in his article in *The Independent* on 13 September 1989, headed 'Freedom will flourish where citizens accept responsibility'.
4. J. Rawls, *A Theory of Justice* (Oxford: Oxford University Press, 1971).
5. D. Gauthier, *Morals by Agreement* (Oxford: Oxford University Press, 1986).
6. This thought is pursued in M. Hollis, 'Honour Among Thieves', *Proceedings of the British Academy* (1990), pp. 163–80.
7. G. Becker, *The Economic Approach to Human Behaviour* (Chicago: Chicago University Press, 1976), pp. 3–14.

8

The individualist premise and political community

IAIN HAMPSHER-MONK

The focus of this essay is on a threat posed to politics which has become increasingly pervasive in the West over the last 25 years or so, a threat which, because of its proximity to the ideal of liberty itself so closely connected with politics is a danger difficult to analyse, and rhetorically, increasingly difficult to articulate. It is the individualist premise.

By targeting the individualist premise I do not wish to attack the broad epistemological conviction that societies comprise a variety of assemblages of natural individuals, nor to denigrate the importance of extensive areas of personal liberty. I refer instead to that particular and narrow conception of the individual as an essentially isolated actor, calculating economic means to ends which are individually identified, autonomously chosen and privately consumed. It is, I believe a conception of the individual which is philosophically unsustainable in itself, and the conceptual incoherence of which gives rise to important and dangerous equivocations when applied to policy issues.[1]

1

Starting from a base in economic theory, the isolated rational egoist has first raided, then successfully annexed large areas of the territories of the surrounding disciplines of politics and international relations, sociology and economic and social history.[2] Even Marxism itself has

A slightly different version of Iain Hampsher-Monk's contribution was published as 'The Individualist Premise and the Practice of Politics' in the volume *Defending Politics, Bernard Crick and Pluralism*, ed. Iain Hampsher-Monk, published by British Academic Press (UK) and St Martin's Press (US and Canada) 1993. British Academic Press is an imprint of I. B. Tauris & Co Ltd. to whom thanks are due for permission to republish the piece.

succumbed: the capitulation of actual Marxist regimes in eastern Europe and their adoption of market forces paralleled the penetration of traditional Marxism as a distinctive theory by market-inspired rational-choice thinking.[3] If not exactly nature imitating art, then at least (and some would say unusually) reality imitating theory. This success, in both academic and political terms, is all the more puzzling when one thinks of the widespread and apparently well-grounded rejection of the isolated individual as an adequate premise in many other, related, but less obviously policy-oriented disciplines.

For example in philosophy, since Wittgenstein, all meaningfulness, from language itself through to complex forms of symbolic action is to be construed as a social form.[4] Indeed since action itself – as opposed to mere behaviour – is defined as meaningful, the very conduct of human life cannot ultimately be understood as the work of an individual agent but only as the deployment of resources which are irreducibly the product of social collectivities.[5] The persistence, and deepening of this view within philosophy can be seen by considering two very influential works on personal identity, P. F. Strawson's *Individuals* (1959), and Derek Parfit's *Reasons and Persons* (1984).

In the first work the self-attribution of personal identity is logically held to be possible only because of the existence of other persons to whom identity is likewise ascribed. The argument, roughly, is that it is impossible to see how, on the basis of only my external and empirical experience of others, I could come to attribute the property of consciousness to *them*, if my understanding of it were originally present only as a form of private self-awareness in *me*, as opposed to being constructed out of mutual interactions.[6] This is a modest enough epistemological embedding of the individual in a social context. It goes no further than Hegel's master-slave dialectic in the *Phenomenology*, even though it approaches the problem analytically and from the *fait accompli*, rather than dynamically and from the postulated absence of self-consciousness.

In Parfit's book, however, personal identity, in the traditional sense, is pronounced an illusion, and its loss is to be seen, not as something about which we might worry, but as a liberation. The relationship between experiences, and even sensations, is not guaranteed by any integrity of the individual, it is more graded and open-textured than anything envisaged by traditional views of the subject. The very identity of a person merges imperceptibly into a social nexus provided by the thoughts and experiences of other persons. Hence, Parfit on his death:

Though there will later be many experiences, none of these experiences will be connected to my present experiences by chains of such direct connections as those involved in experience-memory, or in the carrying out of an earlier intention. Some of these future experiences may be related to my present experiences in less direct ways, there will later be some memories about my life. And there may later be thoughts that are influenced by mine, or things done as a result of my advice. My death will break the more direct relations between my present experiences and future experiences, but it will not break various other relations. This is all there is to the fact that there will be no-one living who will be me.[7]

In critical and literary circles too the individual has been largely written out of the script: deconstructed into her essentially social roles and context(s). Not only the literary character but the actual person is seen as an intersection and bearer of essentially socially constructed relationships, responses and emotions.[8] Even the author is no longer in charge of her text, but is, according to some, rather written, and constructed by and through it. The individual self is no longer a unique or continuous phenomenon, but a plurality derived from the range of contexts in, and by which, they find and (momentarily) define themselves.

Despite 'the new economic history', which does indeed affect neo-classical forms of explanation, our understanding of historical development is again vastly different from that which prevailed when the foundations of economic thinking were being laid. Contrary to contractarian or quasi-contractarian views then widely canvassed, society was never established *from* individuals, rather, individuals were differentiated *out* of social wholes. The establishment of the legal and market social orders so characteristic of the modern state has, in all cases, *supervened* on a pre-existing social whole or wholes, on which it has in many cases been hitherto reliant in establishing limits to the dangers otherwise inherent in unbounded individualism.[9]

This presents us with the paradox that our policy-oriented social sciences are premised on a view of humanity which is contradicted by the findings of philosophical reflection. One might observe that influential accounts of the philosophical premises underpinning economic individualism derive from the discredited logical positivism of the inter-war years, further exemplifying Keynes' dictum about the time-lag in intellectual debts between theory and the policy-sciences. However 'ought' does imply (perhaps more stringently, or merely more accurately *entails*) 'can'. The prescriptions of a coherent moral culture should recognise the basic conditions of human existence, so far, at least, as it understands them at any one time. And on this view the individualist premise is a non-starter.

To this there are two defensive responses that can be made. The first is to remark that whatever the state of philosophy or literary theory, the evidence about what is politically practicable for human beings seems now to be heavily stacked in favour of individualism, both as social policy and perhaps, therefore, also as a premise of theorising. A strident Right has hastily assimilated the demise of communist regimes to the discrediting of social democracy and urged them as evidence against the practicality of the mildest and most limited forms of collectivist endeavour, persuading even some with a long record of dissent from individualist orthodoxies.[10]

The second is to claim, as is often done by apologists for economic individualist explanations, that the method does not purport in any way to model individual psychology, but rather to *explain* social phenomena by using the individualist premise as a way of generating testable hypotheses. The premises of the method are, it is claimed, quite independent of the real motives of those whose behaviour is so modelled.[11]

I shall return to the issue of practicality, but meanwhile I want to consider whether the second claim can be sustained when individualist premises are used to generate policy initiatives, or, more widely, to structure the situation in which the individual makes choices. To put it plainly, can we really sustain agnosticism and indifference as to the realities of moral psychology, whilst operating policies which are premised on, and incentive-geared to reward, individualistic reasoning? To hold such a view is to believe one can create a situation where people will be rewarded for acting *as if* they were rational egoists without believing, indeed denying that they will actually respond by becoming one. Policy initiatives are framed in the *hope* that individuals will respond in the fashion predicted by the hypothesis of rational egoism. This is disingenuous. How is the difference between acting *as if* one were a rational egoist, and actually being one to be sustained? Indeed, if the deconstructivist view of the individual as merely a kind of moment in a hermeneutic force-field is right, then the context provided by policy becomes more, not less, determinative of individual personality.

Doctors and academics, to take a recent example, have been used to working in an environment where their actions are guided by professional norms internalised through long periods of training and socialisation. Policy initiatives in their fields which result from modelling the behaviour of economic agents wishing to economise on money, time and effort, commonly operate through imposing costs on those who seek to maintain professional standards rather than obey the signals carried by pricing mechanisms. Professionals will often seek to maintain their standards, even at some considerable cost to themselves, at least in part, perhaps, because doing so is less a means to an end than it is expressive of their professional – and even personal – identity. However, eventually, if the costs are high enough, the professional ethic will succumb, and individuals' responses will model the theory's originally false egoistic and opportunistic assumptions.[12] This may be thought an idealised story: it is not meant to imply that there are no lazy or opportunistic professionals, merely to illustrate analytically the difference and severe incompatibilities between incentive-driven societies and those which run on the basis of the internalisation of norms.[13]

If individual incentives are, as motives, dominant over internalised, unpoliced, norms, it suggests that where the presuppositions of the rational egoist model are used to construct the social environment they will surely be transformed into the motives of agents. For rational-egoistic and norm-based accounts are not merely competing social explanations, they are, in the end, different possible forms of society, and different senses of the self.

Claims about the strategic dominance of egoism find theoretical support within the axioms of rational choice theory itself through the notion of moral hazard. Imagine an insurance market supervening on a society in which individuals previously bore all their own risk. Standards of care set through norms internalised in the high-risk environment would be high, and claims correspondingly low. However, high standards of care involve costs. Opportunistic policy-holders will gain [time/opportunity/money] through relaxing their previous standards and relying on the insurance cover to remedy any loss. This, however, will result in more claims and consequently higher premiums over the next period. In the absence of any means of identifying high-risk contractors (and to some extent even where there are such means) these higher premiums will be born by all policy-holders and those who maintain the same high internalised standards of care will thus bear both their own monitoring costs *and* the premium rises resulting from the lower care of those claiming on their policies, eventually providing even 'carers' with an incentive to lower their standards too. Obviously insurance companies seek to discriminate different risk categories within their potential market in order to avoid this, but such discrimination is invariably imperfect, and in other manifestations of moral hazard not always possible.

This is particularly the case where, as in modern mass society, strategic defaulters can achieve anonymity. Thus, at an even greater level of generality, one could observe that it is an instance of the universal vulnerability of unpoliced norms to free riding. Take, for example, the erosion of a norm of reciprocity such as that of allowing fellow-drivers to pull into a busy stream of traffic from a side-road. Following such a norm involves an immediate cost to me, with no guarantee of reciprocity. The opportunist will accept invitations to enter streams of traffic himself, whilst not impeding his own progress to offer them to others. In large, impersonal societies, where the identification and sanctioning of defaulters from informal norms is impossible, it is reasonable to conclude that defaulting becomes a 'dominant strategem' – egoistic motivation drives out any generalised, or not immediately reciprocated, or sanctionable exchange.[14] That the market behaviour of rational egoists might constitute a kind of moral 'Gresham's law' undermining and driving out 'good' behaviour is a hypothesis that Hayek has himself acknowledged as a potentially generalisable theorem.[15]

2

The basic idea that human personality is shaped by their social experience is, of course, not a new one. It was a continual preoccupation of republican theory, which is dominated by the issue of discriminating between those political and military experiences of citizens which are supportive and which destructive of virtuous (or *virtú*-ous) civic personalities. However, it is not a view which has been championed by liberal individualists who have characteristically presumed an individual already accoutred with autonomy and rights, entering a pre- and independently existing political arena.[16] As scholars have now made clear to us, one of the crucial problems faced by early defenders of a liberal order, including Adam Smith, was the issue of what effect such a society would have on the political personalities of those living under it, and whether an individualistic commercial order would produce persons capable of sustaining it.[17] But needless to say, the idea that the market structures and moulds individuals' dispositions rather than giving expression to them, although much older, has not recently been prominent in liberal individualist thinking.[18] It comes as some surprise then, if not a nice irony, that the theory of social choice associated with rational egoism itself, and so often used to defend the market as a neutral social institution, also offers a particular explanation of the way that social circumstance feeds back and enters into the formation of individuals' personalities and choices.[19]

For it is, by contrast with the above, claimed by its individualist defenders, that where they are indeed perfect, markets are transparent vectors of consumers' autonomous preferences. In a perfect market the signals carried by prices, the existence of alert entrepreneurs always seeking out and striving to capitalise on unfulfilled desires, and the competitive context in which exchanges take place, in some way guarantees that the aggregate production schedule for a society is the embodiment of individual decisions about how they value and wish to allocate their resources. There is a sense in which the market justifies the social outcome which it generates, because it simply *is* the innumerable expenditure decisions of individuals. For the libertarian individualist the objection to political decisions about allocative issues is that they supervene on allocative decisions the market has *already* made; the issue is thus at least redundant, the activity at best distorting (if you believe the market to be an efficient allocator), and at worst immoral (if you believe that the rights acquired by free transactions between legitimate title-holders are absolute).

However, the market is acknowledgedly bad at supplying certain kinds of goods. Whilst this is notorious, less remarked on are the other ways in which decisions made according to market criteria and via market institutions have all sorts of properties which differentiate them from those made politically.

The most notorious class of goods which the market supplies suboptimally is of course public goods. If individuals act voluntarily, motivated only by their own individual benefit, in pursuit of goods to be privately consumed, how will goods which are intrinsically publicly available and/or can only be supplied collectively come about? The standard example of the lighthouse has it that in the absence of coercion, lighthouses will not be forthcoming because whilst only collective effort can pay for it each individual will reason that their own contribution will not be crucial, since the lighthouse will be built or not depending on whether all the *other* potential contributors perform. Thus each individual, reasoning they may safely 'free ride' on the contribution of the others, will not contribute and the lighthouse will indeed fail to be built.

The goods normally discussed in the now massive literature range from such fairly tangible items as lighthouses through to more abstract goods such as public health, or even, in the case of the rationality of voting, to the good of the persistence of democracy or democratic institutions themselves. There are by now a fairly standard range of solutions to public goods problems, each adapted to the particular properties of the good in question, and of course not unrelated to policy. One popular category of solution, particularly attractive to libertarians, consists in seeking ingenious ways of resolving the public goods into individual goods.

Take, for example, the issue of public health. The prevalence of disease, if the mechanism of transmission is unknown and its incidence is therefore unpredictable, poses a public goods problem. Inasmuch as disease seems to be generated by the general squalor of impoverished city life, and inasmuch as there is no way in which even wealthy inhabitants of the city can avoid contact with that squalor, protection for some becomes inseparably linked with relief for all. However, once the medium of transmission becomes known, and individual means of protection become available – through inoculation for example – the safety of the individual becomes separable from the health of the public.[20] If individuals can protect themselves by private initiative there is no particular reason (on the individualist premise) why they should be protected collectively.

Now this example neatly illustrates the fact that many public goods are public only because, and if, they are non-excludable (that is, not privatisable) at the point of *supply* – as security from the 'miasma' of infection was thought to be. But this is often quite compatible with their being privately *consumed*. For example, unpolluted air is non-excludable but privately consumed, as is the information conveyed by a lighthouse beam to ships negotiating a hazardous reef. Other consumers can't be excluded (given the technology); but it's not that there's anything in the enjoyment of the good that *needs* those others to be included. Their inclusion is, for the individual, a matter of indifference, and as far as the would-be entrepreneurs in the potential market for clean air or safety at sea are concerned, simply a regrettable

aspect of the current technology, or prevailing normative assumptions. One might, for example, envisage scrambled radio direction
beacons, which could only be decoded by those paying a subscription
for a suitable device; or the presumption of a right to breathe clean
air being reversed to create a massive industry in the provision of
personalised breathing apparatus. The analogous move is, in the case
of drinkable tap water, already well under way. The enjoyment of
personal security has been considered a public good because it was
thought it could only be supplied jointly, but can clearly be supplied
on a private basis, as, in a way, it was before Henry VII's abolition of
private retainers, and, increasingly again as security, in various forms is
supplied through private contract.

However, such a solution is not available to one class of public good
which is germane to the argument here. As David Miller has pointed
out, some goods are public because their very goodness consists in
their being jointly *consumed or enjoyed*.[21] He instances many goods
connected with sociability, and ideal-regarding social goods such as
equality. Games such as hockey or squash are irreducibly collective
not only in the way they are supplied, but as they are consumed.
Politics itself is, I urge, such a good. However, in seeking to establish
such a position we must face the other horn of the dilemma on which
liberals, let alone libertarians, seek to impale the advocate of public
goods and exposer of market failure. For, as they point out, the supply
of social goods in Miller's sense is only really possible authoritatively,
that is, authoritarianly. Such solutions entail the imposition of A's
preferences on B, simply because the satisfaction of A's preference
contains reference to some state of B, for example B's greater sociability,
B's involvement in the community, greater equality with A, C, E, F . . .
etc.

To avoid this, claims the liberal, we must rule out *a priori* all
conceptions of the good which involve reference to others' desires, as
part of the individualist premise. Rawls' characterisation of human
beings behind the veil of ignorance, for example, attributes to them a
necessary unconcern (benign or malign) for the preferences of others.
Can space be made for social goods, without abandoning this laudable
concern for the autonomy of others? Arguably it cannot, for without
a shared and thick conception of the good we cannot logically distinguish between benign and malign preferences which include reference
to others' states.

This seems to be an important point. For social goods as defined above do, by definition, entail preferences which refer to the state of being of others.

The alternative case is made by Michael Sandel. In rejecting the individualist premise, he eloquently pleaded the case for the necessary priority of community over rights as constitutive of the individual, on the grounds that on such individualist premises, as, for example, of Rawls,

> a sense of community describes [merely] a possible aim of ante-cedently individuated selves, not an ingredient or constituent of their identity as such. This guarantees its subordinate status. Since 'the essential unity of the self is already provided by the concept of right', community must find its virtue as one contender among others within the framework defined by justice, not as a rival account of the framework itself. The question then becomes whether individuals who happen to espouse communitarian aims can pursue them within a well-ordered society, antecedently defined by prin-ciples of justice, not whether a well-ordered society is *itself* a com-munity in the constitutive sense.[22]

Sandel's question is approximately Miller's one: 'whether com-munitarian aims can be pursued in a society defined by principles of justice', that is, in terms of the priority of liberty rights. His answer is no, or at least only to a vanishingly limited extent. The worry about Sandel's prescription for a thicker sense of community must be that it provides the possibility for the violation of rights in the most brazen fashion, and in doing so it gives tremendous hostages to fortune. For the prioritising of a substantive community validates unpredictable and potentially illiberal forms of ethical life. I do not say this is his intention, his focus is critically directed at Rawls, but it is difficult to see how, short of some Hegelian-type justification for the superior rationality of a *particular* ethical community or tradition, he could evade it.

However, there may be another possibility. The issue is often presented in a way that suggests we are faced with a sharp dichotomy between an anomic libertarianism and a stifling communitarianism.[23] This is premised on the not implausible view that political society must rest on moral consensus, that political conflict can only be kept within bounds if there is a moral consensus on a wide range of issues and that this can only be supplied by a shared moral tradition, and not by rational argument or analysis.[24] But if the adoption of a thick conception of community is a worryingly high (or unattainable) price to pay for the supply of social goods, a conception of limited, *political* community can provide at least a coherent programme for exploring the problem.

The exhortation to pursue or sustain politics as a goal is not necessarily an appeal to altruism, civic virtue, or any such idealised conception of human nature. As powerfully urged recently by Quentin Skinner, the bifurcation between rights-based liberalism and *virtù-* based republicanism, and the related distinction between negative and positive liberty, may be both historically and theoretically pro-crustean.[25] Politics does involve a commitment to a kind of community, although it is a much more exiguous, and in the end procedural commitment, and allows the possibility of a much more diverse community than Sandel seems to have in mind. It is a commitment to, as Bernard Crick has said, 'at least some tolerance of differing truths (and we might add, conceptions of the good), some recognition that government is possible, indeed best conducted, amid the open canvassing of rival interests'.[26] For politics to be conducted in the absence of a homogeneous community it is, moreover, necessary that there be rights, precisely which rights we cannot say, for it will be a matter for political argument – but they will include some notion of free speech and some notion of freedom of association. Conversely, for rights to sustain diverse communities there will need to be some commitment to politics itself as a good, indeed, at least strategically, as the master good. It is not analytically the case that politics in this sense is the master good – there are other possibilities.[27]

However, if politics itself is a public good then its capacity to overcome the sub-optimal supply of such goods resulting from effects in the social environment must be seriously brought in question. One must enquire into the circumstances under which liberty – or politics – can be *practised* – as well as the logical question of what actually constitutes liberty, or politics, moreover one must integrate the two. Recent political theory has been dominated by the latter question almost to the exclusion of the former.

3

As should now be clear, my argument is that one reason why social goods, and politics itself may be under-supplied in a market-oriented society is, not necessarily that people do not value such things, but, as David Miller puts it, that 'a market economy converts preferences into behaviour in a certain sort of way: it gives people differentially strong incentives to act on their various preferences. (For example, it generally gives no incentive at all to act on preferences for public goods).' In pursuing my conception of the good in a market setting, I am constrained by other people's market-channelled behaviour, not by their underlying preference.'[28] Such constraints alter our preferences; preferences are adaptive to persistent thwarting. This claim now requires further elaboration.

One argument in support of such a claim is that it will rarely be the case that individuals would choose politically that allocation of resources which would result from their individual transactions. The effect of imperfect information is clearly one factor here: the assumption of perfect information being one of the most notoriously unrealistic axioms of market theory.

If you asked most people whether it was more important to provide more and better national health care, or a greater variety and choice of biscuits, the evidence suggests that people come down in favour of health care.[29] In fact, however, despite widespread and evidently justifiable concern about the health services there is no evidence of a fall in the variety of available biscuits. Does this falsify the preferences expressed in the questionnaire responses? The fact is that when we buy a packet of biscuits we do not consider the nature of the 'signal' that our purchase may be conveying about the alternative uses to which social resources may be put. By buying the biscuits I do, I undoubtedly express a preference for those I choose over others available, perhaps – although this is more dubious – a preference for biscuits over health care; but nothing can be inferred from numerous such choices (without committing the fallacy of composition), about the preferences those choosers have concerning the socially desired *range* of choice of biscuits. It is just not valid to deduce from the fact that (collectively) shoppers choose from amongst the whole range, that the sum of their expenditure is a collective expression of the value they placed on having that range available. Thus there is no logical link between the individual choices of consumers, and the total social effort put into sustaining that *range of choice*. It is (usually) true, that when I go out to buy a packet of biscuits, I am choosing among biscuits, and not thinking about the health service, or the Third World, or any other possible use of my small change. But even if I were, there is no way in

which I could buy a packet of biscuits at all, without expressing a preference for a particular kind, and so contributing my mite to the apparent
collective endorsement of the value of the current range of choice.

This suggests that the difference between choices expressed through
the market and choices expressed through politics, should not be
construed as two different mechanisms for articulating some already
existing essential public opinion (invariably to the detriment of politics);
rather they should be construed as different activities, involving
different practices and with different (not better or worse) outcomes.
Choosing individually, privately, through the market, simply deprives
each of us of both the knowledge and a context in which we might be
able to make other choices. In this sense freedom has to involve the
public action of free citizens. Acting privately (through the market)
restricts freedom by ruling out the knowledge and capacity to make
certain very important choices.

One way in which the practices of economic and political choice
differ is, as already hinted, in terms of the moral psychology of choice;
and one key consequence of a system of individualistic market choice
seems to be to sever the link between action and moral responsibility.
Now on a utilitarian, or even a consequentialist view, the question of
the morality of an action only arises where a perceptible harmful
consequence results from that action. Where no such consequence
results, or cannot be assigned to an action (or actor) moral issues do
not arise. This is, for example, made the key to one of the distinctions
between negative and positive liberty by Berlin.[30] If infringements on
my liberty which are not assignable to any particular agent are not
truly to be so construed and it follows that only impediments which
can be assigned to specific individuals can be considered the proper
subject of government or legislative action, then government interference in the cumulative effects of market action on individual
liberty is also excluded. The intuitive appeal of this argument derives
from the fact that it does seem to work at the level of moral psychology
through emancipating the individual from considering (or in many
cases even having to be aware of), the consequences of his or her acts.
Thus morally dubious arms sales are justified by statesmen on the
grounds that others will sell if we do not. (No morally different
consequences follow from *our* selling arms as opposed to someone else
– it merely happens to be us that is doing the selling.) And environmentally dubious trade is justified on the grounds that my unilateral
withdrawal will make no difference. (I need a new hardwood front

door, and the destruction of tropical forests will proceed irrespective of whether I buy it or not.) It is, of course, one of the axioms of the perfect market that outcomes are unaffected by the decision of any one actor within it.

These commonplaces of contemporary casuistry are nevertheless highly questionable. Consider the case of the morally squeamish utilitarian torturers who construct an apparatus which enables each one of them to apply pain in increments below the level of perceptibility, yet which collectively delivers such agony as to produce the desired (and quite possibly beneficial) effect. Can we say that the imperceptibility of the consequences of each torturer's acts renders it blameless?[31] Is the imperceptibility of the consequences of each market actor's decisions then also beyond moral censure? The answer to this will depend, both on the facts of the case, and on how, precisely, we formulate the question. But this is not to say it is a semantic issue: it has enormous moral, and, if the argument here is correct, political consequences.

> It is not enough to ask, 'Will my act harm other people?' ... I should ask 'Will my act be one of a set of acts that will *together* harm other people?' The answer may be Yes. And the harm to others may be great.[32]

If this is the correct way to formulate the moral issue, the market does not emancipate us from moral issues. Not even if the *outcome* of market transactions is optimal (notice the squeamish torturers may also be working for a good outcome). If the consequences of our hitherto excusable (because infinitisimal) impacts on the market make a moral difference, we ought to construct ways of ensuring that these outcomes do not eventuate. But since these outcomes are the consequences of *combinations* of individual actions, and not the consequence (or even the intention) of any individual's action, this requires a co-ordinated moral remedy unsuppliable by hidden hands, and the only candidate for such a co-ordinator is politics.

So far the argument has been directed at the incapacity of market decisions to deliver certain kinds of goods, especially those of a moral or collective nature.

However, political decisions are arguably different. Political decisions ask us to step back and to make hard choices about (amongst other things) the relative values of items we would normally regard as incommensurable, between immediate and long-term desires, between wants and values. If taken seriously this not only engenders a kind of awareness not required of market actors, it holds out the possibility of ennobling action.[33] Because, when we make a political decision we are aware that we can in some way be setting a framework within which individual acts and choices can subsequently be made, a different rationale to that open to the choosing individual consumer is both possible, and often forthcoming. For example, given the decline of public transport I might decide as an individual that I need to use a car to get to work; but politically I may (and at the same time) actively support a policy of punitive taxation for motorists to subsidise public transport. As a parent, deploring the lack of resources put into public education might I not decide to pay for my child's schooling (social snobbery, if possible, aside) whilst politically supporting the abolition of private schools and massive re-resourcing of state education? I might politically champion universal, publicly funded health care, yet if I (or my aged parent, or my child) were unable to receive some life-saving treatment on the underfunded National Health Service, and I could afford to do so, I would pay for it privately. Such cases are often read as evidence of hypocrisy: why should they not be read as idealism? If an individual puts time and effort into achieving a political ideal, does it follow that she is hypocritical because she does not sacrifice to it her child's education (if she believes that to be at issue), or her life, or that of her aged parent or child? Does the argument about moral dilution require these sacrifices?

I think these cases point to something else. They point to the *social* nature of the goods being sought, to the fact that such goods, as ideals, can only be realised at the political level, and that that is therefore the level at which they must be addressed. Like the first performer in Hobbes's state of nature, he who does what is right alone 'does but betray himselfe to his enemy'; the rules of sociability, however clearly we may see them 'bind onely to a desire and an endeavour', and politics – not love or religion – is the only means by which that endeavour can be made real.[34] Because market-based societies present to us choices between goods which are, by and large, consumed alone (or in the nuclear family), they tend always to conceal from us the social, or environmental externalities consequent on the aggregation of choices for such goods, and deny us the information, or ability to make the relevant discriminations in our choices.[35] There are few profits to be made from the satisfaction of 'group oriented' desires.

The second point to be made is that politics can resist the processes of individualism and moral dilution only inasmuch as it involves a commitment to sustaining some conception of political community.[36]

It has been remarked that the existence of diverse groups is one of the safeguards of liberty, and of this sense of politics. From Machiavelli's seemingly perverse attribution of Rome's liberty to the contestation between the plebeians and the patricians, through the tremendous eighteenth-century debate on party – of which Madison's reluctant championship of diversity is in some sense the flowering, and Burke's 'little platoon' as the nursery of public affections is the defence – diversity developed *pari passu* with the notion of a liberal and political regime. Since Rousseau, and the French Revolution, Tocqueville, taking his cue from Montesquieu's praise of 'intermediate powers', typified an essentially defensive position in which both (and each of) revolutionary and democratic politics were denounced for their tendency to destroy or erode social groupings, and to atomise the population, a vital element in what we since came to recognise as mass society, and totalitarianism.[37] The existence of intermediate forms of association is vital to the practice of politics. Such associations educate, skill and empower actors, but some do so more than others. The more closely the ends and actions of the association mirror those of the polity the more they will provide a political education. 'All associations', writes Aristotle, 'aim at some good' but the nature of the good sought will largely determine the character of the association.

Are some forms of association threatened by the market or other manifestations of the individualist premise? It is difficult to deny that this is so. The market predictably intervenes to supply many of the selective benefits which, according to Olsonian logic, might help to support association aimed at collective non-excludable goods. For example, social and sports facilities, if truly being used to subsidise the provision of a non-excludable good, can be supplied cheaper by an organisation devoted solely to the business of sports and social facilities. This would logically lead to the demise of collective action groups. Nor has this happened only through the action of the market. A government in the grip of rabidly individualist public policy initiatives has also had the effect of curbing – by a combination of fiat or studied neglect – many forms of association. Notably, for good or ill, those associated with trades unionism, and local government[38] but also many others connected with the provision of social goods – in the health service, for example. The last decade's privatisation policy, driven by at least a rhetoric of individualism, has seen the private expropriation of a mass of wealth and capital accumulated by what were originally, in form, voluntary and local organisations – savings banks, local water boards, etc.

Moreover a part has been played by a perverse puritanism, which, since at least Mandeville, has been the occasional complement to the theorisation of egoism. For ironically, that same rational-egoist premise which in theory argued the implausibility of all forms of association for collective action, led those holding it to mistrust the motives in those associations which they actually found in existence as mere promotional groups, the actions of which distorted the potential of the market to respond smoothly to individuals' needs: all associations to influence politics were potentially a form of rent-seeking behaviour. Existing professional and campaigning groups were therefore sidelined in the policy-making process. All this has been part of a quite explicit drive to replace politics by the market, and to substitute the process of collective, messy and negotiable solutions, with those arrived at impersonally by the individual calculations of isolated consumers.[39]

The success of such a policy involves not only the atomisation of what has ironically been praised so much for its tenuous survival in eastern Europe – civil society; it involves the loss of all that goes with politics – the skills and dispositions of negotiation and accommodation, the diversity of political resources for the individual as well as for society as a whole, together with the political education they entail and require, a practical sense of the limits of what is possible, and the resulting commitment to working within those limits. In 1963 Crick wrote: 'Political compromises are the price that has to be paid for liberty.' The startling claim of the new individualism is that liberty might also exact, as its price, the suppression of politics as compromise, and the means and practices by which it is accomplished.

Is not all this too alarmist? Surely civil society is self-replenishing, there are always new groupings arising? Even a society devoted to the commercial supply of individually consumed goods will throw up forms of association. The drive of humans to associate, even for the bizarre purpose of private consumption, is a strong presumption in favour of our political nature. But we need to discriminate. Machiavelli distinguished between parties based on disputes about liberty and those based on disputes about wealth. This is too crude for our purposes but it is a starting point. A politics which disqualified self-interest as a motive for association would be an exiguous category and an unusual activity. Nevertheless the question of *what* issues groups or parties take up politically is relevant. Fan clubs or associations of train-spotters are unlikely to generate or promote politics. But more contentiously single-issue, want-regarding interest groups may be, in an important sense, less political. Inasmuch as there is one thing that such groups want, their intervention into political activity is one-dimensional, they cannot engage with others in politically creative, interactive, ways, they have no bargaining counters and neither internal diversity, nor other goods to negotiate, no grain with or against which other political actors may work. A group pursuing a complex, ideal-regarding end, however, is not so politically amorphous. Groups seeking complex, principled ends – toleration, cultural or ethnic survival, the alleviation of a complex bad, like poverty – *are* more political. They are more likely to be internally structured, providing points of common agreement and political contact for other groups. They are, or will need to be if successful, more politically educated, they will more likely be enduring.[40] A political society will be rich in groups of the latter kind, whereas an individualist 'market society politics' will predominantly foster groups of the former kind. The prohibition on 'political' activity by ideal regarding charitable organisations not only inhibits their own efficacy, but the depth and wealth of our own polity. In denying politics to such altruistic and ideal-regarding organisations, we deny those qualities to our politics.

To return to my main theme, this is not a puritan argument for a politics of ideals but a reflection on the part this might play in a wider case about the importance of retaining a sense of the value of authentically political decision-making, and the conditions for its survival, and ultimately a warning about the narrowing effects of a politics construed on the model of the economy, on the individualist premise.

NOTES

1. For what I hope is a generalisable analysis and sustained account of one of these worries see my 'The Market for Toleration: A Case Study in an Aspect of the Ambiguity of "Positive Economics"' *British Journal of Political Science*, 21, 1 (1991).
2. The classic works in politics are mostly by émigré economists: Anthony Downs' *An Economic Theory of Democracy*, and Mancur Olsen's *The Logic of Collective Action* (Cambridge, MA, 1965) which, in view of its predominant thesis might be better titled 'the *illogicality* of collective action'. A recent, remarkably astute and synoptic account of the development of this literature as it relates to political

science is to be found in Alessandro Pizzorno's 'On Rationality and Democratic Choice', in Pierre Birnbaum and Jean Leca, *Individualism, Theories and Methods* (Oxford, 1990); for applications to sociology, P. M. Blau, *Exchange and Power in Social Life* (New York: Wiley, 1964) and G. Homans, *Social Behaviour, its Elementary Forms*; on the 'new economic history', which at times seems ready to replace the need for doing any history at all with pure deduction, see Douglas C. North, *Structure and Change in Economic History*, (New York, Norton, 1981); in social history there is the highly suggestive Abram de Swaan, *In Care of the State* (Cambridge: Cambridge University Press, 1988).

3. A seminal article is that of Alan Carling in *New Left Review* 125 (1981); the major work of the school is that of John Roemer, *Free To Lose* (London: Radius, 1988). I would distinguish between rational-choice Marxism and what is sometimes more loosely called 'analytical Marxism' of the G. A. Cohen, Jon Elster school, which, whilst it tries to apply modern standards of linguistic and explanatory rigour to Marx's work, eschews exclusive reliance on rational-choice axioms.

4. Ludwig Wittgenstein, *Philosophical Investigations*, tr. G. E. Anscomb (Oxford, 1963):
    §241 'So you are saying that human agreement decides what is true and what is false? – it is what human beings *say* that is true and false; they agree in the *language* they use. That is not agreement in opinions but in form of life. ...
    §243 ... could we ... imagine a language in which a person could write down or give vocal expression to his inner experience – his feelings, moods, and the rest – for his private use? – Well, can't we do so in ordinary language? – But that is not what I mean. The individual words of this language are to refer to what can only be known by the person speaking; to his immediate private sensations. So another person cannot understand the language.'

5. As forcefully argued and developed by Quentin Skinner.

6. P. F. Strawson, *Individuals, an essay in descriptive metaphysics* (London: Methuen, 1959), p. 102–3.

7. Derek Parfit, *Reasons and Persons* (Oxford, 1984) p. 281. For a recent discussion of the political implications of the deconstruction of the individuality of personality in Parfit and Sandel as responses to Rawls and Nozick, see Michael A. Mosher, 'Boundary revisions: the Deconstruction of Moral Personality' in Rawls, Nozick, Sandel and Parfit', *Political Studies* 39 (1991).

8. 'Haven't you ever been in love, then?' 'When I was younger,' she says, 'I allowed myself to be constructed by the discourse of romantic love for a while, yes.' David Lodge, *Nice Work* (London: Secker & Warburg, 1988) p. 210.

9. Edmund Burke draws attention to this and the attendant dangers of allowing economic motivations to overwhelm the 'manners' under which they grew up and have thrived. See J. G. A. Pocock's 'Burke's analysis of the Political Economy of the French Revolution' in *Virtue Commerce and History* (Cambridge, 1985).

10. Recently rehearsing Hayekian arguments about the incompatibility of non-market orders and liberty, Frank Hahn invites the reader 'to consider what follows with a critical eye in the knowledge that the author would not be displeased to find that he has been mistaken'. Frank Hahn, 'On some economic limits in politics', in J. Dunn (ed.), *The economic limits to modern politics* (Cambridge, 1990) p. 142.

11. For example, Ludwig von Mises, *Human Action: a Treatise on Economics* (London: Hodge, 1949) p. 15; Milton Friedman, *Essays in Positive Economics* (Chicago: University of Chicago Press, 1953) p. 15. The claim exemplifies the logical positivist basis of the methodology.

12. Thus, incidentally, confirming the cynicism of the market-ideologue politician

concerning the efficacy, or even existence of the professional ethic.

13. Felicitously distinguished by Graham Ouchi as 'markets' and 'clans', 'hierarchies' referring to the internal organisation of the conventional firm. G. Ouchi, 'Markets, hierarchies and Clans', *Administrative Science Quarterly*, 25 (1980).

14. See the brilliant and emblematic story of the 'groomer' birds with the variant 'suckers', 'cheats' and 'grudgers' in Richard Dawkins, *The Selfish Gene* (Oxford, 1976), p. 197ff.

15. F. A. Hayek, 'The Uses of "Gresham's Law" as an illustration of "Historical Theory"', p. 318, in F. A. Hayek, *Studies in Philosophy, Politics and Economics* (London: Routledge, 1967) reprinted from *History and Theory*, vol. 1 (1960).

16. For an excellent characterisation of the differences see Pocock, 'Virtue Rights and Manners: A Model for Historians of Political Thought' in *Virtue Commerce and History* (Cambridge, 1985). The optimism often present in liberal individualism was once mischievously characterised by Alan Ryan as the assumption that people were 'parachuted into the world aged twenty-one, white, male, well off, and *terribly* clever'.

17. The works of Donald Winch and Duncan Forbes on Smith and Hume respectively explore these themes.

18. The earliest theorists of modern economics, who understood themselves to be talking, not about an abstraction, but about a particular historical social formation, not only acknowledged, but stressed the moral and epistemological consequences of the spread of commercial transactions in invigorating the mind, enlarging its powers and faculties, and refining tastes. For example, D. Hume, *Essays, Moral, Political and Literary* (Oxford, 1963): 'Of Refinement in the Arts', p. 277, and 'Of Commerce', p. 270. The idea that 'the market' could be construed simply as a set of marginal rates of substitution between any desired goods, derives from 'the marginalist revolution' associated with Edgeworth and Marshall.

19. The neutrality of the market, although a feature of idealised text-book models and political ideologues, is of course by no means uncritically accepted by academic theorists, even those disposed to work within the individualist premise. See, most recently, Robert E. Goodin and Andrew Reeve (eds), *Liberal Neutrality* (London: Routledge, 1989).

20. Indeed, the most analytical treatment of the history of this episode suggests that public health developments in the nineteenth century were driven by an erroneous 'miasmic' theory of infection, which 'dictated a much more radical and effective programme of reform than the essentially individualist approach of contagionists ever could have'. Abram de Swaan, *In Care of the State* (Cambridge and Oxford, Polity, 1988), p. 134. To the extent that this is right we may owe our sewage and water distribution networks to the historical accident that our understanding of the epidemiology of cholera lagged behind the massive growth of the cities by half a century. Third World cities largely manage on the individualist premise, by a combination of spatial separation and private protection.

21. David Miller, 'Market Neutrality and the Failure of Cooperatives' *British Journal of Political Science*, 11 (1981), pp. 326–7. Miller actually distinguishes 'group oriented desires' which require some degree of joint consumption short of social universality, from 'social desires' which require a certain condition of the whole society, such as a degree of equality, or the non-existence of slavery, say. See also chapter 3, 'Market Neutrality' of his *Market, State and Community: the theoretical foundations of Market Socialism* (Oxford, 1989).

22. Sandel, *Liberalism . . .*, p. 64.

23. Or to personalise things: Nietzsche versus Aristotle.

24. As urged for example by Alasdair MacIntyre, *Whose Justice, Which Rationality?* (Oxford, 1988).
25. Quentin Skinner, 'The republican idea of political liberty', in *Machiavelli and the Nature of Republicanism* (Cambridge, 1990), shows how a defence of republican liberty, and a strong conception of politics is quite consistent with a negative, and even egoistic conception of liberty, and indeed that 'if we wish to maximise our own individual liberty, we must cease to put our trust in princes, and instead, take charge of the public arena ourselves.' (p. 308)
26. Bernard Crick, *In Defence of Politics* (Harmondsworth: Penguin, 1962), p. 18.
27. The answer to the question why there has to be 'some tolerance of differing truths', and the public conciliation of rival interests, 'is, of course, that they do not have to be. Other paths are always open. Politics is simply when they are conciliated.' Crick, op. cit., p. 30.
28. Miller, *Market, State and Community*, p. 94, n. 28.
29. The question has never been posed (so far as I am aware) in quite those terms; but there is consistent opinion poll data throughout the eighties supporting increased taxation for more and better social services, and, in particular, for health care.
30. 'I am normally said to be free to the degree to which no man or body of men interferes with my acting.' Whether the market could be construed as *a body* of men seems doubtful, although in the introduction to his 1969 edition Berlin is far more concessive to critics of *laissez faire* as a threat to *negative* liberty than has been acknowledged in the literature: 'the evils of unrestricted *laissez-faire* ... led to brutal violations of negative liberty' and he regretted his earlier neglect to stress the failure of such systems to provide the 'minimum conditions in which alone any degree of significant negative liberty can be exercised by individuals *or groups*' (my emphasis). Isaiah Berlin, *Four Essays on Liberty* (Oxford, 1969), pp. 122 (Two Concepts of Liberty), xlvi (Introduction). Hayek's endorsement of the claim that infringements that result from no deliberate act of an assignable individual are morally irrelevant has been unremitting, *The Fatal Conceit*, in Collected Works, vol. I, ed. W. W. Bartley (London, 1988), esp. Ch. 5 and 6.
31. The example is adapted from Parfit, *Reasons and Persons*, pp. 79–81; 'That imperceptible effects cannot be morally significant' is the fifth of his Five Mistakes in Moral Mathematics, which constitutes Chapter 3.
32. Parfit, *Reasons and Persons*, p. 86.
33. Precisely the opposite is urged by the Collective Choice school – political allocation encourages irresponsibility because it separates the moment of choice in favour of collective provision – voting, from the moment of payment – the incidence of taxation.
34. Hobbes, *Leviathan*, ed. Pogson-Smith (Oxford: Clarendon, 1965) p. 105 [original pagination, p. 68], p. 121 [p. 79]. Not love or religion, because even with the best *will* in the world many of the 'public goods' issues have a large co-ordination problem element.
35. It is of course true that the Green movement has led to an increased *consumer* demand for environmentally friendly goods, and for demands for products to carry relevant information to consumers wishing to discriminate in their favour. But this is not evidence for the triumph of the market as such; it is the result of *political* argument about these issues, and *political* pressure to provide such information, on the part of green and consumer organisations. Sometimes practical considerations make discrimination impossible. Consider, for example, wanting to be supplied with electricity *not* produced by nuclear technology, or very shortly, with food or pharmaceuticals which have at *no point* in their production involved genetically engineered organisms.

36. Which I take to be the essence of Bernard Crick's conception of politics as involving agreement to a specific, limited mode of settling differences by argument, persuasion, bargaining, accommodation, etc.

37. Tocqueville, in the *Ancient Régime* ... remarks on the 'democratic despotism' theorised by the economists of the eighteenth century, and in danger of being realised in the nineteenth-century state: 'abolishing all hierarchies, all class distinction, all differences of rank ... the nation was to be composed of individuals almost exactly alike and unconditionally equal. In this undiscriminated mass was to reside, theoretically, the sovereign power; yet it was to be carefully deprived of any means of controlling or even supervising the activities of its government ... the State was a law unto itself and nothing short of a revolution could break its tyranny. *De jure* it was a subordinate agent, *de facto*, a master.' *The Ancient Régime and the French Revolution*, tr. Gilbert and cited by Crick, op. cit., p. 63.

38. Even by 1986: 'The centralisation from above and decentralisation to markets and consumers below has weakened local government.' D. Kavanagh, *Thatcherism and British Politics* (Oxford, 1987) p. 288. For a period of over ten years, from Margaret Thatcher first taking office until June 1991, there was not a single official meeting at Prime Ministerial level with any representative of the trades unions.

39. For a brisk excursion over the terrain: Bill Jordan, *The Common Good* (Oxford, 1989) Chapters 2 and 3.

40. Jean Leca 'Individualism and Citizenship' in P. Birnbaum and Jean Leca (eds), *Individualism: theories and methods* (Oxford, 1990) p. 154. Leca draws this distinction using the example of membership of Amnesty International, as against the movement against culling baby seals, hinting at a relationship also between public collective issues and private collective issues. Cf. Hegel's interesting distinction in *Philosophy of Right*, between truly public goods and 'private goods that are common to all'.

9

Incentives, inequality and community

G. A. COHEN

... the rulers of mankind ... maintain side by side two standards of
social ethics, without the risk of their colliding. Keeping one set of
values for use, and another for display, they combine, without
conscious insincerity, the moral satisfaction of idealistic principles
with the material advantages of realistic practice.

R. H. Tawney, Equality

The incentive argument, the interpersonal test, and community

1

In March 1988 Nigel Lawson, who was then Margaret Thatcher's
Chancellor of the Exchequer, brought the top rate of income tax in
Britain down, from 60 per cent to 40 per cent. That cut enlarged the
net incomes of those whose incomes were already large, in comparison
with the British average and, of course, in comparison with the
income of Britain's poor people.

How might the Lawson tax cut be defended? Well, economic
inequality is no new thing in capitalist society, so there has been plenty
of time for a lot of arguments to accumulate in favour of it. We hear,
from the political Right, that rich people are entitled to their wealth:
to part of it because they produced it themselves – but for them, it
would not have existed – and to the rest of it because it was transferred
to them voluntarily by others who were themselves entitled to it

This is an abridged version of the Tanner Lecture delivered at Stanford University in May 1991
and published in Grethe Peterson (ed.), *The Tanner Lectures on Human Values*, Volume XIII,
(Salt Lake City: University of Utah Press, 1992).

because they produced it, or because they received it as a gift or in voluntary trade from others who were themselves entitled to it because … (and so on). (Some who hold that view also think that it is because it establishes moral desert that production justifies title, while others find the entitlement story compelling even when the idea of desert plays no role in it.) And then there is the utilitarian proposition, affirmed not only on the Right but in the Centre, that inequality is justified because, through dynamising the economy, it expands the gross national product and thereby causes an increase in the sum of human happiness.

Left-wing liberals, whose chief representative in philosophy is John Rawls, reject these arguments for inequality: they do not accept the principles (entitlement, desert and general utility) which figure in their major premises.[1] But the Right and Centre sometimes offer an additional argument for inequality, to the major premise of which the liberals are friendly. That major premise is the principle that inequalities are justified when they render badly off people as well off as it is possible for such people to be.[2] In one version of this argument for inequality – and this version of it is my topic here – their high levels of income cause unusually productive people to produce more than they otherwise would; and, as a result of the incentives enjoyed by those at the top, the people who end up near the bottom are better off than they would be in a more equal society. This was one of the most politically effective justifications of the unequalising policy of Thatcher Conservatism. We were ceaselessly told that movement contrary to that policy, in a socialist egalitarian direction, would be bad for badly-off people, by advocates of a regime which seems itself to have brought about the very effect against which its apologists insistently warned.[3]

Left-wing liberals deny the factual claim that the vast inequalities in Britain or America actually do benefit the badly off, but they tend to agree that if they did, they would be justified, and they defend inequalities that really are justified, in their view, by the incentive consideration. That is a major theme in John Rawls' work. For Rawls, some people are, mainly as a matter of genetic and other luck, capable of producing more than others are, and it is right for them to be richer than others if the less fortunate are caused to be better off as a result.[4] The policy is warranted by what Rawls calls the difference principle, which endorses all and only those social and economic inequalities that are good for the worst off or, more generously, those inequalities that either make the worse off better off or do not make them worse off: in this matter there is a certain ambiguity of formulation in Rawls, and in what follows I shall take the difference principle in its more generous form, in which it allows inequalities that do not help but also do not hurt the worst off.[5]

Consider, now, socialist egalitarians, who disapprove of policies like the Lawson tax cut. Being to the Left of Left-wing liberals, socialist egalitarians are also unimpressed by the desert, entitlement and utility justifications of inequality. But it is not so easy for them to set aside the Rawlsian justification of inequality. They cannot just dismiss it, without lending to their own advocacy of equality a fanatical hue which they could not themselves on reflection find attractive.

Socialist egalitarians say that they believe in equality. We might well think that they count as egalitarians because equality is their premise. But the structure of that premise is too simple to accommodate the thought that gets them going politically, which is: 'why should some people be badly off, when other people are so *well* off?' That is not the same as the colourless question, 'why should some people be better off than others?' for in that question there is no reference to absolute levels of condition, hence no reference to anyone being badly off, as opposed to just *less* well off than other people are. Maybe some egalitarians would maintain their zeal in a world of millionaires and billionaires in which no one's life is hard, but the politically engaged socialist egalitarians that I have in mind have no strong opinion about inequality at millionaire/billionaire levels. What they find wrong is that there is, so they think, unnecessary hardship at the lower end of the scale. There are people who are badly off and who, they believe, would be better off under an equalising redistribution. The practically crucial feature of the situation is that the badly off are worse off than anyone needs to be, since an equalising redistribution would enhance their lives.

For these egalitarians, equality would be a good thing because it would make the badly off better off. They do not think it a good thing about equality that it would make the well off worse off. And when their critics charge them with being willing, for the sake of equality, to grind everyone down to the level of the worse off, or even lower, they do not say, in response: well, yes, let us grind down if necessary, but let us achieve equality on a higher plane if that is possible. Instead, what they say is somewhat evasive, at the level of principle; they just deny that it is necessary, for the sake of achieving equality, to move to a condition in which some are worse off and none are better off than now. Were they more reflective, they might add that, if levelling down were necessary, then equality would lose its appeal. Either it would make the badly off worse off still, in frustration of the original egalitarian purpose, or it would make the badly off no better off, while others are made worse off to no evident purpose. Relative to their initial inspiration, which is a concern about badly-off people, an inequality is mandatory if it really is needed to improve the condition of the badly off, and it is permissible if it does not improve but also does not worsen their condition.

Accordingly, these egalitarians lose sight of their goal, their position becomes incoherent or untrue to itself, if, in a world with badly-off people, they reject the difference principle and cleave to an egalitarianism of strict equality. (Given the priorities and emphases that I have attributed to them, they should, strictly speaking, affirm as fundamental neither equality nor the difference principle but this complex maxim: make the badly off well off, or, if that is not possible, make them as well off as possible. But, on a modestly demanding interpretation of what it means to be well off, and on a realistic view of the world's foreseeable resource prospects, the practical consequences for the badly off of the complex maxim are those of the difference principle.) We might conclude that the socialist egalitarians that I have in mind should not be called 'egalitarians', since (if I am right) equality is not their real premise. But that conclusion would be hasty, and I shall say more about the propriety of the name 'egalitarian' in a moment.

For my part, I accept the difference principle, in its generous interpretation (see above), but I question its application in defence of special money incentives to talented people. Rawlsians think that inequalities associated with such incentives satisfy the principle. But I believe that the idea that an inequality is justified if, through the familiar incentive mechanism, it benefits the badly off is more problematic than Rawlsians suppose; that, at least when the incentive consideration is isolated from all reference to desert or entitlement, it generates an argument for inequality that requires a model of society in breach of an elementary condition of community. The difference principle can be used to justify paying incentives that induce inequalities only when the attitude of talented people runs counter to the spirit of the difference principle itself: they would not need special incentives if they were themselves unambivalently committed to the principle. Accordingly, they must be thought of as outside the community upholding the principle when it is used to justify incentive payments to them.[6]

Speaking more generally, I want to record here my doubt that the difference principle justifies *any* significant inequality, in an unqualified way. The principle allows an inequality only if the worst off could not benefit from its removal. And I believe that it is in general more difficult than liberals suppose to show that the worst off could not benefit from removal of an inequality, and hence in general more difficult than liberals think it is to justify an inequality at the bar of the difference principle. The worst off benefit from incentive inequality in particular only because the better off would, in effect, go on strike if unequalising incentives were withdrawn. This inequality benefits the badly off only within the constraint set by the inegalitarian attitude, and the consequent behaviour, of the well off, a constraint that they could remove. And an inequality can also benefit the badly off within a constraint set not by inegalitarian attitudes *per se*, but by pre-existing unequal structure. Thus, in a country with state medical provision, the inequality of treatment that comes from allocating a portion of hospital resources to high-fee-paying patients, who get superior care, benefits the badly off when some of the revenue is used to raise standards throughout the service. The unequal medical provision helps poor people, but only against the background of a prior income inequality (which no doubt itself reflects further structural inequality and inegalitarian attitude) that has not, within this argument, itself been shown to benefit them.

The further back one goes, temporally and causally, in the construction of the feasible set, the more one encounters open possibilities that were closed by human choice, and the harder it is to identify inequalities that do not harm the badly off. Bringing the two cases distinguished above together, I conjecture that social inequalities will appear beneficial to or neutral toward the interest of those at the bottom only when we take as given unequal structures and/or inequality-endorsing attitudes that no one who affirms the difference principle should unprotestingly accept.[7]

Now if all that is right, then we might, in the end, in a round-about way, vindicate the application of the term 'egalitarian' to the socialists that I have had in mind, provided that they are willing to tolerate a formulation of their position along lines just foreshadowed. For we might say that a person is an egalitarian if he applies the difference principle in circumstances in which there exist badly-off (as opposed to just less well-off) people *and* he believes that what the principle demands, in those circumstances, is equality itself, if, that is, he believes that in the long run, and prescinding from rooted inegalitarian attitudes and practices, there *are*, in such circumstances, no social inequalities that do not harm the worst off. Equality appears, at first, to be a premise. It is then rejected, *as* a premise, when the reason for wanting equality is clarified: it is rejected in favour of the difference principle (or, strictly, the more complex maxim stated above). But, now grounded in (something like) the difference principle, it re-asserts itself as a conclusion, for our world, in these times, and for the foreseeable future.

2

I now want to focus on Nigel Lawson's tax cut, and on the incentive case against cancelling it, the case, that is, for maintaining rewards to productive people at the existing high level. And I shall consider that case only with respect to those who, so it is thought, produce a lot by exercising skill and talent, rather than by investing capital. Accordingly, the argument I shall examine applies not only to capitalist economies but also to economies without private ownership of capital, such as certain forms of market socialism. Of course, there also exists an incentive argument for high returns to capital investment, but I am not going to address that argument.

Proponents of the incentive argument say that when productive people take home modest pay, they produce less than they otherwise do, and, as a result, relatively poor and badly- off people are worse off than they are when the exercise of talent is well rewarded. Applied against a restoration of the top tax to 60 per cent, the argument runs as follows:

> Economic inequalities are justified when they make the worst-off people materially better off. [Major, normative premise]
>
> When the top rate of tax is 40 per cent, (*a*) the talented rich produce more than they do when it is 60 per cent, and (*b*) the worst off are, as a result, materially better off. [Minor, factual premise]
>
> Therefore, the top tax should not be raised from 40 per cent to 60 per cent.

It is immaterial to present concerns how the circumstance alleged to obtain in part (a) of the minor premise of the argument is supposed to occasion the result described in part (b). One possibility is that the rich work so much harder when the tax rate goes down that the tax take goes up, and more is available for redistribution. Another is that, when the rich work harder, they produce, among other things, (better) employment opportunities for badly-off people.

The critique that follows is not of everything that could be called an incentive, but only of incentives that produce inequality and which are said to be justified because they make badly off people better off. I raise no objection against incentives designed to eliminate a poverty trap, or to induce people to undertake particularly unpleasant jobs. It is not constitutive of those incentives that they produce inequality. My target is incentives conferring high rewards on people of talent who would otherwise not perform as those rewards induce them to do. I believe that the familiar liberal case for incentives of that kind has not been thoroughly thought through.

3

I said that I would criticise the incentive argument by focusing on certain utterances of it. For I believe that, although the argument may sound reasonable when it is presented, as it usually is, and as it was above, in blandly impersonal form, it does not sound so good when we fix on a presentation of it in which a talented rich person pronounces it to a badly-off person. And the fact that the argument undergoes this devaluation when it occurs in that interpersonal setting should affect our assessment of the nature of the society that the incentive justification by implication recommends.

A normative argument will often wear a particular aspect because of who is offering it and/or to whom it is being addressed. When reasons are given for performing an action or endorsing a policy or adopting an attitude, the appropriate response by the person(s) asked so to act or approve or feel, and the reaction of variously placed observers of the interchange, may depend on who is speaking and who is listening. The form, and the explanation, of that dependence vary considerably across different kinds of case. But the general point is that there are many ways, some more interesting than others, in which an argument's value can be speaker-audience-relative, and there are many reasons of, once again, different degrees of interest, why that should be so.

Before describing a form of dependence (of response on who is addressing whom) that operates in the case of the incentive argument, and in order to induce a mood in which we think of arguments in their contexts of delivery, I list a few examples of the general phenomenon:

(a) I can argue that the driver over there should not be blamed for just now making a right turn on a red light, since he does not know that the rules are different outside California. But he cannot, at the moment, make that very argument, entirely sound though it may be.

(b) You want the fishing rod for recreation, and I need it to get my next meal. I know that you are so unstoical that you will be more upset if you do not get to fish than I will be if I do not get to eat. So I let you have the rod, and I cite your hypersensitivity to disappointment as my reason. It would be a lot less good for you to give that as a reason why you should have the rod.

(c) I might persuade my fellow middle-class friend that, because my car is being repaired, and I consequently have to spend hours on the buses these days, I have a right to be grumpy. The same conclusion, on the same basis, sounds feeble when the audience is not my friend but a carless fellow bus passenger who is forced to endure these slow journeys every day.

(d) As designers of advertisements for charitable causes know, our ordinary self-serving reasons for not giving much (we need a new roof, I'm saving for my holiday, I'm not actually *very* rich) sound remarkably lame when we imagine them being presented to those for whom our lack of charity means misery and death.

(e) And such quotidian reasons also sound feeble when they are presented to people whose sacrifice for the cause is much larger than the one the speaker is excusing himself from offering.

(f) Since the pot should not call the kettle black, an employee may be unimpressed when a routinely tax-evading well-heeled superior dresses him down because of his modest appropriations from petty cash.

The examples show that arguments vary in their capacity to satisfy because of variations in people's epistemic (a) or moral (e, f) or social (c) position, or because of issues of tact and embarrassment (c, d, e) and immediacy (d), or because being generous is more attractive than being grabby (b). I shall not here attempt a systematic taxonomy of ways that arguments subside in different sorts of interpersonal delivery. Instead, I pass to a type of case which is of special interest here, since the incentive argument belongs to it.

4

In this type of case, an argument changes its aspect when its presenter is the person, or one of the people, whose choice, or choices, make one or more of the argument's premises true. By contrast with other presenters of the same argument, a person who makes, or helps to make, one of its premises true can be asked to justify the fact that it is true.[8] And sometimes he will be unable to provide a satisfying justification.

For a dramatic example of this structure, consider the argument for paying a kidnapper where the child will be freed only if the kidnapper is paid. There are various reasons for not paying. Some concern further consequences: maybe, for example, more kidnapping would be encouraged. And paying could be thought wrong not only in some of its consequences but in its nature: paying is acceding to a vile threat. You will nevertheless agree that, because so much is at stake, paying kidnappers is often justified. And the argument for paying a particular kidnapper, shorn of qualifications needed to neutralise the counter-vailing reasons mentioned a moment ago, might run as follows:

> Children should be with their parents.
>
> Unless they pay him, this kidnapper will not return this child to its parents.
>
> So, this child's parents should pay the kidnapper.

Now, that form of the argument is entirely third-personal: in that form of it, anyone (save, perhaps, someone mentioned in the argument) might be presenting it to anyone. But let us now imagine the kidnapper himself presenting the argument, to, for example, the child's parents. (What will matter here is that he is doing the talking, rather than that they are doing the listening; the latter circumstance achieves prominence in section 8 below.) The argument that follows is the same as that given above, by an unimpeachable criterion of identity for arguments: its major premise states the same principle and its minor premise carries the same factual claim:

> Children should be with their parents.
>
> I shall not return your child unless you pay me.
>
> So, you should pay me.

Notice, now, that, despite what we can assume to be the truth of its premises and the validity of its inference, discredit attaches to anyone who utters this argument in the foregoing interpersonal setting, even though uttering the same argument in impersonal form is, in most cases,[9] an innocent procedure. And there is, of course, no mystery about why the argument's presenter attracts discredit in the exhibited interpersonal case. He does so because the fact to which he appeals, which is that you will get your child back only if you pay, is one that he deliberately causes to obtain: he makes that true, and to make that true is morally vile.

When he presents the argument, the kidnapper shows himself to be awful, but it is hardly necessary for us to reflect on his utterance of the argument to convince ourselves that he merits disapproval. Independently of any such reflection, we amply realise that the kidnapper's conduct is wrong, and we need not be particularly scandalised by his frank avowal of it. Indeed, in certain instances a kidnapper's presentation of the argument will be a service to the parents, because sometimes his utterance of the argument's minor premise will, for the first time, put them in the picture about how to get their child back. One can even imagine a maybe slightly schizoid kidnapper suddenly thinking, 'Omigod, I've forgotten to tell the kid's parents!' and experiencing some concern for them, and for the child, in the course of that thought.

Yet although what is (mainly) bad about the kidnapper is not his voicing the argument, but his making its minor premise true, he should still be ashamed to voice the argument, just because he makes that premise true. The fact that in some cases he would do further ill not to voice the argument does not falsify the claim that in all cases he reveals himself to be ghastly when he does voice it.

In the kidnapper argument, there are two groups of agents, the kidnapper and the parents, both referred to in the third person in the initial presentation of the argument, and referred to in the first and second persons in its revised presentation. Consider any argument that refers to distinct groups of people, A and B. There are many different ways in which such an argument might be presented. It might be uttered by members of A or of B or of neither group, and it might be addressed to members of either group or of neither. And all of that applies to the incentive argument, with the groups being talented rich people on the one hand and the worst off on the other. In my treatment of the incentive argument I shall mainly be interested in the case where a talented rich person puts it forward, sometimes no matter to whom and sometimes where it matters that poor people are his audience; and at one point I shall consider the opposite case, where a poor person addresses the argument to a talented rich one.

The incentive argument has something in common with the kidnapper argument, even though there are major differences between withholding a hostage and withholding labour until one gets the money one desires. But before looking more carefully at similarities and contrasts between the kidnapper and incentive arguments, I want to explain why the word 'community' appears in my title.

5

In its familiar use, 'community' covers a multitude of conditions, and I shall introduce the particular condition that I have in mind by relating it to the concept of a *comprehensive justification*.

Most policy arguments contain premises about how people will act when the policy is, and is not, in force. Schemes for housing, health, education, and the economy typically operate by altering agents' feasible sets, and their justifications usually say what agents facing those sets can be expected to choose to do.

Consider, then, a policy, P, and an argument purportedly justifying it, one of whose premises specifies how a subset, S, of the population will act when P is not in force, and when it is. We engage in what might be called *comprehensive assessment* of the proferred justification of P when we ask whether the projected behaviour of the members of S is itself justified. And *comprehensive justification* of P obtains only if that behaviour is indeed justified.[10]

'We should do A because they will do B', may justify our doing A, but it does not justify it comprehensively if they are not justified in doing B, and we do not provide a comprehensive justification of our doing A if we set aside as irrelevant the question whether they are justified in doing B. Thus, insofar as we are expected to treat the incentive argument as though no question arises about the justification of the behaviour of the talented rich that its minor premise describes, what we are offered may be a justification, but it is not a comprehensive justification, of the incentives policy.

Now, a policy argument provides a comprehensive justification only if it passes what I shall call the *interpersonal test*. This tests how robust a policy argument is, by subjecting it to variation with respect to who is speaking and/or who is listening when the argument is presented. The test asks whether the argument could serve as a justification of a mooted policy when uttered by any member of society to any other member. So, to carry out the test, we hypothesise an utterance of the argument by a specified individual, or, more commonly, by a member of a specified group, to another individual, or to a member of another, or indeed, the same, group. If, *because* of who is presenting it, and/or to whom it is presented, the argument cannot serve as a justification of the policy, then whether or not it passes as such under other dialogical conditions, it fails (*tout court*) to provide a comprehensive justification of the policy.

A salient way that arguments fail, when put to this test, is that the speaker cannot fulfil a demand for justification that does not arise when the argument is presented by and/or to others. So, to anticipate what I shall try to show, the incentive argument does not serve as a justification of inequality on the lips of the talented rich, because they cannot answer a demand for justification that naturally arises when they present the argument, namely, *why* would you work less hard if income tax were put back up to 60 per cent? The rich will find that question difficult no matter who puts it to them, but I shall often focus on the case where their interlocutors are badly off people, because, in that setting, the question, and the difficulty the rich have with it, may lead to further dialogical development that carries further illumination.

When the justification of policies that mention groups of people is presented in the usual way, with exclusively third-person reference to groups and their members, the propriety of the question why various people are disposed to act as they do is not always apparent. It becomes evident when we picture the relevant people themselves rehearsing the argument, and sometimes more so when the audience is a strategically selected one. The test of interpersonal presentation makes vivid that the justification of policy characteristically depends on circumstances that are not exogenous with respect to human agency.

And so to community. I began by observing that there is more than one kind of community, and I must now specify the kind that is relevant to present concerns. First, though, a few points about the semantics of the word 'community'.

Like 'friendship', 'community' functions both as a count noun and as a mass noun. It is a count noun when it denotes sets of people variously bound or connected (the European community, London's

Italian community, our community) and it is a mass noun when we speak of how much community there is in a certain society, when we say that some action enhances or reduces, or some attitude honours or violates, community, and so on.

A community, one could say, is a set of people among whom there is community: that is how the count-notion and the mass-notion are linked. 'Community' is in this respect like 'friendship': a friendship is a relationship in which friendship obtains. Notice that friends can do and feel things that are inconsistent with friendship without thereby dissolving their friendship. There can be a lapse of friendship in a friendship without that friendship ceasing to be. But there cannot (enduringly) be *no* friendship in a friendship. And all that is also true of community: there can be violations and lapses of community in a community, but there cannot be no community in a community.

In addition to a community in the adjectivally unqualified sense where it is analogous not only in form but also in content to friendship, there are specific types of community, some of which do, while others do not, contribute to community in the just denoted sense. And types of community (mass-wise) distinguish types of community (count-wise). Linguistic community, or community of language, constitutes a linguistic community as such; community of nationality establishes a national community; and community of interest in stamps binds the philatelic community.

The form of community that concerns me here, which I shall call *justificatory community*, prevails in justificatory communities. And justificatory community, though something of a concocted notion, contributes to community *tout court*, that is, to community in the full (adjectivally unqualified) sense sketched a moment ago. A justificatory community is a set of people among whom there prevails a norm (which need not always be satisfied) of comprehensive justification. If what certain people are disposed to do when a policy is in force is part of the justification of that policy, it is considered appropriate, in such a community, to ask them to justify the relevant behaviour, and it detracts from justificatory community when they cannot do so. It follows that an argument for a policy satisfies the requirement of justificatory community, with respect to the people it mentions, only if it passes the interpersonal test. And if all arguments for the policy fail that test, then the policy itself evinces lack of justificatory community, whatever else might nevertheless be said in its favour.

Now, an argument fails the interpersonal test, and is therefore inconsistent with community, if relevant agents *could* not justify the behaviour the argument ascribes to them. What if the agents are actually asked to justify their stance and, for one reason or another, they refuse to do so? Then the argument in question does not necessarily fail the test, for it might be that they could justify their stance. But if their reason for refusing to justify it is that they do not think themselves accountable to their interrogators, that they do not think that they *need* provide a justification, then they are forswearing community with the rest of us in respect of the policy issue in question. They are asking us to treat them like a set of Martians in the light of whose predictable aggressive, or even benign, behaviour it is wise for us to take certain steps, but with whom we should not expect to engage in justificatory dialogue.

To employ the interpersonal test and to regard its failure as indicative of a lack of community is to presuppose nothing about which particular collections of people constitute communities in the relevant sense. Some may think that there is no reason why there should be community between rich and poor in a society, and they may therefore regard failure of the test as uninteresting, or, if interesting, then not because it shows lapse of community. Others, by contrast, might think that community ought to obtain among all human beings, so that it would stain a policy argument advanced by rich countries in North-South dialogue if it could not pass muster in explicit I-thou form.[11] The thesis associated with the interpersonal test is that, if a policy justification fails it, then anyone proposing that justification in effect represents the people it mentions as *pro tanto* out of community with one another. Whether they should be in community with one another is a separate question. That depends on a doctrine, not to be articulated here, about what the proper boundaries of a community are. In my own (here undefended) view, it diminishes the democratic character of a society if it is not a community in the present sense, since we do not make policy *together* if we make it in the light of what some of us do that cannot be justified to others.

It is often said that it is unrealistic to expect a modern society to be a community, and it is no doubt inconceivable that there should be a standing disposition of warm mutual identification between any pair of citizens in a large and heterogeneous polity. But community here is not some soggy mega-*Gemeinschaftlichkeit*. Instead, my claim about the incentive justification is that, to appropriate a phrase of Rawls, it does not supply 'a public basis in the light of which citizens can

justify to one another their common institutions' and that the justification is therefore incompatible with what Rawls calls 'ties of civic
friendship'.[12]

Now some examples of the battery of concepts introduced above.

Under the premiership of Harold Wilson, some economic policies
were justified by reference to the intentions of the so-called 'gnomes
of Zurich', the international bankers who, it was said, would react
punitively to various government decisions. It was a mark of their
foreign status that economic policy had to *placate* those bankers,
and although it might have been thought that they should behave
differently, it would not have been considered appropriate for the
British government to call upon them to do so. But such a call would
surely be appropriate in the case of people conceived as belonging to
our community. Nor should members of our own community need to
be *placated* by our community's policies: when justified, their demands
should be satisfied, but that is a different matter.

An example that for some readers may be close to home: the policy
argument that rates of pay to British academics should be raised, since
otherwise they will succumb to the lure of high foreign salaries. We
can suppose that academics are indeed disposed to leave the country
because of current salary levels. The issue of whether, nevertheless,
they should emigrate is pertinent to the policy argument when they
are regarded as fellow members of community who owe the rest a
justification for decisions that affect the welfare of the country. And
many British academics with an inclination to leave who put the
stated policy argument contrive to avoid that issue by casting the
minor premise of the argument in the third person. They say:
'Academics will go abroad', not: 'We'll go abroad.'

The connection between shared community membership and
being open to requests for justification comes out nicely in an example
of current interest. The Georgian President, Eduard Shevardnadze,
might address the Abkhaz independence movement leaders as
follows:

> Widespread bloodshed is to be avoided. If you persist in your drive
> for independence, we shall intervene forcefully, and there will be
> widespread bloodshed as a result. You should therefore abandon
> your drive for independence.

The Abkhaz leaders might now ask the Georgian government to
justify its conditional intention to intervene forcefully. If the Georgians

brush that question aside, they forswear justificatory community with the Abkhazians.

The Abkhaz leaders might produce a parallel argument:

> Widespread bloodshed is to be avoided. If you intervene forcefully, we shall nevertheless persist in our drive for independence, and there will be widespread bloodshed as a result. You should therefore abandon your plan to intervene forcefully.

And the Abkhazians, too, might feel no obligation to justify their intentions to the Georgians. If, on the other hand, both sides labour under such a sense of obligation, they will enter a justificatory exchange in which each tries to show that the other's minor premise, whether true or not, should be false.

6

The interpersonal test focuses on an utterance of an argument, but what it tests, through examination of that utterance, is the argument itself. If lack of community is displayed when the rich present the incentive argument, then the argument itself (irrespective of who affirms it) represents relations between rich and poor as at variance with community. It follows, if I am right, that the incentive argument can justify inequality only in a society where interpersonal relations lack a communal character, in the specified sense.

Sometimes, as, for example, in the kidnapper case, the interpersonal test will be a roundabout way of proving an already evident point (in the kidnapper case, that there is significant lack of community between the kidnapper and the parents). But in other cases the test will illuminate, and I believe that the incentive argument is one of them. The argument is generally presented in thoroughly third-personal terms and, relatedly, as though no question arises about the attitudes and choices of the rich people it mentions. When, by contrast, we imagine a talented rich person himself affirming the argument, then background issues of equality and obligation come clearly into view and, if I am right, the rich are revealed to be out of community with the poor in respect of the economic dimension of their lives. So we see more deeply into the character of the incentive argument when we cast it in the selected I-thou terms.

Now, an important qualification. I say that the incentive argument shows itself to be repugnant to community when it is offered *on its own* by well-off people. I insert that phrase because the present case against the argument lapses when the argument appears in combination with claims about desert, and/or with Nozick-like claims about a person's entitlements to the reward his or her labour would command on an unfettered market. I do not myself accept that sort of compound justification of incentive inequality, but I do not here contend that it fails the interpersonal test. My target here is the unadorned or naked use of the incentive justification. It is often used nakedly, and with plenty of emphasis that it is being used nakedly. That emphasis occurs when advocates say it is an advantageous feature of the incentive justification that it employs no controversial moral premises about desert or entitlement. (Notice that, since John Rawls rejects use of desert and entitlement to justify inequalities, the Rawlsian endorsement of incentives takes what I call a naked form.)

The sequence of claims that I make goes as follows: The talented rich cannot justify the fact that the minor premise of the (naked) incentive argument is true. If they cannot justify the truth of its minor premise, then they cannot use the argument as a justification of inequality. If they cannot use it as a justification of inequality, then it cannot be used as a justification within community. If it cannot be used as a justification within community, then anyone who uses it (in effect) represents society as at variance with community when he does so.

Testing the incentive argument

7

The kidnapper argument discredits its advocate when the kidnapper puts it forward himself because, as I said, he *makes* it true that the parents get their child back only if they pay, and to make that true is morally vile.

Accordingly, to discredit first-person affirmation of the incentive argument in a parallel way, I must defend two claims. First, that in a sufficiently similar sense, the rich *make* it true that they will not work as hard at 60 per cent tax as they do at 40 per cent: I have to show that the minor premise[13] of the incentive argument owes its truth to their decisions and intentions. (I say *sufficiently* similar, because there undoubtedly are some significant differences here, consequent on the fact that the rich are not an individual but a group, and a group with shifting membership: at the end of this section I address some of the complication which that fact generates.) And it also needs to be shown that, deprived as they here are of recourse to the considerations of desert and entitlement that are set aside in a naked use of the incentive argument, the rich cannot justify making the stated proposition true. I am not, of course, obliged to maintain, even then, that their making it true puts them on a moral par with kidnappers, but just that, if their posture is defensible, then its defence rests on grounds of the sort that a naked user of the incentive argument forgoes.

I turn to my first task, which is to show that the talented rich do make the factual premise of the argument true. Let us ask: if that premise is true, then why is it true? Is it true because the rich are *unable* to work at 60 per cent as hard as they do at 40? Or is it true because they are *unwilling* to work that hard at 60 per cent? If the truth of the premise reflects inability, then we cannot say that, in the relevant sense, the rich *make* the premise true. An inability explanation of the truth of the premise means that the rich could not, by choosing differently, make the premise false.

There are two forms that an inability claim might take. In the first form of the claim, the rich cannot work hard unless they consume things that cost a great deal of money.

Now, it might well be true that without enough money to buy superior relaxation some high-talent performances would be impossible: perhaps the massively self-driving executive does need, to be effective, more expensive leisure between one day's work and the next than he can get living in ordinary accommodation on an average wage. (When I say that he might *need* high-quality leisure, I refer not to his preference ordering or utility function but to what it is physically and/or psychologically possible for him to do. That kind of capacity limitation interacts causally with a person's utility function, but it is not identical with it or an aspect of it.) But the income gap which that consideration would justify is surely only a fraction of the one that obtains even at 60 per cent top tax. The extra money which executives (and so forth) get at 40 per cent can hardly be required to finance whatever luxuries we might imagine that they strictly *need* to perform at a high level: they could afford those necessary luxuries with what they have left even when they pay a 60 per cent tax.

In a different version of the claim that the rich could not work as hard at 60 per cent tax as they do at 40 per cent, what they are said to need is not the goods that only a lot of money will buy but the *prospect* of getting those goods or that money: the high reward is now said to be indispensable to *motivation*, or morale. (You eventually give the biscuit to the performing dog so that the same procedure will work again next time, and not because the dog needs the calories it gets from the biscuit to enable it to go on performing.) This motivation story does not say that, unless they are handsomely paid, the rich will *choose* not to work very hard: the proposition that they have a real choice in the matter is just what the inability claim is designed to contradict. What is rather meant is that the allure of big bucks sustains, and is needed to sustain, the motivational drive required for heavy effort: the rich just cannot *get* themselves to work as hard when they expect to be taxed at 60 per cent as they can get themselves to work when they expect to be taxed at 40 per cent.

Now, in my opinion, there is not much truth in this contention: it represents people of talent as more feeble than, on the whole, they are. It is not likely to be lack of power to do otherwise that causes the rich to take longer holidays, to knock off at five instead of at six, or not to bother trying to get one more order, those being the things that they do when the income tax rises, if the minor premise of the incentive argument is true. The tax rise means that the rich face a new and less appealing schedule of the costs and benefits of alternative courses of action, and they will, of course, find it harder to raise up enthusiasm for choices that now promise smaller rewards. It does not follow that they cannot make, and effectively pursue, those choices.

Still, I say that there is not much, not no, truth in the contention mooted here. For I recognise that a perception that reward is 'too low' can cause, at least somewhat independently of the will, a morose reluctance which operates as a drag on performance. But we should ask what brings about that disabling perception. And if two of its prominent causes were its only causes, then, as I shall now try to explain, the 'motivation' version of the inability contention would be disqualified.

One thing that causes a dispiriting feeling that reward is too low is disappointed expectation. Socialised as they have been in a severely unequal society, the talented rich of course anticipate a handsome return for their exertions. They will therefore be downcast when such return is not forthcoming, even when they do not judge that they deserve or are otherwise entitled to it. But it is not unlikely that they also do make judgements like that. They think that they have a right to golden rewards if they work hard, and so powerful is that belief that it can act as a further cause of low morale: it can make the thought of working hard at 60 per cent tax fill them with a truly disabling dismay.

Now, an inability to work hard at 60 per cent tax (in people who, *ex hypothesi*, routinely work that hard at 40 per cent) that reflects habituated expectation, or judgement of entitlement, or both, cannot count here, in rebuttal of the claim that optional decisions of the talented rich make the minor premise of the incentive argument true. Consider, first, the habituation factor. We are here engaged in a ground-level investigation of a certain justification of inequality. It is therefore inappropriate, by way of contribution to that justification, to cite mere habituation to unequal rewards. Habits can change,[14] and they are therefore beside the point in a fundamental inquiry. And the causal force of belief in the rightness of high reward (which helps to sustain the habitual expectation) must also be ignored here. For we are here envisaging the talented rich uttering the incentive argument in its naked form, in which invocation of entitlement is pointedly eschewed. There would, accordingly, be a kind of pragmatic inconsistency if the rich had to cite their own belief in entitlement when rejecting the claim that the truth of the minor premise of the argument reflects what they are themselves willing and unwilling to do.[15]

If the 'motivation' variant of the inability claim depended entirely on habit and normative belief, we could safely set it aside. We could say that if it is true, it is compromised in the present context by what its truth rests on, that it does not furnish an appropriate reason for saying that talented rich people could not work as hard at 60 per cent tax as they do at 40. The claim might help to silence moralistic charges against the present generation of talented rich people, but it could not contribute to a robust vindication of inequality in human society.

Now I firmly believe that such truth as the inability claim possesses does depend, entirely, on factors of habit and ideology that, for the stated reasons, must here be ruled out. I think it hard to believe otherwise, when one focuses on the inability claim proper, as opposed to the claim, with which it is readily confused, that the talented rich have a *right* not to work as hard at 60 per cent tax as they do at 40 per cent. Nevertheless, I have not shown that there exist no relevant deeper restrictions on motivation, and I acknowledge that there is much more to be said about this matter.[16]

With that *caveat* in place, I now set the motivation claim aside, and I conclude that the reason why the minor premise of the incentive argument is true (if it is true) is that the executive and his like are *willing* to work hard only at a 40 per cent top tax rate.

But, before we ask whether that choice is justified, let me address the complication that, even if each talented individual chooses not to work hard at a 60 per cent tax, no such individual makes the minor premise of the incentive argument true, since its truth requires that many such individuals make similar choices. Here, then, is a disanalogy with the case of the kidnapper, since he makes the minor premise of his argument true all by himself.

In response to this important point, I shall say only two things here. First, notice that an individual talented rich person is relevantly analogous to a member of a large band of kidnappers, who could also truthfully say: it will make no, or not much, difference if I change my choice. Yet, if a member of such a band puts the kidnapper argument in the first-person plural, if he says. 'Giving *us* the money is the only way you will get your child back', then the fact that he is only (a dispensable) one of the 'us' who together ensure that the child is held captive does not make his posture justifiable. And it is similarly true that if what the rich together cause could not be justified if one rich person caused it, then being only one rich person and not all of them would not suffice to make one's behaviour justifiable. One might not be *as* responsible as when one achieves something without assistance, but one also could not say that the result had nothing to do with one's actions.[17]

And whatever the complex truth may be about individual responsibility for a collectively produced result, I am not here primarily interested in commenting on the moral character of rich people. My primary interest is in an argument which, I claim, fails the interpersonal test. Rich people may benefit from a practice on which they have little occasion to reflect. If we here (counter-factually) imagine them trying to justify that practice by recourse to the incentive argument, it is in order to investigate not, in the first instance, how blameworthy they are, but how that argument fares in the light of a norm of justificatory community.

8

In its standard presentation, the incentive argument is put forward as though it is irrelevant to its assessment whether the rich are justified in making its minor premise true, and as though it would be inappropriate to put that question to them. I have protested that the question can be considered inappropriate only if the rich are conceived as inaccessible third persons who do not belong to the society for which the incentive policy is proposed. It does not follow that what the rich do could not be justified, that the neglected question, having been raised, could not be answered satisfactorily. In this section I explore possible answers to it.

The relevant part of the premise (that is, part (a)) says that, if the top tax rises to 60 per cent, the talented rich will work less hard than they do now, when the top tax is 40 per cent. And, so we have concluded, that is because they will then *choose* to work less hard. As a result of that choice, the badly off will be worse off than they were before (by the truth of part (b) of the minor premise of the incentive argument), and, *a fortiori*, worse off than they would be if the talented rich maintained at 60 per cent tax the effort they put in at 40 per cent. On the factual assumptions behind the minor premise of the argument, the ordering of benefit to the badly off from the three work/tax packages just mentioned is as follows:

(a) The talented rich work w at 60 per cent tax
(b) The talented rich work w at 40 per cent tax
(c) The talented rich work $w-x$ at 60 per cent tax,

where w is the amount the rich choose to work at 40 per cent and x the amount by which they reduce their input if the tax rises to 60 per cent.

We must now ask whether the choices of rich people, which make (c) rather than (a) true if the tax rises, and thereby make the badly off worse off than when the tax is low, can be justified, when notions of desert and entitlement are not allowed to figure in justifications.

In certain cases, where working just as hard at 60 per cent tax as one did at 40 per cent would mean an oppressive existence, the choice that the rich make is undoubtedly justified. Think of those harried and haggard Yuppies, or overworked surgeons, who really would lead miserable lives if the massive amount of work that they do were not compensated by the massive amount of income that leads them to choose to work that hard. We can set such 'special burden' cases aside, not because they do not exist, but because of the nature of the justification of the talented rich person's choice in this sort of case.

Let me explain. In the present exercise, the incentive argument is supposed to justify inequality. But when special burden is invoked, what we get is not a justification of an inequality, all things considered, that incentives produce, but a denial that they do produce an inequality, all things considered. That is so because, when we compare people's material situations, we must take into account not only the income they get but also what they have to do to get it. Accordingly, if the talented rich could plausibly claim special burden, the move to the 40 per cent tax which induced them to work harder might also be required for the sake of equality: where work is specially arduous, or stressful, higher remuneration is a counterbalancing equaliser, on a sensible view of how to judge whether or not things are equal. Since I oppose only those incentives that induce unambiguous inequalities, my opposition retires in face of the special burden case, and I acknowledge that, where special burden holds, the rich have a persuasive answer to the question why they make the minor premise of the incentive argument true.

My primary target, as a philosopher, is a pattern of justification, from which the incentive argument deviates when special burden holds. But, as a politically engaged person, I also have another target: the real-world inequality that is actually defended on incentive grounds. And because I also have that second target, I have to claim that the special burden case is statistically uncommon. But I do not find that difficult to do, since I am confident that, if talented rich people were to provide, at 60 per cent tax, the greater effort we are supposing them to supply at 40 per cent, then a large majority of them would still have not only higher incomes but also more fulfilling jobs than ordinary people enjoy.[18]

Since I propose to cast no doubt on the truth of the minor premise of the incentive argument, I must now set aside another case, that in which well-paid talented people so enjoy their work or are so dedicated to making money that they would actually work no less hard after a tax rise. Such people are bluffing if, in the hope of inducing a political effect, they announce that a tax rise would lead them to work less. But in their case, and, *a fortiori*, in the case of talented people whose labour supply curve is in the relevant range not merely vertical but backward-bending, the minor premise of the incentive argument is false, since these people will *not* work less hard if the tax goes up, and this case is therefore out of bounds here.

Summarising and extending the foregoing discussion, I now ask you to look at a table that depicts three positions that the talented rich person might be thought to be in. Of the three cases that appear in the table, two are, for different reasons, irrelevant to our purposes, the special burden case because it poses no problem for the egalitarian point of view (and is in any event not widely instantiated), and the case of bluff, because in that case the minor premise of the incentive argument is false. So, from now on, let us focus on what is called the standard case in the table.

In the table, w denotes the amount which the rich actually work at 40 per cent, and $w-x$ denotes some significantly smaller amount. In all three cases, the rich prefer working w at 40 per cent to working $w-x$ at 60 per cent. This preference may not be readily apparent, but we can demonstrate[19] that they have it. For they choose to work w, rather than $w-x$, when the tax is 40 per cent, and they must prefer $w-x$ at 40 per cent to $w-x$ at 60, since work is the same and income is higher in the first package. It follows that the rich prefer working harder at 40 per cent to working less hard at 60.

Benefit to the (currently) badly off	Preference orderings of the rich across three work/tax packages
	The standard case
2	Work w at 40 per cent
3	Work $w-x$ at 60 per cent
1	Work w at 60 per cent (and be much better off than others are)
	The bluff case
2	Work w at 40 per cent
1	Work w at 60 per cent
3	Work $w-x$ at 60 per cent (and be much better off than others are)
	The special burden case
2	Work w at 40 per cent
3	Work $w-x$ at 60 per cent
1	Work w at 60 per cent (and be worse off than others are as a result)

The preference orderings of the rich are identical in the standard and special burden cases. The differences between those cases (which is formulated in parentheses) lies in the comparison between the lot of the rich and that of other people when the rich are at the bottom of their preference ordering. This comparison reflects both income level and quality of work experience: were they to work as hard at 60 per cent as they do at 40, the rich would in the special burden case be worse off than others are, but in the standard case they would still be much better off than others are. The ordering of benefit to the badly off from the various work/tax packages (which is given by the numbers in the column on the left, and which is the same in all three cases) is based on the assumption that part (b) of the minor premise of the incentive argument is true (so 'w at 40 per cent' ranks above 'w–x at 60 per cent') and on the further assumption that, if the rich worked as hard at 60 as they do at 40, then that would bring still further benefit to the poor (so 'w at 60 per cent' ranks above 'w at 40 per cent').

The interpersonal test has talented rich people *themselves* uttering the incentive argument. Now, for present purposes, the talented rich do not fall under the bluff case, in which the minor premise is false: they really will work less if the tax goes up. And, if we follow a distinction that has found favour with philosophers, the rich do not *threaten* anything if they utter the incentive argument since, in the recommended distinction, you merely *warn* that you will do A when you are bent on doing A independently of the leverage you get from saying that you will do it. Notice that, in the recommended distinction, a kidnapper who likes children merely *warns* if he would actually prefer (for non-strategic reasons) to keep the child if he is not paid: this shows that, under the recommended distinction, non-threatening warnings can be very unpleasant.

So imagine, now, a set of highly paid managers and professionals addressing poorly paid workers, unemployed people, and people indigent for various personal and situational reasons, who depend on state welfare. The managers are lobbying against a rise in tax from 40 to 60 per cent, and this is what they say:

> Public policy should make the worst-off people (in this case, as it happens, you) better off.

> If the top tax goes up to 60 per cent, we shall work less hard and, as a result, the position of the poor (your position) will be worse.

> So, the top tax on our income should not be raised to 60 per cent.

Although these argument-uttering rich may not, for one or other reason, count as *threatening* the poor, they remain people of superior income and form of life who could continue to work as now if the tax rose to 60 per cent, and thereby bring more benefit to the poor, while still being much better off than they are, but who would refuse to do that. They say, in effect: we are unwilling to do what we could do to make you better off and yet still be much better off, ourselves, than you are. We realise that, at the present level of fuel allowance, many of you will be very cold this winter.[20] If the tax went up to 60 per cent and we worked no less hard in response, revenue for fuel expenditure could rise, and some of you would be more comfortable. But in fact we would work less, and you would be worse off, following such a tax rise.

Having presented this argument, the rich are not well placed to answer a poor person who asks: 'Given that you would still be much better off than we are if you worked as you do now at the 60 per cent tax, what justifies your intention to work less if the tax rises to that level?' For these rich people do not say that they deserve a lot because of their prodigious effort, or merit more because of their higher contribution to production. There is in their approach no appeal to such controversial moral premises, and many of them would think that, being free of such premises, their argument is consequently less vulnerable. And they cannot respond by saying that the money inequality which they defend is necessary to make the poor better off, since it is they who make it necessary, and the question put by the poor asks, in effect, what their justification is for making it necessary.

The incentive argument does furnish the poor with a reason to accept the inequality that it recommends. For the poor can take it as given that the rich are determined to sustain the intentions that make the argument work. But the argument cannot operate like that for the rich themselves: since they cannot treat their own choices as objective data, they cannot take it as given that the minor premise of the argument is true. Correspondingly, and unlike the poor, they need a justification not for accepting but for imposing the inequality that the argument defends.

But it might be said that the rich can indeed respond convincingly to the poor, and without advancing the controversial claims about desert and entitlement that are here ruled out. They can say: 'Look, it simply would not be worth our while to work that hard if the tax rate were any higher, and if you were in our shoes you would feel the same way.'[21] Would that not be a good answer to the question the poor pose?

As I shall presently allow, there is some power in this answer. But its rhetorical cast makes it seem more powerful than it is.

Notice, to begin with, that the first part ('Look ... higher') of the quoted plea has no independent interest, no interest, that is, which is independent of the associated claim that the poor, if better placed, would feel (and act) as the rich do now. For it is a presupposition of the challenge which the poor put to the rich that the latter do prefer, and intend, to work less hard if the tax goes up, and in speaking of what is 'worth their while' the rich can only be reminding the poor of those preferences and intentions: they cannot mean, for example, that they are paid nothing, or paid badly, if they work hard at a 60 per cent rate of tax.

So the burden of the rhetorically presented justificatory move is that a typical poor person would behave just as the rich, on the whole, do. But there is something that the poor person can say in reply. He can say: 'Neither of us really knows how I would behave. Not all rich people market maximise as a matter of course, and I hope that, if I were rich, I would not belong to the vast majority that do, especially if I retained a lively sense of what it is like to be in the condition I am now actually in.' (A slave need not be impressed when a master says: 'Had you been born into the slaveholder class, you too would have lived well and treated your slaves like slaves.' Such counterfactual predictions do not show that what people at a certain social level typically choose to do is justifiable.[22])

Suppose now, that the rich abandon the vivid but problematic 'you'd do the same in my shoes', style of justification. Suppose they just just say (this being the content of the text to note 21, without its rhetorical cast) that, even when desert and entitlement are set aside, only an extreme moral rigorist could deny that *every person has a right to pursue self-interest to some reasonable extent* (even when that makes things worse than they need be for badly-off people).

I do not wish to reject the italicised principle, which affirms what Samuel Scheffler has called an 'agent-centered prerogative'.[23] But a modest right of self-interest seems insufficient to justify the range of inequality, the extremes of wealth and poverty, that actually obtain in the society under discussion. Entitlement or desert might justify vast differences between rich and poor: no limit to the inequality they might endorse is inscribed in them. This is particularly clear in the case of the entitlement principle that I am absolute owner of my own labour power. When my power to produce is conceived as fully private property, I may do with it as I will and demand what I may for its use. A proportionately greater attention to one's own interest, as opposed to that of others, is more limited in its justificatory reach, and it seems unlikely to justify the existing contrast of luxury and want.

Now, it might be objected that in characterising the position of the less well off as one of deprivation or want, I am unfairly tilting the balance against the incentive argument. To such an objection I have two replies.

First, I am in this part concerned with a real political use of the incentive argument. Reference to real circumstances is therefore entirely appropriate.

Second, the incentive argument is quite general. It should therefore apply no matter how badly off the badly off are, both absolutely and relatively, to the well off. Accordingly, it is methodologically proper to focus on particularly dramatic cases of its application.

And it is precisely when the condition of the badly off is especially wretched that the *major* premise of the incentive argument can pass as compelling. Where the worst off are not too badly off, it looks more fanatical to assign absolute priority to their claims. But the stronger the case for ameliorating the situation of the badly off is, the more discreditable (if I am right) the incentive argument is on the lips of the rich. So the argument is most shameful where, at first sight, it is most apt.

9

The incentive argument is not problematic (in the particular way that I say it is) when it is thought acceptable to view the rich as outside the community to which the poor belong. But sometimes, in Britain anyway, many of the rich themselves are eager to invoke community, when for example, they react with (real or fake) horror to militant agitation among the poor. (Maybe some of the rich think that 'belong to the same community as' denotes a non-symmetrical relation.)

Of course, particular talented people can affirm the incentive argument without difficulty, by declaring that they personally lack the disposition attributed to members of their class in the argument. But if the argument is going to pass muster as a justification of unequal reward within community, then putting it forward in the first person, and without such disavowal, should not be problematic.

In the third person, the minor premise of the argument just predicts how the rich will behave, and it can show misunderstanding of the speaker's message to demand a justification of that behaviour: the speaker is not reponsible for it, and he might himself be disposed to condemn it. But to affirm the minor premise of the argument with full first-person force is to declare, or, what suffices for present purposes, to manifest, an intention, and a demand for justification is therefore in order. Observe the difference between these two interchanges, each of which follows assertion of the minor premise of the argument to a poor person, in the first case *by* a poor person, or by some third party.

> Poor person: But they, the rich, should not demand so much.
> Reply: That has nothing to do with me. The fact is that they do.

That is a valid reply to the poor person's lament. But now consider an analogous interchange following a first-person presentation of the premise:

> Poor person: But you, the rich, should not demand so much.
> Reply: That has nothing to do with me. The fact is that we (I, and the others) do.

Here the very incoherence of the reply confirms the aptness of the challenge against which it strains.

Finding it difficult to provide a convincing reply, the rich may represent their own optional attitudes and decisions *as* given facts. They might say to the poor, 'Look, we all have to accept the reality of the situation.' Yet it is not an exogenous reality which they are asking the poor to recognise. In this rhetoric of the rich, a declaration of intention masquerades as a description of something beyond choice: the rich present *themselves* in third-personal terms, in alienation from their own agency.[24]

For an analogous self-misrepresentation, consider how absurd it would be for the kidnapper to say: 'Gee, I'm sorry, but the fact is that unless you pay I will not release your child.' If he says that in factual style, and not as a piece of macabre humour, his remark expresses an estrangement from his own intention which means that he is crazy.

And I believe that there is also something weird going on when the will of a class is depicted by its members as *just* a sociological fact. The rich man sits in his living room, and he explains, in a detached style that says that *his* choices have nothing to do with the matter, why the poor should vote against higher taxes on the rich. Here, too, there is alienation, but, because it is less obvious than the alienation of the single kidnapper whom I just portrayed, you do not have to be completely crazy to slip into it. It is easy to slip into *this* alienation because each rich person's individual choice lacks salience, lost as it is among the millions of similar choices typical of members of his class: he participates in a practice so familiar that it gets treated as part of, or on a par with, the course of nature. In a reflective moment he might be appalled by the situation of the badly off, but he reifies the intentions of rich people (his own included), which frustrate their claim to priority, into hard data which social policy must take as parametric. He is unalive to the fact that his own decisions contribute to the condition he describes, a condition which is the upshot of a vast number of personal choices, but which he describes in the impersonal discourse of sociology or economics.

Recall the crazy kidnapper, who says, 'Gee, I'm sorry.' The child's parents might display a corresponding craziness. They do so if they treat the kidnapper's intention as an objective fact not only for them but even for him. And then they think of his demand as just what they happen to have to pay to get their child back, and maybe one of them says to the kidnapper, as to a possibly sympathetic bystander: 'Well, £5,000 *is* a lot of money, as I'm sure you'll agree, but it's less, after all, than what it cost to have Sally's adenoids removed, and, as you've pointed out, it is her *life* that's at stake.'

And these reflections also have a bearing on the incentive argument. I have said that the incapacity of that argument to serve as a justification for inequality when the rich present it to the poor shows that the argument presupposes a lack of community between them. And I have just now also said that when the rich deliver it in a certain cast or tone, they imply that they do not qualify as choosing human agents. In considering that second point, it may be instructive to contemplate a presentation of the incentive argument that we have not yet considered, one in which a poor person addresses a set of rich ones. Now the minor premise will say: if the top tax rises to 60 per cent, *you* will work less hard, and we shall consequently be worse off. If the poor speaker says that in an objective tone of voice, his rich listeners might, as a result, feel the weirdness that comes when someone predicts your behaviour as though you have no control over it. Some of the listeners might even protest: 'Hey, wait a minute. We would like at least to *try* not to work less if the tax rises.' And the poor speaker might counter: 'You're not likely to stick to that resolution. *Please* vote against the tax rise.' In his insistence on the truth of the incentive argument's minor premise, this poor person would be setting his face against community, or against the capacity for agency of his listeners, or against both.

NOTES

1. To be more precise, they reject those principles *at the relevant fundamental level*. The qualification is necessary because Left-wing liberals recognise desert and entitlement as (derivative) rules of legitimate reward in schemes of contribution and compensation which are not *grounded* in notions of desert and entitlement. See John Rawls, *A Theory of Justice* (Cambridge: Harvard University Press, 1971) pp. 103, 310–15; and Thomas Scanlon, 'The Significance of Choice', in *The Tanner Lectures on Human Values*, Vol. 8 (Salt Lake City: University of Utah Press, 1988) pp. 188, 203. For a recent statement of nuanced views on desert and entitlement, see John Rawls, *Justice as Fairness: A Briefer Restatement* (Cambridge: Harvard University, 1989, manuscript), pp. 54, sec. 2, and 57 n. 34; I do not understand the doctrine presented in the latter place.
2. For extensive use of this principle, see F. A. Hayek, *The Constitution of Liberty* (Chicago: University of Chicago Press, 1960), Chap. 3, and esp. pp. 44–49.
3. Strong support for that charge comes from *Punishing the Poor: Poverty under Thatcher*, by Kay Andrews and John Jacobs (London: Macmillan, 1990).
4. See Rawls, *A Theory of Justice*, pp. 15, 102, 151, 179, 546; Rawls, *Justice as Fairness*, pp. 57, 89.
5. Statements of the difference principle display ambiguity along two dimensions. There is the ambiguity remarked in the text above, between inequalities that *do not harm* and inequalities that *help* the badly off, and there is the further ambiguity between *mandated* and *permitted* inequalities. These distinctions generate the following matrix:

	Mandated		Permitted
Helping ones are	1	→	2
Non-harming ones are	3	→	4

Since what is mandated is permitted, and what helps does not harm, there exist the implications among possible interpretations of the principle indicated by the arrows above, and there are five logically possible positions about which inequalities are mandated and which allowed: all are mandated (1,2,3,4); helping ones are mandated, and others forbidden (1,2); none are mandated and only helping ones are permitted (2); none are mandated and all non-harming ones are permitted (2,4); helping ones are mandated and all non-harming ones are permitted (1,2,4). Rationales can be provided for each of these five points of view, and I believe that there are traces of all of them in the letter and/or spirit of various Rawlsian texts. (Although, as I have said, I take the difference principle in a form in which it allows *all* non-harming inequalities, my critique of Rawls is consistent with his holding any of the positions distinguished above: it depends only on his allowing helping inequalities and forbidding harming ones, and that stance is a constituent in each of the five positions.)

6. Although I shall press against Left-wing liberals the thought that community cannot tolerate the inequalities that they endorse, I need not deny that enormous inequalities co-existed with community in pre-market societies. For, if that was indeed true, then the co-existence was possible because of general acceptance, and, more particularly, because of acceptance by the less well off, of ideologies of destiny and place which Left-wing liberals do not countenance. That community can go with inequality when people believe things that liberals regard as false does not show that they can go together in a society possessed of a modern

consciousness.

7. We can also say that inequalities are necessary to improve the condition of the badly off when we take for granted, not, as above, causal, but moral imperatives. Thus incentives can indeed be judged necessary to raise the condition of the badly off when elements of the desert and entitlement rationales that Left-wing liberals reject are affirmed.

8. As opposed to the claim that it is true, which every presenter of the argument can be asked to justify.

9. I express myself in that cautious way because, apart from the case, if you want to allow it, in which the kidnapper himself uses the impersonal form of the argument, referring to himself as 'he', there is the case of a person who puts it forth and conveys (for example, by his tone) that he is quite insensitive to the counter-vailing (if properly overridden) considerations, and/or that he sees nothing untoward in the kidnapper's threat, and/or that he sees human dealings on the model of interaction of impersonal forces.

10. It follows, harmlessly, that penal policies adopted to reduce the incidence of crime lack comprehensive justification. The very fact that such a policy is justi-fied shows that all is not well with society.

11. *In Justice as Fairness* (p. 152, n. 28) Rawls expresses a view which has a bearing on how wide community can be: 'the allegiance to, or the motivational support needed, for the difference principle to be effective presupposes a degree of homogeneity among peoples and a sense of social cohesion and closeness that cannot be expected in a society of states.' This implies that there is sufficient such closeness domestically. (Three further contrasts between the single- and multi-society cases that Rawls sketches in the footnote seem to me to fail, but none of them matter here.)

12. John Rawls, 'Kantian Constructivism in Moral Theory', *Journal of Philosophy* 77, no. 9 (September 1980), p. 561; Rawls, *A Theory of Justice*, p. 536.

13. Or, strictly, part (*a*) of that premise: part (*b*) is true only if others – for example, the government – act in certain required ways. But for simplicity I shall continue to speak of the rich making the factual minor premise (*tout court*) true.

14. If not always at the level of the individual, then certainly at the social level, through reformed structures of education. And even if the relevant habits could not change, that would have more implications for the practice than for the theory of justice. As Rawls says, 'We do not consider the strains of commitment that might result from some people having to move from a favoured position in an unjust society to a less favoured position (either absolutely or relatively or both) in this just society. ... The strains of commitment test applied to cases of hypothetical transition from unjust societies is irrelevant' ('Reply to Alexander and Musgrave', *Quarterly Journal of Economics*, 1974, p. 653, and see Rawls, *Justice as Fairness*, p. 44, on the role of education in sustaining a just society: the relevant strains of commitment are those that survive a socialisation process that instils egalitarian principles in the young).

15. That particular inconsistency would not attach to naked use of the argument by a third party who cites (without endorsing) the belief of the rich in their entitle-ments as what happens to explain the truth of the argument's minor premise. But reference to that belief would nevertheless be unacceptable when the argument for inequality is pitched at a fundamental level. If the rich are unable to work as hard at 60 per cent tax as they do at 40 because they believe that they should be paid more if they work harder, then the stated incapacity cannot, without bizarre circularity, figure in an argument which would justify the proposition that it is *fundamentally right* that they be paid more for working harder.

16. Some of it is said in response to an acute criticism by Samuel Scheffler in paragraphs in the Tanner Lectures that are not reproduced here.

17. For a case which bears on the issue dealt with in the foregoing paragraph, see Derek Parfit's 'harmless torturers' at p. 80 of his *Reasons and Persons* (Oxford: Clarendon Press, 1984). If someone objects that the talented rich are unlike the just-imagined kidnappers in not being an organised group, then, so I believe, reflection on Parfit's case shows that they need not be one for my purposes. And one could also put forward a persuasive case of relevantly unorganised kidnappers, where all that is essential to the analogy is restored, but I shall spare you the rococo detail.

18. Anyone who dissents from that statistical assessment is invited to settle for the following more modest claim, which will suffice here: although it is difficult to tell how much any given individual enjoys or disenjoys his work, it is false that jobs demanding talent are, on the whole, less satisfying. Accordingly, the consideration of burden cannot justify the fact that on the whole they command much more pay.

It is an important point, for Rawls, that the talented are fortunate to be talented, and that is partly because the exercise of talent in work is satisfying. Accordingly, Rawlsians are not well placed to adduce the special burden consideration in support of the justice of incentives. As Robert Nozick remarks, 'Rawls is *not* imagining that inequalities are needed to fill positions that everyone can do equally well, or that the most drudgery-filled positions that require the least skill will command the highest income' (*Anarchy, State and Utopia* [New York: Basic Books, 1974], p. 188).

19. On the usual economists' assumptions, which are innocent here, that choice tracks preference, and that wide choice is preferred to narrow.

20. According to Robin Cook, MP, then Labour spokesman on health, in the severe winter of 1991 there were 4,000 more deaths of old people than are usual in such a period.

21. This piece of dialogue comes from Samuel Scheffler's seminar commentary on these lectures. Scheffler pressed the challenge to which the rest of this section is a response.

22. I have always thought that the right reply to a white South African who says, to an anti-apartheid advocate, 'You would see things differently if you were in my position', is: 'Quite: I'm sure it does blind one's vision.'

23. See his *Rejection of Consequentialism* (Oxford: Clarendon Press, 1982).

24. This is not a return of the inability claim, which we left behind in section 7. That claim acknowledges that the rich form and execute a set of intentions, but denies that they could form and/or execute certain alternative ones. In the motif of alienation, the very fact of intentional agency is concealed, or at least obscured.

Part Four:
The Enrichment of Identities

10

Citizenship and political obligation

BHIKHU PAREKH

In this chapter I intend to explore the nature and especially the content of political obligation. I shall argue that much of the traditional formulation of the problem of political obligation is narrow and biased, and shall reformulate it as an inquiry into the kinds of obligations citizens incur by virtue of their membership of a polity. I shall analyse the nature of the modern state and tease out both the kinds of relationship in which the citizens stand with respect of each other and the sorts of obligations they thereby acquire. Since this is a large inquiry I shall limit myself to a discussion of some of the citizen's important political obligations and say little about how their inescapable conflict can be resolved. And since my central concern is to map out a terrain that has long been ignored, I shall sometimes raise but not tackle large issues, nor push my arguments beyond a certain point, nor pause to counter all possible objections to them.

1

With such notable exceptions as Socrates, Aristotle, Cicero, Rousseau and the civic republicans, a large number of writers on political obligation have concentrated on why the citizen should obey the law or the civil authority.[1] In my view this is a deeply misleading way of approaching the subject. This is not pedantry, for the way we formulate a problem is never philosophically innocent. It crystallises, condenses and conceals important assumptions, and not only determines the questions we ask and the internal balance and orientation of our inquiry but also partially predetermines our answers. Unless we deconstruct it and learn to see or stress what it does not allow us to see or emphasise, we remain trapped within the narrow confines of these assumptions.

I suggest that this is the case with the traditional concentration on why one should obey the law.

First, it is not a question the ordinary citizen and even the political philosopher in his non-philosophical moods ever asks, not even in times of civil war. We know that every organised society requires a structure of authority, which should be generally obeyed if we are to lead peaceful and civilised lives. During a civil war there is by definition neither a civil authority nor the law, and therefore the question of obeying either cannot arise. People either help themselves as best they can or obey the strongest warlord. The questions that worry or should worry a morally sensitive citizen include such questions as what to do about the laws and government policies he disapproves of, whether or not to raise his voice against the injustices and inequalities of his society, whether it should matter to him how his fellow-citizens live, whether he should oppose a dubious war his government might have launched, why he should obey the laws which his rulers violate at will, if he has obligations to those outside his community, and whether he has a duty to participate in the conduct of public affairs. Since the question of why one should obey the law has no context, no basis in the consciousness and experiences of an identifiable body of men, no existential point of reference, and no audience, the discussion of it invariably becomes indeterminate, ill-focused, and unreal. We do not know *who* is asking the question, why, how and where he is situated in history, what his beliefs, values and modes of thought are, and what kind of answer will satisfy him.

Since we can answer an abstract question only in abstract terms, we explain political obligation in terms of such abstract principles as consent, fair play, gratitude and general happiness. And since the hypothetical individual is homogenised, we are required to assume that the basis of political obligation must be the same for all citizens. Not surprisingly, none of the abstract principles used to account for political obligation fully connects either with the social and political reality or with the different political biographies of the citizens.

The difficulties raised by the consent theory are too well known to need reiteration. Although it has been advocated by some of the finest minds in the past and present, none of them has been able to give a satisfactory account of what constitutes consent, how it can be inferred, to whom or to what one consents, why consent matters, what one may or may not consent to, what it entails and commits one to, whether it can ever be free when one is deeply shaped by the polity to which one is supposed to consent, and so on. It is striking that much of the consent-based account of political obligation tends to become quasi-theological, reading hidden meanings into citizens' actions and inactions and involving a good deal of casuistry, a sure sign of a theory lacking roots in reality. Theories based on fair play, gratitude, self-realisation and so on run into similar difficulties, and additionally face those created by the poverty, inequalities and injustices endemic in every society. Thanks to this, our theories of political obligation suffer from a double handicap. Since they fail to address the kinds of question that do or should trouble the morally serious citizen, they do not interest and guide him. And since they abstract away the historical particularities and detach the twin polarities of the individual and the law from the wider social context and the mediating agencies, they remain unable to answer satisfactorily even the abstract question they concentrate on.

Second, the traditional formulation has a statist bias. It assumes that the polity is the sole claimant and object of political obligation, which is why the question why one should obey the law is considered central in the first instance. It ignores the fact that the citizen might also have obligations both to supra-statal entities and agencies and to such non-statal or para-statal groups as his religious, ethnic, cultural and other communities. It is statist also in the sense that it concentrates on the obligations of the citizen and not on those of the state, and largely discusses the latter derivatively and as a matter of secondary importance. This becomes clear if we compare much of the traditional discussion with Pericles' Funeral Oration and especially Socrates' *Crito*. Socrates describes the benefits Athens has consciously and positively conferred upon all its citizens including Socrates himself and made it possible for him to lead a good life. And he does this not to establish some kind of contractual reciprocity between the *polis* and the citizen but to show why the *polis* which does all this is a worthy object of love and gratitude and justly deserves obedience. In his Funeral Oration Pericles refers with pride to how Athens respected and looked after its citizens, took care of the widows of the dead, attended to the needs of the poor, and so on, and suggests that by treating them honourably it had amply earned its citizens' love and loyalty. The other Athenian writers and statesmen too stressed the responsibility of the *polis*, and saw the citizen's obedience to it as a just and legitimately expected moral response.

Yet another respect in which the traditional, especially the post-Hobbesist, discussion is statist consists in uncritically assuming that the state is the highest moral community and that the obligation to it enjoys primacy over all other obligations. Suppose we were to show that the citizen has an obligation to obey the law. Nothing of substance would follow, for one could rejoin that one has obligations to obey one's ethnic, tribal, caste and religious communities as well, and that one would decide what to do when they conflicted with one's political obligation. Rather than explore the bases and the relative weights of the different kinds of obligation, much of the traditional discussion rests on the assumption that the duty to obey the law is the highest obligation and that once it is established, the citizen's course of action is clear.

Third, the traditional formulation rests on an exceedingly narrow view of citizenship and reduces the citizen to a subject. It sees him as a passive and one-dimensional being whose sole or at least primary obligation is to obey the law and of whom nothing more is morally expected. He is not expected to take an active interest in the conduct of public affairs and the quality of public life, to criticise the injustices and inequalities of his society, or to protest against its dubious foreign policies and disastrous wars.

Fourth, the traditional formulation is legalistic and gives a false view of political life. It implies that the law is the central mediating agency between the state and the citizen, and that the state's primary task is to make laws and that of the citizen is to obey them. In actual fact the state acts at many levels and impinges on the citizen at many points that have little to do with the law. It pursues foreign, economic, educational, social and other policies that have profound consequences for the citizen, and about which he generally is and ought to be deeply concerned. Even so far as the law is concerned, its silence is just as important as and sometimes even more important than its utterances. By and large the laws in a reasonably well-ordered polity are passed in consultation with public opinion, and are morally unproblematic. What is often in dispute are the laws the civil authority *refuses to make*, such as those relating to the hours of factory work, working conditions, child labour, environmental pollution and the protection of the weak and vulnerable against the depredation of the rich and powerful. To concentrate on why one should obey the law is to ignore this, and to imply that the citizen's sole concern is to obey or disobey the laws with which the state chooses to confront him.

There are also several other reasons why the traditional formulation is inadequate. It ignores the obligations the citizen might have to the preceding and succeeding generations. It defines politics in narrow terms and ignores the political dimension of many a so-called non-political relationship. It ignores the fact that the citizen might stand in a political relationship with and incur political obligations to those outside his polity. Since the traditional formulation suppresses, distorts or misconceptualises important areas of political life in these and other ways, much of the traditional discussion of political obligation remains unsatisfactory. I suggest that we find a way of re-formulating the problem of political obligation that is less biased and more balanced. In this paper I shall formulate the question of political obligation, not as why one should obey the law, but as what obligations, if any, one incurs by virtue of one's membership of a polity. This formulation is broad enough to include the traditional, but it is free from its ideological biases, locates it in a wider perspective, and allows us to explore obligations that it ignores or marginalises. When so formulated, the question of political obligation invites an inquiry into the nature of the polity, what it means to be a member of it and what obligations, if any, such membership entails.

It would be useful at this stage to explain how the terms polity and obligation are used in this chapter. Since human societies have historically been structured in several different ways such as the Hindu *raj*, the Athenian *polis*, the Roman *civitas*, the medieval kingdom and the modern state, I shall use the neutral term polity to cover them all. A polity is a territorially constituted human collectivity united in terms of its subscription to a system of rules and procedures concerning who is authorised to speak in its name and to take and enforce collectively binding decisions. The rules and procedures constitute and structure it and may be called its constitution. Those authorised and hence entitled to speak and act in the name of the collectivity may be called the civil or political authority.

As for the term obligation, there is an obvious danger against which some of the writers on the subject have not adequately guarded themselves. If our definition of it were to be narrow, ideologically biased or grounded in a specific view of its nature, we would overlook or marginalise a host of actions we feel a citizen ought to undertake. For example, if we were to insist that obligations must be voluntarily undertaken, we would overlook or dismiss those that as it were accumulate behind our backs, are too deep to be easily identified, or are not a matter of choice.[2] Again, if we were to insist that obligations necessarily require coercive sanctions, we would have to conclude that a citizen has no other obligation than to obey the law, this being the only act for failing to do which he is generally coerced by the state.[3] In each case our arbitrary definition of the term 'obligation' prejudices our inquiry and predetermines our answer.

I shall therefore use the term 'obligation' widely to refer to those social actions that the moral agent ought to undertake and his failure to do which reflects badly on him and renders him liable to social disapproval. Obligations relate to actions and not to the states of mind or to moral dispositions. The actions to which they refer affect others' interests, and are in that sense social. Since they are social, the agent is answerable to others and subject to their approbatory or disapprobatory judgement. And since a moral being is expected to take account of others' interests in his socially relevant actions, his failure to discharge his obligations reveals a lack of moral sensitivity, reflects badly on him, and induces or ought to induce in him a sense of guilt. Obligations might be accompanied by sanctions, but they need not be. And when they are, it is not the sanctions that make them obligations. Sanctions are designed to ensure that the obligations are discharged, and presuppose that the latter are autonomous and independent of them.

We acquire obligations in several different ways, and each has a distinct character. Some are acquired by engaging in specific practices such as making promises and entering into contracts. The rule that promises should be kept both specifies what counts as a promise and lays down that the utterances identified as promises should be kept. In making a promise I put myself under the jurisdiction of the rule, and *acquire* the obligation to keep a specific promise. The rule or practice creates the general obligation; my promise individualises the obligation and makes me its unique bearer. By their very nature rule-based or practice-based obligations are specific, concrete, more or less easily identifiable, and are often exhaustively discharged when the requirements of the practice are met.

We also acquire obligations by virtue of our voluntary or involuntary membership of an organisation, a group, or an ethnic, religious, cultural or political community. To be a member of a university, for example, is to be subject to the jurisdiction of its authority, and to acquire obligations to its various levels of authorities, students, staff and colleagues. Some of the organisational obligations involve a measure of choice, especially when the membership is voluntary and the organisation is open to democratic decision making. Others are inherited and *incurred* without a choice, such as the obligations to one's parents, brothers, relatives, in some cases to one's religious or ethnic community, and to some extent to one's polity. Unlike the practice-based obligations, organisational obligations are general, cover a wide variety, cannot be catalogued, depend a good deal on individual interpretation and are subject to well-defined sanctions.

Yet other obligations have little to do with social practices and group membership and are acquired by virtue of being human. In most cultures every human being is believed to have a duty to relieve human suffering within the limits of his abilities. My duty to feed a starving man or to pull a drunken man out of a puddle does not depend on a prior promise or on our membership of a common ethnic or political community. Such obligations are deemed to be *inherent* in our humanity and transcend the man-made boundaries of time, space and culture. Unlike the practice-based and organisationally-derived obligations, these obligations are necessarily vague, lack the focus that the practices and groups provide, depend almost wholly on the moral agent and the society's level of moral consciousness, and are easily overlooked or ignored.

Obligations are discharged for a number of reasons. I have an obligation to look after my children. I might discharge it because I love them, and do all that I ought to do as an expression of my love for them. Or I might discharge the obligation because I have a sense of pride or honour, and would feel demeaned if I were to fail to look after my children. Or I might discharge it because I am a conscientious person, a good Kantian, who discharges all his obligations out of a sense of obligation or duty unsullied by such natural feelings as a sense of joy, pleasure, honour and even love. Or I might look after my children because I fear my neighbour's or friends' likely criticisms, the long arm of the law, or God's wrath. My motive for discharging the obligation, or rather the spirit in which I discharge it, reveals the kind of person I am, and is of importance to others and even to me as a basis for predicting whether or not I can be depended upon to discharge it in difficult situations.

Political obligations refer to obligations entailed by one's membership of a polity. As such they are a species of organisational obligation, and are discharged by different individuals in different spirits. The question as to what obligations an individual incurs by virtue of his membership of a polity is not amenable to a simple answer, for both the quality of the membership and the nature of the polity are capable of great variety. Let us take each in turn.

The membership of a polity can take several forms and admits of degrees. Some, such as the temporary residents, are its partial and temporary members and enjoy limited rights and obligations. Some, such as the resident aliens, have a right of indefinite residence but are not qualified to be or have chosen not to become full citizens. Some, such as non-resident citizens, have chosen either temporarily or permanently to settle abroad, but continue to enjoy all the rights of citizenship including the right to vote and stand in national elections. Some others acquire citizenship by virtue of their birth, but have never lived and do not intend to live in the country of their birth, and are *de jure* but not *de facto* citizens. Some others might not be citizens of a country, but they might belong to its dominant ethnic or religious group and enjoy the rights of full potential membership. The diasporic Jews are not Israeli citizens, but they enjoy the right to acquire its citizenship whenever they choose to do so. The Indians settled abroad, the so-called non-resident Indians, do not have the right to settle and vote in India, but they enjoy the right to buy land, invest money and to set up industries on the same terms as, and sometimes on even better terms than, Indian citizens, and are. emerging as super or what the indigenous Indians call deluxe citizens. The overseas Chinese have an even more complex relationship with China. It would seem that a new and historically unprecedented category of diasporic citizenship is beginning to emerge, presenting the paradox of a body of men and women who potentially or actually enjoy all the rights but none of the obligations of citizenship including the traditional obligations to pay taxes and to fight and die for their country.

All this means that, unlike earlier writers, we can no longer go on talking about citizenship as if it were a simple and homogenous concept. The different categories of members mentioned above stand in different kinds of relationship to and have different kinds of obligations to their polity. A fully considered theory of political obligation relevant to the modern polity will need to spell out the bases of and the differences between these and other kinds of obligation. In this paper I concentrate on full and normally resident members, whom I shall call 'citizens'.

Like its membership, the polity too admits of diversity of forms. Some polities, such as the traditional Hindu polities, were socio-centric. They were societies topped up with a government, whose job it was to preserve the existing social order. In these societies political and social status, or citizenship and caste-membership, were inseparable. The polity did not represent a separate sphere of existence, and to be a good citizen was also to be a good caste-member. Further-more, the obligations of the citizens varied with their caste. The members of a warrior caste had an obligation to die for their country, whereas other castes had different obligations. In such societies politi-cal obligation was one of the several dimensions of the wider social obligation to preserve the caste-based social order, and there was no distinct obligation called *political* obligation.

Classical Athens represented a very different kind of polity. The birth of the *polis* marked the reconstitution of the pre-existing tribes, and represented an autonomous order of existence enjoying pre-eminence over all others. This led to the emergence of citizenship as a distinct status and a novel identity. The *polis* referred not to an ethnic community as in India and China, nor to a territorial unit as in many a medieval European kingdom, not to a set of impersonal institutions as in the modern state, but to the citizens viewed collectively, 'Where two Athenians meet, there is the *polis*.' To be a citizen was to partici-pate in the life of the community including its sports, public festivals, rituals and the conduct of public affairs. In such a close-knit and inti-mate community, the citizen was brought up to love it and to cultivate appropriate virtues. He was expected to be guided by such sentiments as piety, the love of order, the desire to be useful (*chrésimos*), and above all the love of honour and a zealous ambition on behalf of his community (*philotimia*). 'You, men of Athens, differ from the rest of humanity in behaving piously towards the gods, dutifully towards your parents, and *philotimas* towards your homeland.' Since to be a good citizen was to be guided by the love of the polis, the sentiment of piety, *philotimia* and so on, the language of virtue and not the relatively impersonal language of obligation best expressed the citizen's relation to his *polis*. This is how Socrates discusses his attitude to Athens in the *Apology* and especially in the *Crito*, in both of which the language of obligation is more or less absent.[4] We might say that the classical Athenian discharged his political obligations not out of a sense of obligation but out of the love of his community.

The traditional African societies, the medieval European kingdoms, the modern state, and so on represent yet other kinds of polities. In each case political obligation has a different basis, texture, structure and form. In this paper I concentrate on the modern state.

The modern state is a distinct and historically specific mode of constituting the polity. Although it shares a number of features in common with the pre-modern polities, it articulates, relates and structures them differently and additionally possesses several novel features of its own. To be a citizen of it is to be related to other citizens and to the civil authority in a certain manner, and that pattern of relationship gives rise to specific obligations. I shall therefore begin with a brief sketch of the central features of modern citizenship, and explore how each of them, either singly or in conjunction with others, generates specific obligations.

2

Modern citizens have multiple identities. They are not just citizens but also members of families, clans, tribes and specific ethnic, religious and cultural groups. Since the modern state is abstracted from society and enjoys an autonomous mode of existence, citizenship is an autonomous identity in the sense that one does not need to belong to a specific ethnic, cultural or religious group in order to become a citizen. In practice, of course, some states do privilege some of these groups and award their citizenship on a preferential basis, but this is not a universal practice and is invariably condemned. As bearers of several identities, modern men and women are involved in different kinds of relationships with different individuals, and have multiple obligations. Although their political obligation is very important, it is only one of their many obligations, and is expected to respect the demands of and compete with the others for their allegiance.

The modern individual's multiple identities are of several different kinds. Some are contingent, detachable, and largely marginal. The fact that one is a neighbour, fellow-golfer or a colleague often means little. Some identities such as those derived from the membership of a class, an occupation or a political party, have deeper roots. They are more durable, express the allegiance of the bearer, and partially shape him. Yet other identities are central to one's very being and go to make one the kind of person one is. The familial, political, cultural, ethnic, religious and other identities belong to this category. They are inherited and thus inescapable, an integral part of oneself and thus non-detachable, catch one young and permanently set the tone and structure of one's personality, shape one's deepest thoughts and values, and constitute one as a specific kind of person. Since they strike such deep roots in one's being and consciousness, they generally arouse considerable loyalty and affection.

The modern individual's complex relation to his differently structured social identities has not proved easy to theorise. Many liberals have conceptualised the individual as a socially transcendental being for whom social identities are contingent and external, do not penetrate and structure his innermost world, and are basically like 'roles' or social 'positions' rather than modes of being or forms of self-articulation. While the liberals are right in relation to some social identities, they are, as we saw, wrong with respect to the others which strike deeper roots. And while they are right to highlight the important fact that the individual has an inner world that is uniquely his own, they are wrong to see it as a kind of transcendental and archimedean point unaffected by the social world.

The communitarian is strong where the liberal is weak. He rightly stresses that the individual is social to the very core of his being, and that he is not an abstract centre of transcendental self-consciousness freely choosing his values, modes of thought, objects of affection and attachments but is profoundly shaped by his society. However, the communitarian exaggerates and misinterprets this valuable insight. There is nothing called *the* society or *the* community of which one is supposed to be a member and by which one is constituted. The individual is a member of several communities, each with its own distinct history and character, each shaping her in a unique manner and evoking unique loyalties, and all sometimes pulling in different directions. Since she is shaped by several communities, she is not constituted by any one of them. And since she is a reflective being, she is able to use the space created by her plural identities to take a critical and larger view of each and, over time, of *all* of them and to reconcile their conflicting demands in her own unique way. As she negotiates her way through her different communal identities, she both evolves a more or less coherent self and *reconstitutes* the various communities of which she is a member. Even as these communities constitute her, she too constantly redraws their internal and external boundaries and reconstitutes them. The relationship between the individual and the community is far more complex and dialectical than the simple-minded communitarian view implies.

When the communitarian talks about *the* community, he often has the state in mind. Not surprisingly the communitarian is often an ardent supporter of the state, and communitarian discourse is often a thinly disguised statist and even nationalist discourse. The communitarian is right to think of the state as a *community* for, contrary to the liberal understanding of it, the state is, as we shall see, bound together by deep ties of common moral, cultural and material interests. However, it is only *a* community, one among many existing within its borders, and not necessarily the most profound and powerful in its impact. Furthermore, although one's political community does shape one deeply, this is so partly because it acts through these other communities, and its direct contribution is often limited. And although it is certainly an object of one's affection and loyalty, this is partly because it allows the other communities to exist and flourish. Like Hegel and the British Idealists the communitarian mistakenly equates the state with the totality of the communities that happen to exist within its boundaries, and attributes to it a moral character which it partially derives from and shares with them. A person's significant social identities then are not 'roles' she acquires and discards at will, but nor do they singly or collectively exhaust her. The self is basically like Hegel's concrete universal, whose humanity is articulated in and realised through its social relations but which is nevertheless not exhausted in them and retains the capacity to view them all critically. Citizenship is a significant social identity, but it is neither the only one nor always the most important.

The individual acquires, sustains and balances his social identities because he possesses or is capable of acquiring the capacity to enter into and appreciate the demands of the corresponding forms of social relationship. This capacity inheres in him as a human being, and is integral to what makes him human. Animals lack this capacity, not contingently but necessarily, that is, by virtue of being who they are. My society does, of course, shape and structure my distinctively human capacities, but it does not create them and can only change them within certain limits. My multiple social identities therefore presuppose my humanity, my status as a human being. To respect them is to respect me not only as their bearer but also as a human being, as someone uniquely capable of becoming their bearer. Now as a human being I am a member of the human species and stand in a relationship of equality with other human beings. I am human in exactly the same sense as you are. And if I make certain claims on the basis of my humanity, others may make them too, and I am logically committed to respecting their claims. Since my social identities presuppose my humanity, and since my humanity commits me to recognising other human beings as my equals, my social identities are subject to the fundamental constraint of not requiring me to behave in a manner that ignores or tramples upon the claims of other human beings. Citizenship is one social identity and is subject to this constraint. In being a citizen I do not cease to be a human being; on the contrary, my citizenship expresses and articulates my humanity. My citizenship cannot therefore absolve me from moral obligations to other human beings wherever they might happen to live. A state that requires me to treat outsiders as subhuman, as of no moral significance, denies my own humanity and compromises or even forfeits any claim to my allegiance. This is not to deny my special relationship with and my strong obligations to my polity. Rather it is to claim that these obligations cannot exclude and must be balanced against my obligations to outsiders. Just as my political obligations must respect and not lightly override the obligations generated by my familial, ethnic, religious and other identities, they must not ignore the constraints of the universal obligations of my humanity.

Citizens are moral agents, that is, persons capable of choice and autonomy and responsible for the consequences of their actions. Although moral agency is the necessary presupposition of every polity, which simply cannot exist unless its members are acknowledged to be capable of understanding and conforming to its demands, it is uniquely central to the modern state. The modern state recognises only the individual as its basic ontological and moral unit, and invests her with rights and obligations, expects her to make choices, and holds her uniquely responsible for her actions. When she commits a crime, she alone and not her family, caste, clan or village is held responsible and punished. Earlier polities viewed the individual as a member of a family, caste, clan or tribe, to be held causally and morally co-responsible for the acts of other members of these collectivities. Again the modern state sets great store by the principle of non-interference and requires its citizens studiously to refrain from interfering with each other. In so doing it presupposes that each individual is equipped to run his life himself and that his moral dignity demands that others should leave him free to do so. The centrality of moral agency in the modern state has important implications for political obligation.

Since citizens are moral agents and responsible for the consequences of their actions, they cannot be expected uncritically to obey the civil authority. They have an obligation to judge its laws and policies and to satisfy themselves that these do not require them to do outrageous deeds. Indeed one can go even further. Since the state treats them as free moral agents in all *its relations with them*, it cannot consistently require them not to behave as one in *their relations with it*. It requires them to accept responsibility for their actions. Obeying it is one of these actions. And therefore the state must respect their right and duty to examine its laws and policies, and freely to decide if they are prepared to accept the responsibility for the consequences of doing what it requires them to do. Moral agency works both ways. It renders the citizen liable to punishment for his failure to obey the law. But equally it renders the state liable to his critical judgement, censure and even disobedience in extreme cases.

Hobbes, who was one of the first to notice the dual nature of moral agency, sought to avoid its uncomfortable implications by rejecting both the possibility and the need for the citizen to judge his sovereign. He ruled out the former by insisting that since the citizens' judgements diverged, the very existence of the civil society required that the sovereign should be exempt from such judgements. And he ruled out the need by arguing that if the sovereign ever required the citizen to act immorally, the responsibility and the guilt were wholly his, the citizen being merely a passive instrument of his will. After suitable modifications, Hobbes' view was recently reiterated by Michael Oakeshott.[5]

Neither of Hobbes' two arguments is convincing.[6] As we shall see later they rest on a deeply flawed view of the nature of citizenship. But even within the Hobbesian framework of thought, the arguments lack force. As he sees it, the civil society exists to create a peaceful, stable and commodious existence for its members, and the sovereign's authority is conditional on his ability to achieve this objective. Since the objective provides a collectively agreed public standard, the citizens can evaluate their sovereign in terms of it, and ask if he is achieving it without endangering their future security or causing the polity an excessive long-term damage. It is likely that they will disagree, but the answer to that lies in making institutional arrangements for resolving their disagreements, not in denying them the right to judge the sovereign in matters relating to their vital interests.

Hobbes' second argument is even less convincing. As a moral being a citizen cannot avoid deciding whether or not what he is asked to do is moral. And if he acts immorally, he cannot hide behind the argument that he was only carrying out his sovereign's commands. If the sovereign asks me to kill an innocent person, he is certainly wrong to command such an action, but I am equally wrong to comply with him. And if I do comply, not he alone but both of us are morally guilty. Hobbes' argument is a version of the more recent 'superior order' argument invoked by the ex-Nazi war criminals, and is no better.

As moral agents then the citizens have an obligation to ensure that the civil authority does not require, or place them in a situation in which they feel required, to act immorally. Although they should respect and trust its judgement, especially in matters about which they are unlikely to be fully knowledgeable, and although they should appreciate the fallibility of their consciences and moral judgements, they cannot abdicate their unique and inextinguishable personal responsibility for their actions. If they feel convinced after calm reflection that a law confronts them with unacceptable demands or is likely to cause serious harm to the community, they have an obligation to criticise and protest against and even perhaps to disobey it.

Furthermore, the relationship between authority and obligation is dialectical in nature and far more complex than is suggested by many a writer on political obligation. At one level authority generates obligation, in the sense that for a citizen to accept a government as a legitimately constituted authority in his or her polity is to acknowledge an obligation to obey it. However, we need to explain how it acquires the authority in the first instance. The authority of a government is not a once and for all endowment or the inherent property of an office; it is based on and sustained by the constant acknowledgement and acceptance of its citizens. It is a common experience that even a duly constituted government loses its authority when for some reason its citizens cease to recognise an obligation to uphold and maintain it. In obeying its laws they do not passively respond to a pre-existing authority but also continually ratify, reinforce and indeed create it. Like its authority, the government derives its power too from the support and co-operation of its subjects. Ultimately, its power consists in nothing other than their willingness to extend it their energetic support. To obey a law is to empower the government, to increase its ability to execute its will.

Since the government's authority and power are built up by means of its citizens' daily acts of obedience and support, citizens need to ask if it wisely uses the authority and power which their support confers upon it. No civil authority is free from the temptation to misuse power, to cut legal corners, to yield to pressures of sectional interests, to submit to the influence of the self-interest and dogmatism of those in power. Citizens therefore have an obligation to keep an eye on it and to ensure that it does not become arrogant, ignore the public interest, stifle dissent, or acquire a degree of authority and power likely over time to threaten their rights and liberties.

The civil authority in the modern state derives its authority from and acts in the name of its citizens. It carries their collective *persona*, and when it speaks and acts they are deemed to be speaking and acting through it. Furthermore, the civil authority is charged with the task of pursuing their collective interests, and is expected to justify its actions in terms of them. The highest, indeed the sole justification a government can offer of its actions is that they were necessary in the interest of the community. The collective interest of the community is invoked to legitimise almost everything, including the most horrendous wars, deception, lying, the brutal repression or expulsion of the minorities, and even state-sponsored terrorism.

Since the civil authority speaks and acts in their name and justifies its actions in terms of their interests, its citizens are doubly implicated. Since it speaks in their name, they need to ask themselves if they are prepared to own its actions and accept them as their own. Since it justifies its actions in terms of their interests, they need to ask if they are willing to have their interests so defined and pursued and to bear the moral responsibility for the ensuing consequences. The extent of their responsibility obviously depends, among other things, on their ability to influence the government. It is at a minimum, although not wholly absent, in a totalitarian society in which they lack the requisite political power, information and the opportunity for organised action, and it is at a maximum in a democratic society where these preconditions of political responsibility are amply present. Although a democratic government is the *immediate* author of and thus *primarily* responsible for its actions, it undertakes them with the authority and knowledge of and in broad consultation with its citizens. They are therefore co-authors of and co-responsible for its actions.

If on reflection the citizens feel that these actions are ill-advised, outrageous or likely to cause enormous suffering to the outsiders and that they cannot own them, they have a duty to try to dissuade the government from undertaking them. And if they fail, they have a duty to find ways of publicly or privately dissociating themselves from its actions and, when necessary, protesting against them. It is a common experience that every government pushes the limits of its freedom as far as it can get away with, and that its definition of collective interest is sometimes grossly mistaken and perverse. Sectional interests sometimes masquerade as common interests, and narrow electoral considerations inspire wars or policies that do grave long-term damage to the community. Morally responsible citizens need to keep their government on a short leash and to subject its definition and pursuit of their collective interest to constant and searching scrutiny.

3

The modern state is not a chance collection of men and women who happen to live together, nor a loose collectivity made up of self-contained communities, but a reasonably cohesive polity. Its members share a way of life in common and are tied together by countless moral, cultural and material bonds. They share common collective memories, myths, territory, customs, traditions, values, language and a manner of conducting their collective affairs. Their current rights and opportunities are a precipitate of common struggles and their material and cultural resources are a product of their collective efforts. Their interests and aspirations are closely linked and they share a common future. For these and other reasons they constitute and recognise themselves as forming part of a collective 'we', and their political identity is an important element in their conception of themselves.

Their sense of community can, of course, be easily exaggerated. No known polity is free of class, ethnic and other conflicts, divergent moral traditions, memories of bitter internecine warfare and past exploitation. No known polity is free of grave injustices and inequalities either. And no polity has such a strong sense of community that the bulk of its members feel troubled when their fellow citizens starve, sleep in cardboard boxes, die prematurely, suffer from avoidable accidents or lead lives of bleak despair. In spite of all this no polity that has lasted for long can avoid developing some sense of common identity, some common loyalties and affections, and some sense of mutual concern. As such, its members feel entitled to make claims on one another and on their collective resources. The claims might be and sometimes are ignored in practice, but they are rarely rejected as preposterous or misconceived. However thin it might be, their sense of belonging to a shared community forms an ontological basis of, or at least an ontological background to, their mutual moral claims. When a section of them suffer material hardships and injustices or lack opportunities for growth, this is not just their personal misfortune which it is their own responsibility to resolve but a structural defect in their community, a common misfortune, which it is their common responsibility to redress.

At a deeper level, the fundamental interests of the members of a polity substantially overlap. Since they share a common collective environment and their lives criss-cross at countless points, their personal and collective lives cannot be disjoined. Crimes by a small group of them create a general sense of insecurity and affect the lives of them all. Fraud and deception by a few heighten mutual suspicions, lower the threshhold of trust and civility, and call for cumbersome measures that cause hardship to all. When a section of the community is degraded or unjustly treated and full of resentment and hatred, the rest are not only deprived of the benefits of their potential contributions but are also made to bear the moral, psychological and financial cost of repairing the damage they do to themselves and to others. As beings endowed with a moral sense and a capacity of self-reflection, human beings cannot brutalise and maltreat others without hardening themselves, building up distorted systems of self-justification and suppressing their doubts and finer impulses, thereby lowering both their own and the general level of humanity. There is a limit to the extent to which the privileged groups can withdraw from the rest of the society and live behind protective walls. Even if their ghettos are physically secure, they breed their own moral privations and distortions. In short, individuals cannot easily lead rich and fulfilling lives except in a rich and lively society. The point becomes clearer if we take an example.

Each of us lives in a self-chosen part of the town. The place where we live is not located on an island; it is adjacent to other houses which collectively form a street and share a road in common. Since each house is affected by the others, their occupants have a common or collective interest in the way their houses are structured, their lawns kept, the road attended to, and so on. We do not thus live in a house; we also live in a street. And we do not use the road merely as a means to get from one place to another, it is an integral part of where we live and has a non-instrumental significance to us. This is why we feel concerned about the street just as we do about our own house. We deplore or admire its aesthetic quality, the way it both separates and relates us, the manner in which it reflects and nurtures our relationships with each other, and the atmosphere it creates. At a different level we also feel this way about the city in which we live. We share in common its roads, streets, parks, lakes, and so on; they are not only common to us but among us. Each city has a definite atmosphere, a character, a feel, an intangible quality which we may admire or loathe. Some cities are a joy to live in and walk around, creating feelings of pleasure, confidence and well-being, and evoking certain types of emotional and even moral responses from us. Others are the Devil's invention.

What is true of such 'physical' entities as streets, roads and cities is no less true of such human associations and institutions as the family, the university, a club, a commercial concern, and the neighbourhood communities. They are not means to something external to them, rather they represent the way we have chosen to live and relate to each other. They reflect and reinforce our self-conceptions and aspirations, shape our innermost being and give a distinct tone to our social and personal life. Their rules, practices, rituals and traditions therefore have a non-instrumental and expressivist significance. They do not merely help achieve specific objectives with more or less efficiency and economy, but also create a distinct atmosphere and ethos, bringing out either the best or the worst in us, encouraging a climate of trust and harmony or of suspicion and conflict, enhancing a sense of well-being or generating spirals of resentment and frustration. Since social organisations and their rules are an integral part of the ontology of life, their structure and maintenance make great demands on their members' sense of collective responsibility.

A political community is no different from other associations, although its size and complexity prevent us from fully appreciating its communal nature. We share our political institutions and practices, and their nurture and improvement is our common concern. They are our collective assets which we hold in trust and which organise us into a single and specific type of political community. We have a collective interest in preserving and improving them, not as private individuals but as members of the community in question. As individuals we might find a practice or a law burdensome, but as members of the community we may not violate them without impoverishing the moral quality of collective life. Our shared institutions and practices generate an irreducible ethos or atmosphere that vitally shapes our conceptions of ourselves and our conduct. They might bring us together in a spirit of co-operation or divide and fragment us, draw us out of ourselves and lift us to a new level of being or reinforce our helplessness and isolation, and evoke and nurture our sense of mutual concern or appeal to our narrow personal interests and encourage selfish and aggressive attitudes.

The political community also generates its own distinctive emotions and sentiments which can only be experienced as members of a community, along with others not as private individuals. Such emotions as national self-respect, national shame, a sense of elation at the country's achievements or depression at its mean policies, a sense of pride in one's way of life and a feeling of comradeship in struggling for a common cause are all inherently public and shared, and incapable of being enjoyed by isolated individuals in the privacy of their homes. A man might feel depressed when his wife dies and ashamed when he or she is caught stealing. He might also feel depressed when innocent men and women die in a war launched by his country, or ashamed when his government is caught trying to topple a foreign government or murder an inconvenient head of state. The qualities and structures of the emotions of depression and shame are quite different in the two cases, and mutually irreducible.

Thanks to the domination of the subjectivist view of politics, we have only a dim awareness of these and other crucial aspects of political life. We do not fully appreciate that political life is a shared life and that, whether we like it or not, we pay taxes, fight in wars and make sacrifices for those whom we shall never see. The state is the institutionalisation of sympathy in space and time, and its members are related by the ties of *objective* sympathy. Contrary to much of the liberal mythology, our lives are never our own. We are constantly and often deeply affected by the way others lead their lives, making it existentially impossible for any of us to lead his life the way he likes. If the middle classes were to withdraw from an area, the working classes would be ghettoised against their will. And if the whites withdrew their children from racially mixed schools, the black children would be forced into segregated schools against their wishes. In the first case the working classes did not choose their radically changed environment; the middle classes imposed it on them. In the second, the black parents did not choose all-black schools for their children; the white parents chose it for them. In the context of a shared way of life, I necessarily choose *both* for myself and for others, and my choice is your coercion. I do not run my life myself, you run it too. And I live not just my own life but also a part of yours. To talk about choice in the abstract and to equate it with freedom is to be blind to its inseparable coercive shadow. Since this is so easily seen, the blindness is not inadvertent but wilful and designed to promote obvious ideological interests.

Since the citizen's ability to lead a good life depends on his fellow citizens and on the quality of the collective life, he acquires several obligations. He has an obligation to ensure that his fellow citizens enjoy full access to the material and cultural resources of their community and are able to lead satisfying and socially valuable lives. He also has an obligation to highlight and speak up against the poverty, the injustices, the grotesque inequalities and the various forms of oppression that tend to accumulate in every society. He has a particular obligation to stand up for those too demoralised, confused and powerless to fight for themselves, and to help create a society in which no oppressed group feels a political orphan. When poverty and injustice are allowed to fester and the cry of the victims goes unheard, their smouldering anger tends to turn into rage and their bitterness is likely to degenerate into mindless nihilism. Both self-interest and morality require that no citizen should allow such a situation to develop.

As we saw, the integrity of the public realm, high standards of public morality, the climate of civility, the sense of justice, the habit of complying with the law, the intolerance of hypocrisy and humbug in public life, the culture of public protest against patently partisan and ill-conceived laws, and so on are shared public goods and constitute the moral and political capital of the community. Although the citizens do not fully realise this, they constantly draw upon that capital, and would not flourish or even survive for long as a community in its absence. Its constant upkeep and enrichment is therefore one of their highest political obligations.

Moral and political capital are not such that can be built up once and for all, or left in the care of a few. Such capital exists only in so far as it is lived; it is preserved only in so far as it is constantly actualised in the thoughts and actions of citizens. The culture of civility exists in so far it is woven into the fabric of collective life, and is maintained if citizens behave towards each other and conduct their collective affairs in a civil manner. The general climate of respect for the law exists and is preserved only to the extent that citizens respect and obey the law. There is nothing mysterious about this, for this is equally true of all moral and especially spiritual goods. Love and friendship, for example, can be said to exist when, and only last as long as, those involved habitually behave towards each other in the spirit of love and friendship. Citizenship is no different. As Aristotle observed, the *polis* is actualised in and has no identity independently of the way its citizens relate to each other in their public lives. The citizen was, as the ancient Athenians put it, a *polités*, a *polis-person*. Isocrates captured the point well when he called *politeia* (citizenship) the *psukhé* of the city, its 'beating heart' or 'life and soul'.

4

Every polity exists in time, and is aware of doing so. Its present is a product of its past, and the two together shape its future. Although all polities have a sense of both the past and the future, the relative importance they assign them varies greatly. For a variety of reasons the pre-modern polities had a stronger sense of the past than of the future. Since, among other things, they were far less subject to constant change than their modern counterparts, their present was continuous with their past and they expected the future to be little different. The past for them was not 'dead' but living; it was vividly and deeply inscribed in every area of their life in the form of traditions, customs, deities and a relatively stable natural and social environment. Since they daily lived their past, which is very different from living *in* the past, they experienced no hiatus between the past and the present.

The early modern polity reacted against the cultural and spatial constraints of its past and present, and sought to reconstitute itself on a radically different foundation. It became obsessed with the future, to which the present was seen as a mere means and the past largely as a hindrance. Once industrialisation and modernisation got under way and the pace of change increased, they created a sense of rootlessness, disorientation and discontinuity. Besides, in a rapidly changing world, each new generation brought with it very different ideas and values, raising the question as to how it was to be integrated into the ongoing social whole. Social and economic divisions, increased immigration, and so on raised similar problems. For these and related reasons the polity began to turn to its past for stability and roots. It reconstructed and reinterpreted its past in the light of both its present and the hoped-for future, and sought to integrate all three into a more balanced sense of historical time. Whereas geography was politically important and widely taught in the early modern period – marked by the great voyages of exploration – it was history that acquired this status in the nineteenth century and attracted considerable official and unofficial attention. Not space but time now acquired political salience. A common view of the past was used to give the polity a moral and historical depth and to unite its citizens on the basis of a shared sense of national identity.

The modern state, then, is a uniquely historical entity, and is acutely aware of being one. It is not just a succession of generations but an ongoing whole bound together by shared memories and hopes. The modern citizen knows that his way of life, modes of thought, practices, habits, institutions and material conditions are products of the efforts, choices and sacrifices of countless men and women in the past. And he knows too that his generation will in turn shape the world of its successors. The generations are also linked at a deeper ontological level, which again is far more characteristic of the modern state than of its earlier counterparts. We live and act in the belief that our polity will survive us, that our grandchildren and their grandchildren will continue to be born, that our achievements will not perish with us. Without such a belief we would see no point in raising families, building homes, saving money, writing books, or constructing monuments. We thus build up expectations about the future generations and count on them to preserve and build on the world we have created. The present is the future of the past, and the previous generations had similar expectations of us. Each generation thus depends on its successors to help it give meaning to its life, and derives its sense of significance from, among other things, their anticipated responses. The future is not only in the future; it is conceptually a part of, and partially constitutes, the present. Unlike most pre-moderns who sought to resemble and be worthy of their ancestors and largely sought meaning in the past, moderns at least partly turn to the future for their sense of meaning and worth.

Since we depend so heavily on succeeding generations, the living wield considerable power over the dead. They decide whether or not and how to remember the past, which past buildings and monuments to preserve or destroy, which past achievements to cherish, which dead individuals to declare non-persons, and in general which past to preserve or kill. The dead continue to live through our memories of them. And while some are too powerful to be defeated by our attempts to wipe out their memories, most are too fragile to survive our forgetfulness. In one sense human beings are mortal; in another far more important sense they can live for ever if the living so decide.

Since the modern state is a profoundly and self-consciously historical polity, to be a member of it is to participate in an ongoing historical process and be linked to the collective narrative of a specific community. Citizenship thus is not just a legal or a political but also a historical status; it entails not just legal and political but also historical rights and obligations; and it confers not just a legal and political but also a historical power. To be a citizen is to shape the world the succeeding generations will inherit and to exercise a considerable power over them. To be a citizen is also to wield power over the preceding generations and to decide what parts of their world will continue to last. The notorious communist tendency periodically to rewrite history books, to destroy old monuments and to build new ones, to rename cities and streets, to rearrange the museums, and so forth is the most striking example of the power the living exercise over the dead. But this was not unique to them, and in one form or another it occurs in all societies including our own.

Since different generations are linked together, exercise power over each other and affect each other's vital interests, they stand in a moral relationship and incur mutual obligations. The present generation has obligations both to its predecessors and to its successors. It has the former because they created the world, warts and all, of which it is a beneficiary. It has obligations also because they lived and acted in the expectation that the world they built as well as their deeds and achievements will not die with them, and counted on the goodwill of their successors. Finally, the obligation to the preceding generations derives from the more general fact that the way a generation treats its predecessors shapes the way it will in its turn be treated by its successors and helps create a climate of inter-generational trust.

Obligations to preceding generations are discharged in several ways, of which I shall mention two by way of example. First, we owe them the duty of remembrance. Immortality is the highest gift the living can confer upon the dead and which the latter are able to receive. And memory is the only source of immortality available to mortals. Every polity consciously or unconsciously acknowledges this obligation and honours its dead by declaring national holidays on their birth or death anniversaries, naming streets and cities after them, building monuments for unknown soldiers, telling stories about them, and cherishing their deeds.[7] In almost all polities such a collective remembrance is often deeply partial. It is reserved for their heroes and ignores the contributions of 'ordinary' men and women.

It is also partial in its choice of heroes, largely concentrating on kings, queens, politicians, explorers and military generals to the neglect of rebels, trade unionists, community leaders, local activists and others. We owe the latter too a deep obligation of gratitude and need to rediscover, reconstruct and cherish their memories. Local histories, the history from below, the subaltern studies and so on have at least partly sprung from this concern. Collective remembrance is an expression of what the classical Athenians and especially the Romans called piety, and is a highly political act. It honours and expresses the community's gratitude to its benefactors. By reassuring contemporaries that their achievements, however small, will not be forgotten and that posterity will do them the justice that may be denied them during their lifetime, it inspires them to do noble deeds. By honouring past rebels as well as rulers, it builds up a sense of collective solidarity and keeps alive the tradition of political protest. And by helping create the spirit of collective piety and historical continuity, the acts of collective remembrance give the polity a moral and spiritual depth and a sense of wholeness.

Second, just as we benefit from the good our predecessors have done, we also inherit the evil they have perpetrated. They might have engaged in such practices as slavery, colonialism, untouchability, ruthless economic exploitation and a tyrannical repression of minorities. The present generation often materially benefits from the consequences of these practices. It also benefits socially in the sense that its sense of racial, cultural or gender superiority, and the power and prestige associated with it, are often derived from these practices. But even when no such benefits accrue, we have a duty to rectify the injustices the previous generations might have perpetrated either inadvertently or in all good intentions. In doing so we redeem their honour and good name and reduce the moral burden of their deeds. More importantly, we clear the name of our polity to which both they and we belong and of which all generations are custodians. Contrary to much of the liberal view, the generations are not abstract, isolated and reified entities living in their own time; they are nothing more than the polity as it is humanly composed at arbitrarily abstracted points in time. They are basically its past, present and future members and represent its different historical moments or stages. As such the relations between them are not external but grounded in and mediated by their membership of a common polity. The continuity of the polity in the midst of the unceasing generational changes explains why its treaties, legal obligations, debts, commitments and contracts remain binding on those who were not a party to it. This is very like what happens in clubs, corporations, universities and other organisations in all of which privileges and liabilities are involuntarily inherited and enjoyed or suffered. It is therefore logically incoherent to say that *we* in the present generation did not engage in slavery, colonialism or genocide or class oppression. Our polity did, and as its current members we cannot disown all responsibility for the consequences of what its previous members did. The nature, basis, extent and limits of inter-generational obligations raise many important questions, but they are not relevant to our discussion.[8]

Every generation enters the flow of history at a particular point in time and inherits a past with its painful and pleasant memories. Although it cannot undo the past and disown the burden of painful memories, it can lighten their weight by mitigating at least some of the effects of the past actions. In so doing, it civilises the past, reduces its moral burden, and bequeaths to the succeeding generations a better past and a less fractious society. That all this is not too high-minded or moralistic is evident in the fact that this is how we cope with the past in our individual and collective lives. We sometimes feel guilty about our past unjust, immoral or foolish deeds and make appropriate amends to those involved or to others. We feel troubled by some of the things our parents might have done in their own interest or ours, and we seek to redeem their honour and good name in whatever ways we can. Many colonial powers, especially the Dutch, felt this way about their imperial history and did much to help their ex-colonies. Even Britain, which apparently feels morally less troubled than most about its imperial history, recognises its historical obligations to its colonial immigrants, and for several years allowed them an unrestricted entry and gave them the full rights of citizenship on arrival. This was also how the Germans felt about the Jews after the Second World War. Although only a handful of them had worked in the concentration camps or been involved in rounding up the Jews, most Germans felt deeply ashamed of their past and sought ways of redeeming their parents' and especially their country's good name. Rightly or wrongly, their unstinting economic and political support for the state of Israel is an expression of that sentiment.

Just as we have political obligations, that is, obligations derived from our membership of a specific polity, to our predecessors, we have even more extensive and stringent obligations to the future generations.[9] The obligations are derived from several interconnected sources of which I shall mention two. First, as moral beings we have a duty to reciprocate the benefits others confer upon us. The reciprocity need not be undirectional. My parents brought me up as best they could. And I reciprocate their love and kindness partly by looking after them in their old age and partly, especially if they are dead, by giving the best I can to my children. Reciprocity consists in ensuring that I do not merely receive benefits but also confer them on others. There is no reason why my benefactor and the recipient of my benefit should both be the same person; indeed if that were so, countless benefits in life would go unreciprocated, our social life would be impoverished, and our moral life crushed by unpaid moral debts. In fact we do not define reciprocity in this way. You hold open the door for me, and I hold it open for someone else. I would be mad if I insisted on opening it only for you and waited until the opportunity occurred. The point is well captured in the notices in many a British Rail lavatory urging the user to leave the seat as clean as he would like to find it. The same complex principle of reciprocity governs the relations between generations.

Second, we have obligations to future generations because they consist of human beings who, as we saw, enjoy a basic equality with us and have equal rights to the good life. Besides, our actions shape the world they will inherit and affect their life chances. As moral beings we have a duty to take full account of the likely consequences of our actions on them.

Our obligations to the future generations are both negative and positive, requiring us not to harm and, whenever possible, to promote their interests. We may not therefore use up vital natural resources and gravely impoverish them, or run up huge debts to solve our short-term economic problems, or discourage savings and fail to build up capital, or spoil the environment. At the political level we may not destroy the integrity of the public realm by corrupting our political institutions, or oppress vulnerable groups and leave behind a legacy of bitter memories, or engage in populist gimmicks to solve our short-term political problems and set dangerous precedents, or follow a foreign policy that leaves the country friendless. To solve our problems by aggravating those of our successors is to be a historical free-rider. As the history of every modern state demonstrates and as the contemporary cases of the developing countries clearly show, a stable, peaceful, cohesive and just polity requires the co-operation of several generations, each of which has an obligation to play its full part in this common historical task. The earlier generations often have to make the greatest sacrifices in order to build up both vital economic and political infrastructures and habits of hard work, civility and self-discipline. This is obviously unfair but inescapable. And its only redeeming feature is that the earlier generations have the unique advantages of occupying pride of place in the history of their community and enjoying their successors' grateful remembrance.

5

Thanks to the development of the world economy, of rapid transport and communication, of international movements of labour, capital, cultures and ideas, and so on, every modern state is increasingly being drawn into a global economic, political and cultural order. No country's economic interests for long remain unaffected by the economic policy of another. A civil war in one country precipitates legal and illegal migration, and it is very difficult to keep people out without resorting to devices that corrupt the moral and political life of the receiving countries. Diseases recognise no national boundaries, nor do the effects of environmental pollution. Ideas, cultures, institutions and practices travel freely and set up homes in new and sometimes inhospitable countries. As economic and political systems, patterns of consumption, lifestyles and moral and political beliefs have begun to come closer, there is an increasing cultural homogenisation of the world, to which much of the rhetoric of religious fundamentalism and national identity is an understandable but ultimately impotent reaction.

Thanks to the interdependence and convergence of human interests, beliefs and values, and the consequent realisation that the destinies of all states are interlocked, the old and long familiar concept of *mankind* is evolving into a novel and historically specific concept of *human community*. Men and women the world over are beginning to see each other not just as members of a common species and bearers of equal moral claims, but also as fellow-members of a large and diffuse, yet real and recognisable human community bound together by ties of mutual interest and concern. The inevitably slow and tentative trans-formation of the human species into a human community, of human equality into human fellowship, is a significant moral achievement, and gives depth, context and urgency to the universality of the moral obligation discussed earlier.

The emergence of the human community is evident at several levels. We tend to see the great artistic, architectural, literary and other achievements of different societies not as their exclusive property with which they may do as they like, but as a *common* human heritage which we all have a shared duty to preserve. We see nature too as mankind's *common* environment which we have a collective duty to nurture, so that no state may do what it likes with its forests and various species of plants and animals. We feel that certain basic rights and liberties are *common* human entitlements and that no state may deny them to its citizens. The idea of humanity as a collective moral subject is evident in the 1979 United Nations Convention on the Moon and the other Celestial Bodies and the 1992 United Nations debate on the Earth Charter, as also in the concept of crimes against humanity introduced at the Nuremberg trials. When there are natural and man-made disasters in other parts of the world, many feel involved and offer such help as they can. Many men and women are troubled by the living conditions and the truncated lives of their fellow humans in other parts of the world, and feel diminished and distressed at their own or their government's failure to do much about it. When a foreign government invades or bullies another, our own interests are not directly affected. Yet we feel concerned at the violation of the norms of international justice and morality of which we increasingly see ourselves as custodians. The slow and hesitant but unmistakable emergence of the consciousness of human community, which is both expressed in and sustained by these and countless other cases, has no historical parallel. No previous age felt an obligation to help the victims of disasters or the poor in other countries, nor saw their culture and environment as their common human heritage. There was no doubt, acknowledgement of a duty to help fellow Christians or members of the Islamic *umma*, but this was a very restrictive sense of the moral duty and, in any event, it was largely left to the efforts of individuals and mostly ignored in practice.

The state plays and will continue to play a vital role in holding its citizens together, giving their lives a stable framework, ensuring a measure of civility, and giving them a sense of rootedness and individuality. However it cannot continue in its current form. It contains several different ways of life and is no longer a cohesive moral unit. It is subject to constant external influences, and is not and cannot be culturally stable and autonomous. Many of its citizens are acutely aware of the demands of the human community and expect the state to respect these. The economic, political, moral, environmental and other interests of the state are deeply bound up with those of other states and cannot be pursued in isolation. States today face common problems and challenges, and these require global co-operation and planning. In an increasingly interdependent world, the actions of a state directly or indirectly affect the well-being of human beings elsewhere, and it cannot remain morally indifferent to their consequences.

This means that the modern state as we have known it for the past three centuries can neither go on as it is nor be declared historically obsolete. It still has vital moral, political, cultural and other functions to perform, but their character and context are changing radically. Its citizens therefore face unprecedented challenges and dilemmas. They need so to restructure the state that it is both cohesive and open, defines and pursues its interests in a way that damages neither its own citizens nor the so-called outsiders, and remains a community without losing sight of the larger human community of which it is increasingly becoming an integral part. They need to appreciate that even as they share many interests in common with the citizens of other polity, they also share many interests in common with the citizens of other polities. The global context in which the state functions today adds a global dimension to political obligation.

Since the interests of the citizens the world over are interlinked, and since the moral agent has obligations to his fellow-humans wherever they happen to live, citizenship today needs to be defined in global terms. Not that we are all now 'citizens of the world', for the world is not a polity and a shallow and rootless cosmopolitanism runs the grave danger of feeling exempted from concretely caring for anyone in the name of an abstract love of all. Rather that as citizens of our respective polities, we are developing sufficiently strong bonds to constitute us into a worldwide community of citizens. The human community is not a super-polity but a community of communities, regulating and limiting but not replacing the constituent political communities. We are not global citizens, rather our citizenship has a global dimension and orientation.

Citizens the world over therefore have a duty to be concerned about how their counterparts in other polities lead their lives. No state is the business of its citizens alone, and conversely no state may treat its citizens any way it likes. Even as no individual can lead a good life unless others do so too, no state today can ensure its citizens the conditions of a good life in an unstable, unjust and warring world. It might, of course, try to build fortresses around its frontiers and leave the poorer and violent states to their fate. But such a ghettoisation has its own privations, diminishes the humanity of the rich and powerful, and is precarious. It also leads to much dishonesty and hypocrisy for, although a state might ignore the claims of its less privileged counter-parts when it suits it to do so, it rarely hesitates to interfere with them when its interests are affected by their actions, as they invariably are in an interdependent world. A country cannot for long keep out the most wretched refugees and asylum-seekers, or watch images of unbearable human suffering, or hear daily stories of ethnic cleansing, brutality and rape without damaging its own moral sensibility. In the ultimate analysis human degradation and brutalisation are indivisible. Either we all grow and flourish together or none will.

6

I have argued that political obligation refers to the obligations citizens incur by virtue of their membership of a polity, and that their character and content change with the changes in the nature and context of that polity. Some of these obligations are too deeply embedded in the structure of our political relationship to be easily identified and require patient investigation. Contrary to much of the traditional discussion of the subject, being a good citizen is like being a good father, friend, Christian or academic, that is, a demanding and morally serious relationship involving a wide variety of obligations. These obligations include the duty to comply with the law, to respect and uphold civil authority, to take an active part in the conduct of public affairs, to speak up against prevailing injustices and inequalities, to accept responsibility for the deeds of our predecessors, to be mindful of the interests of our successors, and to help our fellow humans in other parts of the world. These obligations do not exhaust all the obligations of citizenship, and are only intended to show how complex and multi-farious they are. For reasons stated earlier, I have called them obligations, but it does not matter how we describe them as long as we agree that a morally serious citizen ought to respect their demands and may not ignore them without good reasons, a sense of guilt and a measure of social disapproval. The fact that little guilt and social disapproval are associated with the neglect of many of these obligations shows how little we value and understand our moral status as citizens.

NOTES

1. For a fuller discussion see my 'A Misconceived Discourse on Political Obligation', in *Political Studies*, 51 (June, 1993).
2. Carole Pateman, *The Problem of Political Obligation: A Critique of Liberal Theory* (Oxford: Polity Press, 1985).
3. This is the commonest way of defining political obligation, and is partly responsible for the inadequacy of much of the traditional discussion of the subject.
4. The ancient Greeks had no word for duty or obligation. Their nearest equivalent meant what one *must* do or what is the *proper* thing to do.
5. Michael Oakeshott, *On Human Conduct* (Oxford: Clarendon Press, 1975), pp. 154ff., especially p. 158.
6. For a perceptive critique of Hobbes' view, see Preston King, *The Ideology of Order* (London: Allen & Unwin, 1974) pp. 237ff. For King's outline of an alternative theory of political obligation, see ibid. pp. 277ff.
7. It was to celebrate and commemorate the Athenians who had died for their *polis* that the institution of the *epitaphios* had been originally devised around 460 BC.
8. I have discussed some of these issues in 'A Case for Positive Discrimination' in Bob Hepple and Erika M. Szyszezak (eds), *Discrimination: The Limits of Law* (London: Mansell, 1992).
9. For a valuable discussion of this complex issue, see Brian Barry's 'Justice Between Generations' in his *Liberty and Justice, Essays in Political Theory 2* (Oxford: Clarendon Press, 1991).

11

Transnational justice: permeable boundaries and multiple identities

ONORA O'NEILL

Political philosophers have traditionally said little about the legitimacy of boundaries. Of course, there have been attempts (not always impressive attempts) to argue that certain boundaries are natural, or needed for the security of certain nations or states. (Ireland's 'natural' boundary includes the entire island; Israel's security demands a boundary that includes the Golan Heights.) Such arguments presuppose that boundaries can be legitimate; they query the justice of placing boundaries here rather than there, but not the justice of boundaries as such. Here I shall set aside arguments about the placing of boundaries in order to look at arguments about the legitimacy of the institution of boundaries.

These arguments are seldom made explicit either in philosophical or in political or in daily discussion. Yet although boundaries are not one of the classical topics of political philosophy, many positions are committed to rather strong claims about boundaries and their legitimacy. For example, any argument that can justify an account not merely of state power, but of the powers of states, must also justify boundaries between states. This may seem trivial until we note that any plurality of states that are thought of as occupying exclusive territories, as they usually are, will sanction, indeed demand, boundaries that segment human lives and societies, and hence rights and entitlements, at certain spatial demarcations and so may obstruct universal standards of justice.

Liberal political philosophers in particular have devoted great efforts to justifying the limits of legitimate state power, but hardly any to justifying the limits of states. Often it is taken for granted that if we can justify the state, we can justify states. Yet this is far from obvious, for states are many and intrinsically particular, yet liberals suppose that justice is one and intrinsically universal in the sense that it applies to all. However, modern states stop at well-defined territorial boundaries, and it is not obvious why the distinctions which those boundaries establish between the rights, expectations and life chances of those whom they divide are to be justified within a political tradition that insists, as liberalism does, that principles of justice have universal scope. How can such principles be tied to particular territories?

One liberal argument in favour of this line is offered by Alan Gewirth, who writes:

> The territorial circumscription of states and their laws is not anti-thetical to their being justified by the universal principles that all persons' rights to freedom and well being must be equally and impartially secured. That the minimal state secures rights only for persons living within its territory is a practical limitation deriving from the fact that the state's functions must operate in relation to persons who are physically present in a specific physical area, although the development of international law may help to mitigate this limitation. But the universal principle also justifies that there be a multiplicity of such states so that all persons' rights are equally secured.[1]

Several objections spring to mind. First, it is simply false that state boundaries discriminate between those who are inside and those who are outside their boundaries. Membership is not reducible to location. Aliens who are inside state boundaries will have different, usually lesser, claims on the state where they find themselves and on its citizens. Citizens abroad will retain special claims on their state. Moreover, access to membership is jealously curtailed by most states, and in par-ticular by rich states. These are not trivial matters in a world in which many people lead lives, or long stretches of life, without full member-ship in states where they find themselves. Refugees, Gastarbeiter, resident aliens, illegal immigrants do not share the claims to state pro-tection either of liberty or of well-being that citizens enjoy. These commonplace observations suggest at least that any philosophical arguments about the legitimation of state power that is relevant in a world of many states would be helped by an explicit approach to the legitimation of boundaries.[2]

Most political debate is no more explicit about boundaries than are philosophical debates. It treats the state system as the background and context of politics, and boundaries as a parameter rather than a theme of political discourse. Rights and justice are mainly to be sought within bounded states. To secure justice is to ensure that each state measures up to certain standards, rather than to work towards a common structure, let alone towards a world state, which would abolish both boundaries and the plurality of states. And yet, on the surface, boundaries seem an affront to any conception of justice that asserts that there are universal human rights or universal standards of justice. For boundaries limit, indeed prohibit, the activities that may be undertaken by those whom they exclude. 'Outsiders' may find that various components of justice are routinely denied them by states which exclude them: they are variously denied rights to travel, to take up abode, to own property, to work, to receive welfare benefits, as well as rights of political participation within states of which they are not members or citizens. These exclusions are commonplace and generally seen as legitimate.

Parallel oversights are common in everyday discussion. Boundaries are generally seen as legitimate, except when they are thought to be wrongly located. We take it that political units must tessellate the earth, dividing its entire surface into discrete territories whose bounded unity may best be mapped by distinct, abutting patches of colour. Older maps might show us that this is not inevitable, for they left many boundaries fuzzy or undefined and classified some regions (sometimes disingenuously) as *terra incognita* or *no man's land*. Equally, we often take for granted that for political purposes we must divide other human beings neatly into fellow citizens and aliens, and that those who live where they are not citizens are variously anomalous, being, for example, resident aliens, guest workers or illegal immigrants.

This political classification of 'outsiders' is sharper than most cultural classifications, which tend to arrange others along axes of gradually increasing foreignness rather than dividing them exhaustively into mutually exclusive groups. For example, many in the UK will think of Australians as not wholly foreigners, while well aware that they are not citizens, and of the Irish as different but hardly foreigners. Or again, Russians have coined the phrase 'near abroad' to refer to parts of the former USSR that are neither Russia nor 'really' foreign.

This suggests that cultural and national classifications may not have to be as complete, as sharp or as permanent as the standard distinctions of political philosophy, of politics and of daily discussion. A boundary is after all, merely an institutionalised way of limiting specified activities by specified people at a certain point. My front door is a boundary for the activities of those whom I do not invite in; town limits are a boundary for the collection of rubbish by municipal dustmen; the outer boundaries of the EU are a limit for certain sorts of duty free movements of goods. The world is full of boundaries, many of them evidently tied to quite specific activities and permeable to some but not to others who seek to undertake those activities. I am free to travel beyond the municipal limits, but there may be a certain amount of trouble if I try to collect rubbish there, even if this is something that I am authorised to do within those limits.

The familiar state boundaries of the modern period, which are depicted on maps and taken for granted in so many ways, are in fact not typical boundaries, but, as it were, 'supernormal' boundaries, at which a multiplicity of functions of a state and multiple obligations and entitlements of all whom it recognises as its citizens end abruptly, and beyond which the functions of another state and the obligations and entitlements of its citizens begin. *What is distinctive about the supernormal boundaries modern states have erected is that they are formed by the organised coincidence of many different more specific sorts of boundaries all of which are (super)imposed and policed by state power.*

This organised coincidence of distinguishable boundaries is in no way inevitable, as can be seen from the many ways in which they may disintegrate. A favoured, but misleading, image of changing boundaries is the 'fall' of the Berlin wall. In this case an evidently supernormal boundary, that was designed to be impermeable for most activities by most of those whom it separated, was abolished. Today this boundary has vanished, and East and West Berlin are a single jurisdiction; only a few transitional arrangements differentiate the rights and entitlements of those who live in the city's two halves. A quite different, and more typical, image of changing boundaries is provided by the numerous less spectacular ways in which they alter without 'falling' or being abolished, as a result of decisions to alter their permeability for various activities by specific categories of persons. For example, today's boundaries within the European Union follow the exact lines of the boundaries of forty years ago, but have a wholly different significance. Forty years ago passport inspections and customs searches, exchange controls and frontier guards policed and maintained these supernormal boundaries with strenuous rigour. Today these boundaries are far more porous to the movement of people, money and goods. Yet it would be quite misleading to speak of these boundaries as having been abolished, or having fallen. Evidently they still demarcate jurisdictions, with distinct laws, institutions and different citizens; moreover, the external boundaries of the European Union remain relatively impermeable to many outsiders. The change is that the internal boundaries of the European Union have become porous for many activities by many persons for whom and for which they would previously have been impermeable so that the boundaries of fewer activities now coincide at these locations.

This suggests that if we want to think about the arguments for legitimating boundaries, we should pay attention to arguments for making them more or less permeable in specific ways, rather than confining attention to arguments for the creation, abolition or redefinition of states. In decisions about the ways in which movements of people, goods and money may be restricted, regulated and eased, the boundaries of states and the significance of sovereignty can be transformed without either boundaries or states being abolished. In attending to these questions we may also come to think of the regimentation of boundaries characteristic of a world of sovereign states as one end of a spectrum of possible ways of segmenting human life. In the transition from a feudal mosaic with countless dispersed demarcations, sovereign states made their internal boundaries more and more permeable, and their external boundaries more and more impermeable. Internal and external sovereignty were sharply defined in modern states, and demanded porous internal but impermeable external boundaries.

If today we are moving away from supernormal forms of state sovereignty, this may be properly reflected neither in the abolition nor in the redrawing of boundaries but in quite varied changes that make specific boundaries more and less porous for specific activities and for specific people, and insists less on a concentration of all boundaries at a very limited number of demarcations.

Multiple identities

This way of thinking about the boundaries of states allows a wide range of political debates, that are often treated as quite distinct, to be connected in that they all raise questions about ways in which state boundaries should be made more and less permeable. Trade policies determine the ways and the degree to which boundaries are permeable to goods. Refugee, immigration, employment and social policies determine who can flow through which frontiers for which purposes. Policies to restrict, attract or direct foreign investment and to regulate currency convertibility and speculation as well as access to financial services, make boundaries more, less or differently porous to flows of money and capital.[3]

However, actual debates about these policies usually take the legitimacy of actual boundaries for granted. Their legitimacy is assumed in the very terms of discourse, which distinguish home-produced from foreign goods, citizens from aliens, domestic from foreign investment and currencies. When these distinctions are taken for granted, so too is the legitimacy of the state boundaries that define them. If boundaries and the terms of discourse which presuppose them are to be justified we must then look beyond discussions of current policies. Yet it is surprisingly unclear where we should look.

In the rest of this paper I shall leave aside arguments for and against modifying the permeability of existing boundaries in order to consider some well entrenched views about the ultimate source of legitimacy of boundaries. A clear appreciation of these arguments may shed light on reasons for and against altering the permeability of boundaries.

The longest standing arguments for the legitimacy of boundaries base political justification on supposed cultural reality. Boundaries, hence a plurality of states and jurisdictions, are said to be legitimate, or even required for just and ordered societies, because they enable culturally distinct groups, in particular peoples and nations, to build and share common political institutions within which they can do things in their own way, and preserve, cultivate and transmit their own traditions. Although there is often a functional strand in these arguments (culturally homogeneous states are said to be politically more stable or more likely to secure democratic legitimation), the main weight of such arguments lies in the thought that cultural identities provide a fundamental sort of legitimation, by which the exclusion of foreigners and their activities can be justified.

This appeal to the boundaries of nations as justifying the boundaries of states is far from straightforward because the boundaries of nations are territorially chaotic.[4] It is rarely possible to draw a boundary that includes all and only those who recognise themselves or are recognised by others as sharing a single national identity. Very few actual states are nationally homogeneous. Very few such states could be created except by drastic and drastically unjust policies such as ethnic cleansing, deportation or forced relocation, forced assimilation or irredentism.

Hence the appeal to national identity to justify boundaries is standardly modified by allowing that there will be minorities within given boundaries. The universalistic aspirations of theories of justice and human rights are adapted to – perhaps compromised by – the realities of intermingled nations. Nations are said to have rights of self-determination; but minorities (minority nations?) only rights to be protected. Whether a given minority is a nation, so can invoke a right to self-determination, and with it a right of secession, is left obscure. Evidently the claim that cultural identities can justify state boundaries runs into countless *practical* difficulties in any world in which nations are territorially mingled.

The strategy of justification may, however, run into much more elementary difficulties. The basic idea behind a cultural justification of political boundaries is the thought that cultural identities are deep, singular and permanent in a way that political structures are not; that we begin by being members of nations in a way that is much more profound than our citizenship of states, hence that (national) identities can justify bounded states. However, cultural, including national, identities may be neither singular nor unalterable features of human beings.

In the first place, nations too have their histories, and these histories are often formed rather than simply expressed by the histories of states. States often engage in programmes of nation-building, by which they seek to form and reform the identities of their citizens. Nation-building policies are common not only in newly formed states, but in established states which feel the need to woo, steer and consolidate their citizens' loyalties. Such programmes may be a response to experience or fears of separation or disaffection (e.g. postwar cultural policies in Alsace and Lorraine), or a way of assimilating immigrants of disparate origin (US or Israeli nation-building).

There is much to be said for such policies: the citizens whose sense of self and identity they transform or consolidate may be more committed, more closely bound to one another and less open to secessionist appeals. However, the very use of these strategies shows that national identity is not an unquestionable, singular and non-negotiable given for every individual which provides a foundation for political legitimation, including the legitimation of state boundaries.

The strategy of justifying state structures by appeals to national or other identities is also undercut by other considerations. Identities are not only historically malleable; they can be multiple. A single individual may have more than one identity; many will have a self-understanding which makes them members of more than one nation. Although it is often denied, it is not hard either to find counter-examples, or to trace some of the sources of denial.

It is well recognised that an individual can have (for example) a religious, a national and a regional identity: it is possible to be Lutheran, German and Saxon. But it is often supposed that certain combinations of cultural identity and any two national identities must be mutually exclusive. For example, it will be commonly held that nobody can be liberal and communist, or French and Swedish.

Certain supposed examples of dual identities are indeed unconvincing. The 'hyphenated' combined national identities claimed by certain US citizens (German-Americans, Italian-Americans) – or by sociologists who write about them – are not convincing examples of multiple national identity. These people are avowedly American, if with an inflection. Their German or Italian identity may be something which is paraded but not preserved. Indeed, members of these groups are often eager to shed the distinctive features of their claimed identity of origin, whose language and culture they do not preserve and sometimes make haste to lose. Another marginal case of multiple national identity is provided by individuals of mixed provenance who may feel and be seen by others as having more than one national identity. However, if these were the only convincing examples of dual national identity they might be thought of as unimportant exceptions to the claim that each person can have only one national identity.

Yet the most significant case of multiple national identities occurs where many people simply see themselves as having a plurality of national identities. Some such cases are regarded as unproblematic: it is uncontroversial today to be Lombard and Italian, Scots and British, Bavarian and German. These cases are seen as unproblematic because they are often pigeon-holed as combinations of national and provincial identity, where the latter is seen as a special case or inflection of the former. We have no trouble in acknowledging the possibility of multiple national identities that are hierarchically organized. Equally we have no problem in acknowledging the possibility of multiple religious or political identities, provided that they can be thought of as dealing with different aspects of life.[5]

However, these convenient ways of pigeon-holing cases of ostensibly dual identity overlook the fact that both the hierarchical structure (by which dual national identities are made to seem unproblematic) and the separation of spheres of life (by which different religious or political identities may be combined) may both depend on temporary, changeable, indeed fragile, accommodations. Multiple identities that seem coherent and compatible at one time may be brought into tension, conflict and even contradiction at others. Once upon a time it was easy to be German and Jewish; once upon another time it became impossible. Once upon a time it was easy to be Irish and British; latterly it has been easy (and even then not wholly easy) only for those of Irish origin living in Britain. There are possible worlds in which it might no longer be possible to be Breton and French, or Scots and British, and in the actual world it has become harder to be Quebecois and Canadian. There have been actual worlds in which one could not be Christian and liberal, or communist and existentialist, and others in which these combinations have been prized. Where tension is slight, identities that are more or less easily combined will be thought of as hierarchically related (e.g. local or regional and national identity) or as pertaining to different aspects of life (e.g. religious and national identity, religious and political identity). But when tension rises, pairs of identities that can no longer be readily combined will no longer be thought of either as hierarchically related or as pertaining to different aspects of life.

None of this is too surprising if one thinks closely about identity, including national identity. Not long ago discussions of these matters in English would have spoken not of *identities* but of *senses of identity*. The older terminology is less misleading. To have a sense of identity is to have a certain constellation of views of oneself, of whom one recognises as one's own and whom one recognises as other, of who will recognise one as fellow countryman or woman or as foreign, as of the faith or as infidel, and to feel appropriate sentiments of affiliation and its lack. In short, to have a (sense of) (national) identity is to have certain beliefs and sentiments. No doubt these beliefs and sentiments will often be deeply cherished and hard to change; still, like other beliefs and sentiments they are both relatively indeterminate and open to change.

It is the *indeterminacy* of (senses of) identity that makes multiple identities possible. To be Protestant and Italian, for example, is unusual but possible because neither sense of identity is sufficiently determinate to preclude the other (once upon a time things were different). Only if a sense of identity were fully determinate, if it could saturate lives, would it be incompatible with all other senses of identity.

It is the *malleability* of (senses of) identity that make it possible to change (combinations of) senses of identity. To change or modify one's (sense of) (national) identity is not a matter of losing one's sense of self, let alone one's life, but simply a matter of changing and modifying some range (perhaps a large range) of beliefs and sentiments about one's relations of affiliation and of distance to others. Such changes in beliefs and sentiments may be difficult or easy, welcome or unwelcome, matters of pride or of shame; but they need not involve any sort of affront to integrity or to the continuities of life, let alone intrinsic inconsistencies. Countless stories of assimilation and aliena-tion bear witness to the mundane fact that changes of national and other identity, even when stressful and reluctant, may pose neither threat nor peril to whose who live through the change.[6]

Once we realise that (national) identities are constellations of beliefs and sentiments we can also shed some light on the conditions under which multiple identities may be possible, indeed normal, and the conditions under which they may become stressful or even impossible. Evidently *any* two beliefs or sentiments or principles may *sometimes* create conflicts for those who are attached to both. However, some of these conflicts are occasional and contingent: family loyalty and patriotic duty are often readily combined.[7] Other conflicts of identity and loyalty may be systematic and irresolvable, so that sooner or later one or the other (sense of) identity and its loyalties have to give. There was a time, long gone, when to be English and Catholic was impossible because a conception of Englishness prevailed which was deeply and systematically hostile to Catholicism; revisions in conceptions both of Englishness and of Catholicism have made this combination of identi-ties readily supportable. Conversely, it is imaginable that pairs of identities which appear entirely compatible today could undergo changes by which it may become hard or impossible to maintain both identities. There are imaginable future worlds in which one can no longer be Scots and British, or Catalan and Spanish, or in which one can no longer be Christian and capitalist, or Muslim and socialist.

None of this suggests that identities, including national identities, are unimportant. On the contrary, a cursory reading of political his-tory since 1789, let alone of events since 1989, suggests that identities, and especially national identities, are both culturally and politically important. Policies and polities that do not take account of (national) identities, loyalties and traditions are likely to run into deep problems.

Nevertheless, national identities are not fundamental to the legitimation of permanent political structures such as states and their boundaries, for two quite distinct but individually sufficient reasons. First, boundaries (as noted above) can rarely be fashioned to provide nations with states of their own, except by denying other nations that are territorially fragmented into minorities states of their own. Second, even if the territorial realities were less awkward, or if we thought that it was possible for states to be non-territorial, or less territorial (perhaps by establishing consociational structures) appeals to identity would have limited justificatory potential. This is because claims that state boundaries can or should be adjusted to take account of (national) identities can be countered by claims that (national) identities can or should be adjusted to take account of state boundaries. More generally, once we realise that the national and other identities are neither singular nor historical constants, and won't provide any bed-rock for justificatory arguments, we will have to acknowledge that arguments from identities of any sort to the justification of state boundaries can be countered by arguments from the realities of state boundaries to the revision of identities. Nations may claim states of their own, and equally states may seek to forge nations of their own.

In our world, where states with supernormal boundaries and exorbitant powers have recently maimed many lives, the appeals of nations to states of their own often seem more alluring than any appeal of states to forge nations of their own. Secession can seem safer than more imperialism. However, appeals of either sort might seem both less alluring and less alarming if placed in the context of a less exaggerated view both of boundaries and of (national) identities, which acknowledges that both can be permeable and variable. If boundaries can be made more and less permeable, and (national) identities can be reshaped, reformed and recombined, it may be possible to devise political forms that take account of varying sorts and combinations of identity without treating either identities or states and their boundaries as foundational. Taking (national) identities seriously enough does not mean that we need to take over-seriously mythical claims that states should be homogeneous nation states, or that nations should have rights of self-determination or of secession. Taking boundaries seriously enough does not mean that we need suppose that states must have supernormal forms of internal or external sovereignty. The malleability and permeability of (senses of) identity may be best acknowledged by policies that also acknowledge the variable permeability of boundaries.

NOTES

1. Alan Gewirth, 'Ethical Universalism and Particularism', *Journal of Philosophy*, 85, (1988), p. 300. See also John Simmons, *Moral Principles and Political Obligation* (Princeton University Press, 1979) p. 31.
2. For examples of ways in which boundaries and the plurality of states are taken for granted, consider Rawls' assumption that we can begin an account of justice by considering the case of a bounded society (see *A Theory of Justice*, Cambridge, MA: Harvard University Press, 1971, p. 8) as well as communitarian assumptions that the starting point for political reflection can be the convictions of 'our' community or 'our' tradition.
3. For linkages between restrictions on the movements of money and of people see Brian Barry and Robert E. Goodin (eds), *Free Movement: Ethical Issues in the Transnational Migration of People and of Money* (University of Pennsylvania Press, 1992).
4. See Onora O'Neill, 'Justice and Boundaries' in C. Brown (ed.), *Political Restructuring in Europe: Ethical Perspectives* (Routledge, 1993).
5. In practice there is often a lot of controversy whether certain positions can genuinely pertain to different aspects of life – for example, whether anyone can be simultaneously communist and Christian, Marxist and existentialist, communitarian and post-modernist.
6. For this reason, identities cannot themselves provide unchallengeable starting points for ethical or political arguments of the sort some Wittgensteinians and communitarians have hoped to find.
7. But not always: witness Sartre's student who was torn between filial and patriotic duty. His dilemma arose not from lack of moral codes but from the fact that he was committed to two which (in his particular situation, but not in all) made conflicting demands.

Index